LEX AQUILIA

ON GIFTS BETWEEN HUSBAND AND WIFE

LONDON : HUMPHREY MILFORD
OXFORD UNIVERSITY PRESS

LEX AQUILIA

(Digest IX, 2, Ad Legem Aquiliam)

TEXT, TRANSLATION, AND COMMENTARY

ON GIFTS BETWEEN HUSBAND AND WIFE

(Digest XXIV, 1, De Donationibus inter Virum et Uxorem)

TEXT AND COMMENTARY

BY

JAMES B. THAYER

CAMBRIDGE

HARVARD UNIVERSITY PRESS

1929

PRINTED AT THE HARVARD UNIVERSITY PRESS
CAMBRIDGE, MASS., U. S. A.

CONTENTS

AD LEGEM AQUILIAM

ABBREVIATIONS

A. G. . . . . *Archivio Giuridico.*
Arch. . . . . *Archiv für die Civilistische Praxis.*
Arch. P. . . . . . *Archiv für praktische Rechtswissenschaft,* 3 Folge, vol. 3.

Beseler . . . . . . *Beiträge zur Kritik der Römischen Rechtsquellen.*
Biondi, A. N. . "Actiones Noxales," in *Annali del Seminario Giuridico,* Palermo, 1925, vol. 10.
Buckland . . . . *A Textbook of Roman Law.*
Bull. . . . . *Bullettino dell' Istituto di Diritto Romano.*

De Francisci . . *Studii sopra le Azione Penale e la loro Intransmissibilità Passiva.*
De Medio . . . . "La Legittimazione Attiva nell' Actio Legis Aquiliae": *Studi in onore Vittorio Scialoja,* vol. 1.

E. G. I. . . . . . . Ferrini in *Enciclopedia Giuridica Italiana, s. v.* Danni.
Esp. . . . . Ferrini in Pessina's *Enciclopedia del Diritto Penale,* vol. 1.

Girard . . . . *Manuel Élémentaire de Droit Roman,* 6 ed.
Grueber . . . . . *The Lex Aquilia* (references are to the commentary).

K. V. I. . . . . . . *Kritische Vierteljahrschrift für Gesetzgebung und Rechtswissenschaft.*

Lenel . . . . *Das Edictum Perpetuum,* 2 Aufl.
Levy . . . . *Konkurrenz der Actionen und Personen.*

Mommsen . . . *Beiträge zum Obligationenrecht,* F. Mommsen.
Monro . . . . *Lex Aquilia.*

Naber . . . . *Observatiunculae de jure Romano,* Mnemosyne, N. S.

Pernice . . . . . . Labeo, vol. 2, 2 ed., 1895, 1900.
Pernice, S. . . . *Sachbeschädigung.*

Rabel . . . . "Grundzüge des Römischen Privatrechts," Holtzendorff, *Enzyclopädie,* 7th ed., vol. 1, 399 ff.
Rotondi . . . . . *Rivista del Diritto Commerciale,* 1916, vol. 1.
Rotondi, S. G. *Scritti Giuridici,* vol. 2.

Schulz....... Fritz Schulz, *Einführung in das Studium der Digesten.*

von Tuhr.... *Zur Schätzung des Schadens in der Lex Aquilia.*

Vangerow ... *Lehrbuch der Pandekten*, 7 Aufl.

Windscheid... *Lehrbuch der Pandekten*, 9 Aufl.

Z............ *Zeitschrift der Savigny Stiftung*, Romanistisches Abteilung.

References to other fragments of this title are given without preliminary numbers.

J. means the Institutes; the Digest is meant if no letter is appended.

Any mention of the *Basilica* or the *Scholiast* refers to Heimbach's edition, Lib. 60, Tit. 3.

A history of the transformation of Aquilian liability into that of the modern civil law for damage to property is given by Rotondi, *R. D. C.*, 1917, vol. 1, 236 ff.; copious references to the great scholars of earlier times, like Cujas, Noodt, and Suarez, of whom so much modern exegesis is a more or less conscious echo, may be found in Castellari, 22 A. G. 305 ff.

AD LEGEM AQUILIAM

IX. 2

1. ULPIANUS *libro octavo decimo ad edictum* Lex Aquilia omnibus legibus, quae ante se de damno iniuria locutae sunt, derogavit, sive duodecim tabulis, sive alia quae fuit: quas leges nunc referre non est necesse. 1. Quae lex Aquilia plebiscitum est, cum eam Aquilius tribunus plebis a plebe rogaverit.

2. GAIUS *libro septimo ad edictum provinciale* Lege Aquilia capite primo cavetur: 'ut qui servum servamve alienum alienamve quadrupedem vel pecudem iniuria occiderit, quanti id in eo anno plurimi fuit, tantum aes dare domino damnas esto': 1. et infra deinde cavetur, ut adversus infitiantem in duplum actio esset. 2. Ut igitur apparet, servis nostris exaequat quadrupedes, quae pecudum numero sunt et gregatim habentur, veluti oves caprae boves equi muli asini. sed an sues pecudum appellatione continentur, quaeritur: et recte Labeoni placet contineri. sed canis inter pecudes non est. longe magis bestiae in eo numero non sunt, veluti ursi leones pantherae. elefanti autem et cameli quasi mixti sunt (nam et iumentorum operam praestant et natura eorum fera est) et ideo primo capite contineri eas oportet.

3. ULPIANUS *libro octavo decimo ad edictum* Si servus servave iniuria occisus occisave fuerit, lex Aquilia locum habet. iniuria occisum esse merito adicitur: non enim sufficit occisum, sed oportet iniuria id esse factum.

4. GAIUS *libro septimo ad edictum provinciale* Itaque si servum tuum latronem insidiantem mihi occidero, securus ero: nam adversus periculum naturalis ratio permittit se defendere. 1. Lex duodecim tabularum furem noctu deprehensum occidere permittit, ut tamen id ipsum cum clamore testificetur: interdiu autem deprehensum ita permittit occi-

ON THE AQUILIAN LAW

IX. 2

1. The *Lex Aquilia* partially repealed all preceding laws of every kind, including the Twelve Tables, which related to wrongful damage to property. These need not now be mentioned.

1. The *Lex Aquilia* is a plebiscite, as Aquilius, their tribune, proposed it to the *plebs*.

2. The first chapter of the *Lex Aquilia* reads: if anyone wrongfully kills another's slave of either sex, or his four-footed beast, let him be condemned to pay to the owner whatever was its greatest value in the past year.

1. And later it is provided that the action shall be for double against a defendant who denies liability.

2. So it appears that to our slaves are assimilated the four-footed beasts which are classed as "cattle" because they are kept in herds, like sheep, goats, cows, horses, mules, or asses. And as to the question whether pigs are counted as cattle, Labeo rightly answers that they are. But the term does not include dogs, nor *a fortiori* wild animals, like bears, lions, and panthers. However, elephants and camels are so to speak "mixed" and, though their nature is wild, as they do the work of draft-animals they should be included in the first chapter.

3. If a slave of either sex is wrongfully killed, the *Lex Aquilia* applies. It is rightly added that the killing shall be wrongful; killing does not suffice unless it is done unlawfully.

4. Hence if I kill your slave, while he is lying in wait intending to rob me, I shall not be liable, for natural reason permits self-defense against danger.

1. The Twelve Tables allow the killing of a nocturnal thief if he is caught in the act, provided that warning is first given by a shout; but if the thief is caught in the daytime he may be

dere, si is se telo defendat, ut tamen aeque cum clamore testificetur.

5. ULPIANUS *libro octavo decimo ad edictum* Sed et si quemcumque alium ferro se petentem quis occiderit non videbitur iniuria occidisse: et si metu quis mortis furem occiderit non dubitabitur, quin lege Aquilia non teneatur. sin autem cum posset adprehendere, maluit occidere, magis est ut iniuria fecisse videatur: ergo et Cornelia tenebitur. 1. Iniuriam autem hic accipere nos oportet non quemadmodum circa iniuriarum actionem contumeliam quandam, sed quod non iure factum est, hoc est contra ius, id est si culpa quis occiderit: et ideo interdum utraque actio concurrit et legis Aquiliae et iniuriarum, sed duae erunt aestimationes, alia damni, alia contumeliae. igitur iniuriam hic damnum accipiemus culpa datum etiam ab eo, qui nocere noluit. 2. Et ideo quaerimus, si furiosus damnum dederit, an legis Aquiliae actio sit? et Pegasus negavit: quae enim in eo culpa sit, cum suae mentis non sit? et hoc est verissimum. cessabit igitur Aquiliae actio, quemadmodum, si quadrupes damnum dederit, Aquilia cessat, aut si tegula ceciderit. sed et si infans damnum dederit, idem erit dicendum. quodsi inpubes id fecerit, Labeo ait, quia furti tenetur, teneri et Aquilia eum: et hoc puto verum, si sit iam iniuriae capax. 3. Si magister in disciplina vulneraverit servum vel occiderit, an Aquilia teneatur, quasi damnum iniuria dederit? et Iulianus scribit Aquilia teneri eum, qui eluscaverat discipulum in disciplina: multo magis igitur in occiso idem erit dicendum. proponitur autem apud eum species talis: sutor, inquit, puero discenti ingenuo filio familias, parum bene facienti quod demonstraverit, forma calcei cervicem percussit, ut oculus puero perfunderetur. dicit igitur Iulianus iniuriarum quidem actionem non competere, quia non faciendae iniuriae causa percusserit, sed monendi et docendi causa: an ex locato, dubitat, quia levis dumtaxat castigatio concessa est docenti: sed lege Aquilia posse agi non dubito:

killed only if he defends himself with a weapon, warning also being given by a shout.

5. So if one kills another who is attempting to attack him with a sword, the killing is not held wrongful; and if in mortal fear one kills a thief, there is certainly no Aquilian liability. On the other hand, if one prefers to kill, when it is possible to arrest the thief, by the better view it is a wrongful killing; hence there is also liability under the *Lex Cornelia*.

1. We must understand *injuria* not as an insult of some kind, as in the *actio injuriarum*, but as that which is done unlawfully, that is, contrary to law, as when the killing is culpable; hence both actions, that of the *Lex Aquilia* and that for insult, will sometimes concur, and there will be double assessment of damages, one for damage and one for insult. Thus we interpret *injuria* as damage caused culpably even by one who did not intend the injury.

2. Hence the question whether there will be an Aquilian action for damage done by a lunatic; Pegasus denies it: "What fault can there be in one who is not in his senses?" which is quite true. So the Aquilian action fails, as it would if an animal had done the damage, or a tile had fallen. And the same must be said if a child does the damage; but if he were over seven Labeo says that as he is held for theft he must be liable for the Aquilian action, to which I agree, if he were capable of distinguishing between right and wrong.

3. If a teacher in the course of instruction wounds or kills a slave, is he held under the *Lex Aquilia*, on the ground that he committed wrongful damage? Julian writes that one is liable for putting out a pupil's eye in the act of disciplining him, so that liability for killing follows *a fortiori*. These are the facts of the case reported by him: he says that a cobbler, because a pupil, a freeborn *filius familias*, ineptly performed his appointed task, struck his head with a last, putting out his eye. Here Julian holds that there is no liability for insult because the blow was not given for that purpose but to correct and instruct, and he doubts whether the action on the contract will lie, because slight punishment is permitted to a teacher. I, however, have no doubt that the action of the *Lex Aquilia* can be brought,

6. PAULUS *libro vicensimo secundo ad edictum* praeceptoris enim nimia saevitia culpae adsignatur.

7. ULPIANUS *libro octavo decimo ad edictum* Qua actione patrem consecuturum ait, quod minus ex operis filii sui propter vitiatum oculum sit habiturus, et impendia, quae pro eius curatione fecerit. 1. Occisum autem accipere debemus, sive gladio sive etiam fuste vel alio telo vel manibus (si forte strangulavit eum) vel calce petiit vel capite vel qualiter qualiter. 2. Sed si quis plus iusto oneratus deiecerit onus et servum occiderit, Aquilia locum habet: fuit enim in ipsius arbitrio ita se non onerare. nam et si lapsus aliquis servum alienum onere presserit, Pegasus ait lege Aquilia eum teneri ita demum, si vel plus iusto se oneraverit vel neglegentius per lubricum transierit. 3. Proinde si quis alterius impulsu damnum dederit, Proculus scribit neque eum qui impulit teneri, quia non occidit, neque eum qui impulsus est, quia damnum iniuria non dedit: secundum quod in factum actio erit danda in eum qui impulit. 4. Si quis in colluctatione vel in pancratio, vel pugiles dum inter se exercentur alius alium occiderit, si quidem in publico certamine alius alium occiderit, cessat Aquilia, quia gloriae causa et virtutis, non iniuriae gratia videtur damnum datum. hoc autem in servo non procedit, quoniam ingenui solent certare: in filio familias vulnerato procedit. plane si cedentem vulneraverit, erit Aquiliae locus, aut si non in certamine servum occidit, nisi si domino committente hoc factum sit: tunc enim Aquilia cessat. 5. Sed si quis servum aegrotum leviter percusserit et is obierit, recte Labeo dicit lege Aquilia eum teneri, quia aliud alii mortiferum esse solet. 6. Celsus autem multum interesse dicit, occiderit an mortis causam praestiterit, ut qui mortis causam praestitit, non Aquilia, sed in factum actione teneatur. unde adfert eum qui venenum pro medicamento dedit et ait causam mortis praestitisse, quemadmodum eum qui furenti gladium porrexit: nam nec hunc lege Aquilia teneri, sed in factum. 7. Sed si quis de ponte aliquem praecipitavit, Celsus ait, sive ipso ictu perierit aut continuo submersus est aut lassatus vi

6. for excessive brutality on the part of a teacher is considered to be culpable.

7. Julian maintains that in this action the father may recover for the loss of his son's services caused by the destruction of his eye, as well as the expenses incurred in caring for him.

1. We should hold that there is a killing whether the attack be committed with a sword, a stick, or any other implement, or the hands, as in a case of strangulation, or with the foot, the head, or in any other manner.

2. If one who is overloaded throws down his burden thereby killing a slave, the Aquilian action will lie, because it was in his power not to load himself in that way. For even if one slips and crushes another with his burden, Pegasus says that he will be liable under the *Lex Aquilia*, provided that he loaded himself unduly or carelessly walked through a slippery place.

3. Similarly, if one has done damage by being pushed by another, Proculus writes that neither the one who pushed can be held because he did not kill, nor the one who was pushed because he did not do wrongful damage; in which case an action *in factum* should be given against the one who pushed.

4. If one kills another in wrestling or in the pancratium, or in a sparring match, or in any public exhibition, there is no Aquilian liability, since the damage seems to be committed in the cause of honor and valor, not wrongfully. But this does not hold in the case of a slave, since only freemen are accustomed so to contest; it does hold if a *filius familias* is wounded. Obviously the Aquilian action will lie if the plaintiff is wounded after he has given in, or if a slave not a party to the contest has been killed, but there is no action if his master has entered the slave in a private match.

5. If one gives a slight blow to a sick slave thereby killing him, Labeo rightly says that he will be liable to an Aquilian action, because what will not kill one man may well kill another.

6. However, Celsus says that it is very important whether the defendant killed or furnished the cause of death; in the latter case he is held not in an Aquilian action but in an action *in factum*. Thus he mentions one who gives poison under the guise of medicine and says that he furnished the cause of death, like him who gives a sword to a lunatic, the latter being liable not to an Aquilian action but to one *in factum*.

7. If one throws another off a bridge, whether he dies from the impact, or is immediately drowned, or dies from exhaus-

fluminis victus perierit, lege Aquilia teneri, quemadmodum si quis puerum saxo inlisisset. 8. Proculus ait, si medicus servum imperite secuerit, vel ex locato vel ex lege Aquilia competere actionem.

8. GAIUS *libro septimo ad edictum provinciale* Idem iuris est, si medicamento perperam usus fuerit. sed et qui bene secuerit et dereliquit curationem, securus non erit, sed culpae reus intellegitur. 1. Mulionem quoque, si per imperitiam impetum mularum retinere non potuerit, si eae alienum hominem obtriverint, vulgo dicitur culpae nomine teneri. idem dicitur et si propter infirmitatem sustinere mularum impetum non potuerit: nec videtur iniquum, si infirmitas culpae adnumeretur, cum affectare quisque non debeat, in quo vel intellegit vel intellegere debet infirmitatem suam alii periculosam futuram. idem iuris est in persona eius, qui impetum equi, quo vehebatur, propter imperitiam vel infirmitatem retinere non poterit.

9. ULPIANUS *libro octavo decimo ad edictum* Item si obstetrix medicamentum dederit et inde mulier perierit, Labeo distinguit, ut, si quidem suis manibus supposuit, videatur occidisse: sin vero dedit, ut sibi mulier offerret, in factum actionem dandam, quae sententia vera est: magis enim causam mortis praestitit quam occidit. 1. Si quis per vim vel suasum medicamentum alicui infundit vel ore vel clystere vel si eum unxit malo veneno, lege Aquilia eum teneri, quemadmodum obstetrix supponens tenetur. 2. Si quis hominem fame necaverit, in factum actione teneri Neratius ait. 3. Si servum meum equitantem concitato equo effeceris in flumen praecipitari atque ideo homo perierit, in factum esse dandam actionem Ofilius scribit: quemadmodum si servus meus ab alio in insidias deductus, ab alio esset occisus. 4. Sed si per lusum iaculantibus servus fuerit occisus, Aquiliae locus est: sed si cum alii in campo iacularentur, servus per eum locum transierit, Aquilia cessat, quia non debuit per campum iaculatorium iter intempestive facere. qui tamen data opera in eum iaculatus est, utique Aquilia tenebitur:

tion overcome by the power of the current, Celsus says that the *Lex Aquilia* applies, just as if one hurls a child against a rock.

8. Proculus says that if a doctor unskillfully operates on a slave, either the action on the contract or that on the *Lex Aquilia* will lie.

8. The law is the same if the wrong use is made of a drug; likewise a defendant who operates properly but omits further treatment will not escape but will be held guilty of negligence.

1. So, too, if a mule-driver through inexperience is unable to hold in his mules so that they run over another's slave, he is usually held on the ground of negligence. This is true even if he could not prevent the advance of the mules on account of weakness; and it is not inequitable that weakness should be counted a fault since one ought not to embark on an enterprise in which one knows or ought to know that his weakness will be dangerous to others. The law is the same for one who from inexperience or weakness cannot hold in the horse on which he is riding.

9. Likewise if a midwife gives a drug from which the patient dies, Labeo draws this distinction: if she did it with her own hands, she is held to have killed; but if she offered it so that the patient took it herself, the action is *in factum;* and this is correct, for in the latter case the defendant furnished the cause of death, rather than killed.

1. If, by force or suasion, one administers a drug to another, orally or by injection, or if one massages him with a poisonous preparation, one is liable, like the midwife, to an Aquilian action.

2. If one kills a slave by starvation, Neratius holds him liable *in factum.*

3. If my slave is riding a horse and by frightening the horse you cause him to be thrown into a river so that he perishes, Ofilius writes that the action is *in factum*, as where my slave is lured into an ambush by the defendant and there killed by a third person.

4. If a slave is killed by those who are throwing javelins for sport, the *Lex Aquilia* applies, but if men are throwing javelins in a field and the slave crosses it, there is no action, because he ought not unseasonably to make his way over the playing field. Nevertheless, one who hit the slave on purpose would be liable under this statute,

10. Paulus *libro vicensimo secundo ad edictum* nam lusus quoque noxius in culpa est.

11. Ulpianus *libro octavo decimo ad edictum* Item Mela scribit, si, cum pila quidam luderent, vehementius quis pila percussa in tonsoris manus eam deiecerit et sic servi, quem tonsor habebat, gula sit praecisa adiecto cultello: in quocumque eorum culpa sit, eum lege Aquilia teneri. Proculus in tonsore esse culpam: et sane si ibi tondebat, ubi ex consuetudine ludebatur vel ubi transitus frequens erat, est quod ei imputetur: quamvis nec illud male dicatur, si in loco periculoso sellam habenti tonsori se quis commiserit, ipsum de se queri debere. 1. Si alius tenuit, alius interemit, is qui tenuit, quasi causam mortis praebuit, in factum actione tenetur. 2. Sed si plures servum percusserint, utrum omnes quasi occiderint teneantur, videamus. et si quidem apparet, cuius ictu perierit, ille quasi occiderit tenetur: quod si non apparet, omnes quasi occiderint teneri Iulianus ait, et si cum uno agatur, ceteri non liberantur: nam ex lege Aquilia quod alius praestitit, alium non relevat, cum sit poena. 3. Celsus scribit, si alius mortifero vulnere percusserit, alius postea exanimaverit, priorem quidem non teneri quasi occiderit, sed quasi vulneraverit, quia ex alio vulnere periit, posteriorem teneri, quia occidit. quod et Marcello videtur et est probabilius. 4. Si plures trabem deiecerint et hominem oppresserint, aeque veteribus placet omnes lege Aquilia teneri. 5. Item cum eo, qui canem irritaverat et effecerat, ut aliquem morderet, quamvis eum non tenuit, Proculus respondit Aquiliae actionem esse: sed Iulianus eum demum Aquilia teneri ait, qui tenuit et effecit ut aliquem morderet: ceterum si non tenuit, in factum agendum. 6. Legis autem Aquiliae actio ero competit, hoc est domino. 7. Si in eo homine, quem tibi redhibiturus essem, damnum iniuria datum esset, Iulianus ait legis Aquiliae actionem mihi competere meque, cum coepero redhibere, tibi restituturum. 8. Sed si servus bona fide alicui serviat, an ei competit Aquiliae actio? et magis in factum actio erit danda. 9. Eum, cui vestimenta

10. because even a game, if dangerous, is culpable.

11. Mela gives another case: if a ball game was going on and a player hitting the ball knocked it against the hand of a barber so that the throat of the slave being shaved by the barber was cut by the razor, whoever of them was negligent will be held under the *Lex Aquilia*. Proculus holds that the barber was at fault; and truly, if he was doing business near a place usually devoted to sport or where there was heavy traffic, he is partly responsible; but there is much to be said for the view that he who engages as a barber one who has set up his stool in a dangerous place has only himself to blame.

1. If one holds a slave and another kills him, the former is liable *in factum* for having furnished the cause of death.

2. But if several strike a slave, let us consider whether all are held for killing. If it can be shown who gave the mortal wound, he will be liable for killing; if not, Julian says that all are liable for killing; and if one has been sued, the others are not released, for what one pays under the *Lex Aquilia* does not relieve another, as a penalty is involved.

3. Celsus writes that if one gives a slave a mortal wound and another later kills him, the former will not be held for killing but for wounding, since the slave died from another wound; the latter will be held for killing; Marcellus agrees and it is the better view.

4. For the same reason if several let fall a beam and crush a slave, the ancients held that they were all liable under the Aquilian statute.

5. Proculus also gave an opinion that the Aquilian action lies against one who, even though he was not holding his dog, angered it, causing it to bite another; but Julian says that he would be liable under this statute only if he was holding the dog when he caused it to bite another; otherwise, that is, if he was not holding it, an action *in factum* lies.

6. The right to bring the Aquilian action belongs to the *erus*, that is, the owner.

7. If wrongful damage is done to the slave which I am about to "redhibit" to you, Julian says that I acquire the Aquilian action, but I must cede it to you when I attempt to "redhibit" the slave.

8. If a slave is in the power of a *bona fide* possessor, will the latter be able to exercise the Aquilian action? He ought rather to be granted an action *in factum*.

commodata sunt, non posse, si scissa fuerint, lege Aquilia agere Iulianus ait, sed domino eam competere. 10. An fructuarius vel usuarius legis Aquiliae actionem haberet, Iulianus tractat: et ego puto melius utile iudicium ex hac causa dandum.

12. PAULUS *libro decimo ad Sabinum* Sed et si proprietatis dominus vulneraverit servum vel occiderit, in quo usus fructus meus est, danda est mihi ad exemplum legis Aquiliae actio in eum pro portione usus fructus, ut etiam ea pars anni in aestimationem veniat, qua nondum usus fructus meus fuit.

13. ULPIANUS *libro octavo decimo ad edictum* Liber homo suo nomine utilem Aquiliae habet actionem: directam enim non habet, quoniam dominus membrorum suorum nemo videtur. fugitivi autem nomine dominus habet. 1. Iulianus scribit, si homo liber bona fide mihi serviat, ipsum lege Aquilia mihi teneri. 2. Si servus hereditarius occidatur, quaeritur, quis Aquilia agat, cum dominus nullus sit huius servi. et ait Celsus legem domino damna salva esse voluisse: dominus ergo hereditas habebitur. quare adita hereditate heres poterit experiri. 3. Si servus legatus post aditam hereditatem sit occisus, competere legis Aquiliae actionem legatario, si non post mortem servi adgnovit legatum: quod si repudiavit, consequens esse ait Iulianus dicere, heredi competere.

14. PAULUS *libro vicensimo secundo ad edictum* Sed si ipse heres eum occiderit, dictum est dandam in eum legatario actionem.

15. ULPIANUS *libro octavo decimo ad edictum* Huic scripturae consequens est dicere, ut, si ante aditam hereditatem occidatur legatus servus, apud heredem remaneat Aquiliae actio per hereditatem adquisita. quod si vulneratus sit ante aditam hereditatem, in hereditate quidem actio remansit, sed cedere ea legatario heredem oportet. 1. Si servus vulneratus mortifere postea ruina vel naufragio vel alio ictu maturius perierit, de occiso agi non posse, sed quasi de vulnerato, sed si manumissus vel alienatus ex vulnere periit, quasi de occiso

9. Julian says that one to whom clothes have been lent cannot bring the Aquilian action if they are torn, but the owner may do so.

10. Julian deals with the problem whether the usufructuary or the usuary may bring the action; I consider that an *actio utilis* had better be granted in these circumstances.

12. If the owner of the property wounds or kills a slave in whom I have the usufruct, I should be given an action against him on the analogy of the *Lex Aquilia* for the proportion of my usufruct, so that the part of the year even before the creation of my usufruct will be reckoned in assessing the damage.

13. A freeman has a "*utilis*" Aquilian action on his own account, he has not the direct action because no one can be held to be owner of his own limbs. The owner has an action on account of a fugitive slave.

1. Julian writes that if a freeman in good faith acts as my slave, he is liable to me under the *Lex Aquilia*.

2. If the slave of an unclaimed inheritance is killed, it is a question who may bring the Aquilian action since the slave has no owner. Celsus says that the statute intended to indemnify the owner, therefore the inheritance will be considered the owner; hence the heir may sue after entry upon the inheritance.

3. If a slave left as a legacy is killed after the inheritance has been entered upon, the legatee may bring the Aquilian action, if he did not accept the legacy after the slave's death; but if he refused it, Julian holds that the result will be that the action belongs to the heir.

14. Moreover, if the heir himself kills the slave, it must be held that the legatee has an action.

15. From Julian's view it would follow that if the bequeathed slave is killed before entry is made upon the inheritance the Aquilian action acquired by the inheritance remains with the heir, but if the slave is wounded under these circumstances, the action remains with the inheritance, but the heir should cede it to the legatee.

1. If a slave is mortally wounded, but his death is accelerated by the fall of a house, a shipwreck, or another blow, an action cannot be brought for killing, but for wounding; but if he dies from the wound after he has been manumitted or

agi posse Iulianus ait. haec ita tam varie, quia verum est eum a te occisum tunc cum vulnerabas, quod mortuo eo demum apparuit: at in superiore non est passa ruina apparere, an sit occisus. sed si vulneratum mortifere liberum et heredem esse iusseris, deinde decesserit, heredem eius agere Aquilia non posse,

16. MARCIANUS *libro quarto regularum* quia in eum casum res pervenit, a quo incipere non potest.

17. ULPIANUS *libro octavo decimo ad edictum* Si dominus servum suum occiderit, bonae fidei possessori vel ei qui pignori accepit in factum actione tenebitur.

18. PAULUS *libro decimo ad Sabinum* Sed et si is qui pignori servum accepit occidit eum vel vulneravit, lege Aquilia et pigneraticia conveniri potest, sed alterutra contentus esse debebit actor.

19. ULPIANUS *libro octavo decimo ad edictum* Sed si communem servum occiderit quis, Aquilia teneri eum Celsus ait: idem est et si vulneraverit:

20. IDEM *libro quadragensimo secundo ad Sabinum* scilicet pro ea parte, pro qua dominus est qui agat.

21. IDEM *libro octavo decimo ad edictum* Ait lex: 'quanti is homo in eo anno plurimi fuisset.' quae clausula aestimationem habet damni, quod datum est. 1. Annus autem retrosus computatur, ex quo quis occisus est: quod si mortifere fuerit vulneratus et postea post longum intervallum mortuus sit, inde annum numerabimus secundum Iulianum, ex quo vulneratus est, licet Celsus contra scribit. 2. Sed utrum corpus eius solum aestimamus, quanti fuerit cum occideretur, an potius quanti interfuit nostra non esse occisum? et hoc iure utimur, ut eius quod interest fiat aestimatio.

22. PAULUS *libro vicensimo secundo ad edictum* Proinde si servum occidisti, quem sub poena tradendum promisi, utilitas venit in hoc iudicium. 1. Item causae corpori cohaerentes aestimantur, si quis ex comoedis aut symphoniacis aut gemellis aut quadriga aut ex pari mularum unum vel unam occiderit: non solum enim perempti corporis aestimatio facienda

alienated Julian says that an action may be brought for killing. The difference follows from the fact that you killed him at the time when you gave him the wound, although this was not proved till he died; but in the former case the accident did not allow it to be proven whether you killed him. If you order a mortally wounded slave to be free and heir and he dies after you, his heir cannot bring the Aquilian action,

16. because in that case the affair has reached a point where an action could not have arisen.

17. If the owner kills his slave, he will be liable in an action *in factum* to a *bona fide* possessor or pledgee.

18. If the pledgee kills or wounds the slave, he can be sued in the Aquilian action and that upon pledge, but the plaintiff must be content with either action.

19. If one kills a slave owned in common, Celsus says that he is liable under this statute, which is equally true if he wounds him,

20. that is, for the value of the share which belongs to the plaintiff.

21. The statute says: "Whatever was the highest value of the slave during that year," which clause gives the rule for the valuation of the damage committed.

1. The year is reckoned backwards from the time of killing, but if he was mortally wounded and died only after a long interval, according to Julian we shall compute the year from the date of the wound, although Celsus is of the contrary opinion.

2. But do we merely assess the value of the slave as it was when he was killed, or rather consider the interest of the plaintiff in his not being killed? And our practice is to estimate the plaintiff's interest.

22. Thus if you have killed a slave whom I have promised to deliver under a penalty, my interest therein will be considered in the judgment.

1. Elements of value inherent in the object are considered, as where one kills a member, male or female, of a band of actors or singers, of twins, a chariot team, or a pair of mules; for the valuation should be made not only of the object de-

est, sed et eius ratio haberi debet, quo cetera corpora depretiata sunt.

23. Ulpianus *libro octavo decimo ad edictum* Inde Neratius scribit, si servus heres institutus occisus sit, etiam hereditatis aestimationem venire. 1. Iulianus ait, si servus liber et heres esse iussus occisus fuerit, neque substitutum neque legitimum actione legis Aquiliae hereditatis aestimationem consecuturum, quae servo competere non potuit: quae sententia vera est. pretii igitur solummodo fieri aestimationem, quia hoc interesse solum substituti videretur: ego autem puto nec pretii fieri aestimationem, quia, si heres esset, et liber esset. 2. Idem Iulianus scribit, si institutus fuero sub condicione 'si Stichum manumisero' et Stichus sit occisus post mortem testatoris, in aestimationem etiam hereditatis pretium me consecuturum: propter occisionem enim defecit condicio: quod si vivo testatore occisus sit, hereditatis aestimationem cessare, quia retrorsum quanti plurimi fuit inspicitur. 3. Idem Iulianus scribit aestimationem hominis occisi ad id tempus referri, quo plurimi in eo anno fuit: et ideo et si pretioso pictori pollex fuerit praecisus et intra annum, quo praecideretur, fuerit occisus, posse eum Aquilia agere pretioque eo aestimandum, quanti fuit priusquam artem cum pollice amisisset. 4. Sed et si servus, qui magnas fraudes in meis rationibus commiserat, fuerit occisus, de quo quaestionem habere destinaveram, ut fraudium participes eruerentur, rectissime Labeo scribit tanti aestimandum, quanti mea intererat fraudes servi per eum commissas detegi, non quanti noxa eius servi valeat. 5. Sed et si bonae frugi servus intra annum mutatis moribus occisus sit, pretium id aestimabitur, quanto valeret, priusquam mores mutaret. 6. In summa omnia commoda, quae intra annum, quo interfectus est, pretiosiorem servum facerent, haec accedere ad aestimationem eius dicendum est. 7. Si infans sit occisus nondum anniculus, verius est sufficere hanc actionem, ut aestimatio referatur ad id tempus, quo intra annum vixit. 8. Hanc actionem et heredi ceterisque successoribus dari constat: sed in heredem vel ceteros haec

stroyed, but account must also be taken of the amount by which the value of the other members is depreciated.

23. On this subject Neratius writes that if a slave, instituted as heir, is killed, the value of the inheritance will come into account.

1. Julian says if a slave is killed who was ordered to be free and heir, neither the substituted nor the legitimate heir in the Aquilian action may recover the value of the inheritance, which would not have been permitted to the slave; which opinion is correct; and therefore he says that only the market value of the slave will be computed, because the substitute seems to have no other interest; but I do not think that even the market value will be estimated, because if the slave had been heir he would also have been free.

2. Julian also writes that if I am instituted heir on condition that I manumit Stichus, and Stichus is killed after the death of the testator, I may even recover as damages the value of the inheritance, for by the killing fulfillment of the condition became impossible; but if the slave was killed in the lifetime of the testator, the value of the inheritance will not be allowed, because the highest value is judged retrospectively.

3. Continuing, Julian writes that the value of the slave who was killed is decided as of the time in the past year when it was the highest; hence if the thumb of a very valuable painter is cut off and within a year from that time he is killed, when the Aquilian action is brought his value will be judged as of the date before he lost his thumb and his skill.

4. But if my slave is killed who had committed great frauds in connection with my property, and whom I was about to put to torture in order to discover his accomplices, Labeo well says that my damages will include the interest that I had in discovering the frauds that he had committed, and not merely the value of harm that he had done.

5. If a thoroughly worthy slave whose habits have changed within the year is killed, his value will be judged as it was before the change of character.

6. In short, all the advantages which may have increased the value of the slave within a year from the time he is killed must be held to be added to the damages.

7. If a child under a year old is killed, the better view is that this action will suffice to permit the value to be judged with reference to the part of the year when he lived.

8. It is settled that the action belongs to the heir and other

actio non dabitur, cum sit poenalis, nisi forte ex damno locupletior heres factus sit. 9. Si dolo servus occisus sit, et lege Cornelia agere dominum posse constat: et si lege Aquilia egerit, praeiudicium fieri Corneliae non debet. 10. Haec actio adversus confitentem competit in simplum, adversus negantem in duplum. 11. Si quis hominem vivum falso confiteatur occidisse et postea paratus sit ostendere hominem vivum esse, Iulianus scribit cessare Aquiliam, quamvis confessus sit se occidisse: hoc enim solum remittere actori confessoriam actionem, ne necesse habeat docere eum occidisse: ceterum occisum esse hominem a quocumque oportet.

24. PAULUS *libro vicensimo secundo ad edictum* Hoc apertius est circa vulneratum hominem: nam si confessus sit vulnerasse nec sit vulneratus, aestimationem cuius vulneris faciemus? vel ad quod tempus recurramus?

25. ULPIANUS *libro octavo decimo ad edictum* Proinde si occisus quidem non sit, mortuus autem sit, magis est, ut non teneatur in mortuo, licet fassus sit. 1. Si procurator aut tutor aut curator aut quivis alius confiteatur aut absentem vulnerasse, confessoria in eos utilis actio danda est. 2. Notandum, quod in hac actione, quae adversus confitentem datur, iudex non rei iudicandae, sed aestimandae datur: nam nullae partes sunt iudicandi in confitentes.

26. PAULUS *libro vicensimo secundo ad edictum* Puta enim, quod qui convenitur fateatur se occidisse et paratus sit aestimationem solvere, et adversarius magni litem aestimat.

27. ULPIANUS *libro octavo decimo ad edictum* Si servus servum alienum subripuerit et occiderit, et Iulianus et Celsus scribunt et furti et damni iniuriae competere actionem. 1. Si servus communis, id est meus et tuus, servum meum occiderit, legi Aquiliae locus est adversus te, si tua voluntate fecit: et ita Proculum existimasse Urseius refert. quod si non voluntate tua fecit, cessare noxalem actionem, ne sit in potestate servi, ut tibi soli serviat: quod puto verum esse. 2. Item si

successors in title, but the action is not allowed against the heir or successors, as it is penal, unless it happens that the heir is enriched by the damage.

9. If a slave is killed maliciously, it is obvious that the owner may also prosecute under the Lex Cornelia, and if he has brought the Aquilian action, the decision should be postponed until after that in the criminal cause.

10. Our action is for ordinary damages against one who confesses, for double if one deny.

11. If one falsely confesses to killing a living slave and later attempts to prove that he is alive, Julian writes that the Aquilian action fails, although he confessed to the killing; for the action upon a confession relieves the plaintiff only of the burden of proving that the defendant killed the slave, nevertheless the slave must have been killed by someone.

24. This is clearer in an action for wounding a slave, for if one confess that he did the wounding and the slave is not wounded, for what kind of a wound shall we compute the damages, or to what date shall we reckon back?

25. Thus if the slave was not killed yet is dead, the better opinion is that one is not liable for the dead slave even though one may have confessed.

1. If an agent, a tutor, a curator, or anybody else confesses that the absent defendant did the wounding, an *actio utilis* should be permitted against those who confessed.

2. It should be noted that in this action against the confessor, the judge is appointed not to decide the liability but to assess the damages, none of the elements of a law suit are present when one confesses.

26. For suppose that the defendant confesses to the killing and is ready to pay the damages, but his adversary claims an excessive amount.

27. If a slave carries away and kills another slave, Julian and Celsus write that the actions for theft and wrongful damage are available.

1. If a common slave, that is, of you and me, kills my slave, I have an Aquilian action against you if he did it with your consent; which Urseius declares to have been the view of Proculus. He adds that if it was without your consent there is no noxal action lest it should be in the power of the slave to serve you alone; to which I agree.

servus communis meus et tuus sit occisus a servo Titii, Celsus scribit alterum ex dominis agentem aut litis aestimationem consecuturum pro parte aut noxae dedi ei in solidum oportere, quia haec res divisionem non recipit. 3. Servi autem occidentis nomine dominus tenetur, is vero cui bona fide servit non tenetur. sed an is, qui servum in fuga habet, teneatur nomine eius Aquiliae actione, quaeritur: et ait Iulianus teneri et est verissimum: cum et Marcellus consentit. 4. Huius legis secundum quidem capitulum in desuetudinem abiit. 5. Tertio autem capite ait eadem lex Aquilia: 'Ceterarum rerum praeter hominem et pecudem occisos si quis alteri damnum faxit, quod usserit fregerit ruperit iniuria, quanti ea res erit in diebus triginta proximus, tantum aes domino dare damnas esto.' 6. Si quis igitur non occiderit hominem vel pecudem, sed usserit fregerit ruperit, sine dubio ex his verbis legis agendum erit. proinde si facem servo meo obieceris et eum adusseris, teneberis mihi. 7. Item si arbustum meum vel villam meam incenderis, Aquiliae actionem habebo. 8. Si quis insulam voluerit meam exurere et ignis etiam ad vicini insulam pervenerit, Aquilia tenebitur etiam vicino: non minus etiam inquilinis tenebitur ob res eorum exustas. 9. Si fornicarius servus coloni ad fornacem obdormisset et villa fuerit exusta, Neratius scribit ex locato conventum praestare debere, si neglegens in eligendis ministeriis fuit: ceterum si alius ignem subiecerit fornaci, alius neglegenter custodierit, an tenebitur qui subiecerit? nam qui custodit, nihil fecit, qui recte ignem subiecit, non peccavit: quid ergo est? puto utilem competere actionem tam in eum qui ad fornacem obdormivit quam in eum qui neglegenter custodit, nec quisquam dixerit in eo qui obdormivit, rem eum humanam et naturalem passum, cum deberet vel ignem extinguere vel ita munire, ne evagetur. 10. Si furnum secundum parietem communem haberes, an damni iniuria tenearis? et ait Proculus agi non posse, quia nec cum eo qui focum haberet: et ideo aequius puto in fac-

2. Again if a slave owned by you and me in common is killed by a slave of Titius, Celsus writes that if either owner sues he ought to obtain the value of his share or else noxal surrender of the whole, because the latter expedient is not divisible.

3. The owner is held if a slave kills, but not the *bona fide* possessor. It is a question whether the owner is liable to the Aquilian action on account of a fugitive slave. Julian holds that he is, which is perfectly true, since even Marcellus agrees.

4. The second chapter of this statute has become obsolete.

5. In the third chapter the *Lex Aquilia* reads: Regarding all other things except slaves or cattle killed, if anyone does damage to another, by wrongfully burning, breaking, or injuring, whatever was the value thereof within the last thirty days, so much let him be condemned to pay to the owner.

6. If, therefore, one has not killed but has burnt, broken, or injured a slave or a quadruped, it is certain that an action may be brought under these terms of the statute. So if you throw a torch at my slave and scorch him, you will be liable to me.

7. Thus if you set fire to my woods or my country house I shall have the Aquilian action.

8. If one intended to burn my tenement and the fire spreads to that of a neighbor, the latter will also have the Aquilian action, as well as the tenants on account of any of their movables that have been destroyed.

9. If the tenant's slave is detailed to look after a furnace but goes to sleep and the house burns down, Neratius writes that the tenant is liable for damages under the contract, providing he was negligent in choosing his laborers; however, if one lights a fire in a furnace, and another negligently watches it, will the former be held? for he who watched it did nothing, and he who correctly lit the fire was not at fault. What is the conclusion? I should say that there is an *actio utilis* both against him who went to sleep at the furnace and him who carelessly watched the fire; nor can anyone claim as to the former that he underwent a natural experience common to all mankind, because his duty was either to extinguish the fire or prevent it from escaping.

10. If you have an oven against a wall held in common with your neighbor, will you be liable for wrongful damage? And Proculus says there can be no action, as there would be none against one who had a fireplace; yet I consider it more equitable to allow an action *in factum* that is, if the wall is

tum actionem dandam, scilicet si paries exustus sit: sin autem nondum mihi damnum dederis, sed ita ignem habeas, ut metuam, ne mihi damnum des, damni infecti puto sufficere cautionem. 11. Proculus ait, cum coloni servi villam exussissent, colonum vel ex locato vel lege Aquilia teneri, ita ut colonus possit servos noxae dedere, et si uno iudicio res esset iudicata, altero amplius non agendum. sed haec ita, si culpa colonus careret: ceterum si noxios servos habuit, damni eum iniuria teneri, cur tales habuit. idem servandum et circa inquilinolegis Aqulae personas scribit: quae sententia habet rationem. 12. Si, cum apes meae ad tuas advolassent, tu eas exusseris, legis Aquiliae actionem competere Celsus ait. 13. Inquit lex 'ruperit.' rupisse verbum fere omnes veteres sic intellexerunt 'corruperit.' 14. Et ideo Celsus quaerit, si lolium aut avenam in segetem alienam inieceris, quo eam tu inquinares, non solum quod vi aut clam dominum posse agere vel, si locatus fundus sit, colonum, sed et in factum agendum, et si colonus eam exercuit, cavere eum debere amplius non agi, scilicet ne dominus amplius inquietet: nam alia quaedam species damni est ipsum quid corrumpere et mutare, ut lex Aquilia locum habeat, alia nulla ipsius mutatione applicare aliud, cuius molesta separatio sit. 15. Cum eo plane, qui vinum spurcavit vel effudit vel acetum fecit vel alio modo vitiavit, agi posse Aquilia Celsus ait, quia etiam effusum et acetum factum corrupti appellatione continentur. 16. Et non negat fractum et ustum contineri corrupti appellatione, sed non esse novum, ut lex specialiter quibusdam enumeratis generale subiciat verbum, quo specialia complectatur: quae sententia vera est. 17. Rupisse eum utique accipiemus, qui vulneraverit, vel virgis vel loris vel pugnis cecidit, vel telo vel quo alio, ut scinderet alicui corpus, vel tumorem fecerit, sed ita demum, si damnum iniuria datum est: ceterum si nullo servum pretio viliorem deterioremve fecerit, Aquilia cessat iniuriarumque erit agendum dumtaxat: Aquilia enim eas ruptiones, quae

burnt down; but if you have not yet injured me, but use your fire in a manner which makes me apprehensive of damage, I think the security against threatened damage will suffice.

11. Proculus says that if the slaves of a tenant have burnt down the house the tenant is held either on the contract or under the *Lex Aquilia*, with the privilege of noxal surrender, and if one action has become *res judicata*, the other may no longer be brought. This is upon the assumption that the tenant was not at fault; if he employed obviously irresponsible slaves, he ought to be held for so doing in a direct action for wrongful damage. He observes that the same is true for persons working for the tenant of an apartment, which opinion is sound.

12. If you burn my bees which have flown over to join yours, Celsus says that the Aquilian action lies.

13. The statute says "*ruperit.*" Almost all the ancients take this to mean "*corruperit*" (spoils).

14. So Celsus decides that, if you scatter weeds or wild oats into another's cornfield, so that the crop is spoiled, the owner may bring not only the interdict *quod vi aut clam*, and the tenant, if the field is rented, but also the action *in factum;* and if the tenant brings the proceeding, he must give security against a repetition of the suit, that is, lest the owner also recover; for it is one kind of damage to spoil or alter the object so that the *Lex Aquilia* will apply, but another where there is no alteration, but something is inserted which makes separation difficult.

15. Celsus says that the Aquilian action clearly lies against one who contaminates wine, or pours it away, or turns it into vinegar or spoils in any other way, because pouring off or turning sour are included in the term "*corrumpere*" (spoil).

16. And he admits that burning and breaking are included in this term, but he adds that it is nothing new that a statute, after enumerating some special cases should append a general word including the cases already provided for, which opinion is correct.

17. We shall all agree that "*rumpere*" includes wounding or striking a slave, with a switch, a whip, the fists, a weapon, or anything else, so as to break the skin or make a bruise, but this is providing that pecuniary damage follows the wrong, for if the slave has not depreciated either in value or usefulness, the *Lex Aquilia* does not apply, though there may be an action for insult; this statute dealing only with cases of spoil-

damna dant, persequitur. ergo etsi pretio quidem non sit deterior servus factus, verum sumptus in salutem eius et sanitatem facti sunt, in haec mihi videri damnum datum: atque ideoque lege Aquilia agi posse. 18. Si quis vestimenta sciderit vel inquinaverit, Aquilia quasi ruperit tenetur. 19. Sed et si quis milium vel frumentum meum effuderit in flumen, sufficit Aquiliae actio. 20. Item si quis frumento harenam vel aliud quid immiscuit, ut difficilis separatio sit, quasi de corrupto agi poterit. 21. Si quis de manu mihi nummos excusserit, Sabinus existimat damni iniuriae esse actionem, si ita perierint, ne ad aliquem pervenirent, puta si in flumen vel in mare vel in cloacam ceciderunt: quod si ad aliquem pervenerunt, ope consilio furtum factum agendum, quod et antiquis placuit. idem etiam in factum dari posse actionem ait. 22. Si mulier pugno vel equa ictu a te percussa eiecerit, Brutus ait Aquilia teneri quasi rupto. 23. Et si mulum plus iusto oneraverit et aliquid membri ruperit, Aquiliae locum fore. 24. Si navem venaliciarum mercium perforasset, Aquiliae actionem esse, quasi ruperit, Vivianus scribit. 25. Si olivam inmaturam decerpserit vel segetem desecuerit inmaturam vel vineas crudas, Aquilia tenebitur: quod si iam maturas, cessat Aquilia: nulla enim iniuria est, cum tibi etiam impensas donaverit, quae in collectionem huiusmodi fructuum impenduntur: sed si collecta haec interceperit, furti tenetur. Octavenus in uvis adicit, nisi, inquit, in terram uvas proiecit, ut effunderentur. 26. Idem et in silva caedua scribit, ut, si immatura Aquilia teneatur, quod si matura interceperit, furti teneri eum et arborum furtim caesarum. 27. Si salictum maturum ita, ne stirpes laederes, tuleris, cessare Aquiliam. 28. Et si puerum quis castraverit et pretiosiorem fecerit, Vivianus scribit cessare Aquiliam, sed iniuriarum erit agendum aut ex edicto aedilium aut in quadruplum. 29. Si calicem diatretum faciendum dedisti, si quidem imperitia fregit, damni iniuria tenebitur: si vero non imperitia fregit, sed rimas habebat vi-

ing which cause some loss. Therefore even if the value of the slave is not reduced but expenses are incurred in curing or caring for him, these seem to me a loss, hence the Aquilian action may be brought.

18. If one tears or spots another's clothes, he is liable on the ground of "*ruptio*" (spoiling).

19. If one throws my corn or millet into the river, the Aquilian action is available.

20. So if one mixes sand or anything else with grain so that it is hard to separate them, an action will lie, as it were, for spoiling.

21. If one knocks coins out of my hands, Sabinus thinks that the direct action lies if they are lost so that nobody else has obtained them as where they fall into a river, the sea, or a sewer, but if another has obtained them, an action lies for aiding and abetting a theft, as the ancients held. He adds that the action *in factum* may be brought.

22. If a slave woman or a mare has had a miscarriage caused by your blow, Brutus says you will be liable to an Aquilian action for "*rumpere*."

23. If one overloads a mule and breaks one of its limbs, this statute applies.

24. One who scuttles a trading vessel is liable to an Aquilian action for "*rumpere*," as Vivianus writes.

25. If one picks unripe olives, or cuts corn or grapes prematurely, he is liable under this law; but if they are ripe, the Aquilian action does not lie, for there is no injury, since he has presented you with the expenses which are involved in gathering such a crop; if he removes them after they are gathered, he is liable for theft. As for the grapes, Octavenus adds the proviso that they must not be thrown upon the ground so that they burst.

26. Vivianus says the same about a thicket; if the twigs are not ready for cutting the Aquilian action lies, but if they are taken when ripe the actions for theft and secretly cutting down trees are applicable.

27. If you cut pollard willows without injuring the trunk, there is no Aquilian action.

28. If one castrates a slave boy, thus increasing his value, Vivianus holds that this statute does not apply, but one should bring the action for insult, or that on the edict of the aediles, or the one for quadruple the value.

29. If you give a cup to a jeweller to be filigreed and he breaks it through lack of skill, he is liable for wrongful dam-

tiosas, potest esse excusatus: et ideo plerumque artifices convenire solent, cum eiusmodi materiae dantur, non periculo suo se facere, quae res ex locato tollit actionem et Aquiliae. 30. Si cum maritus uxori margaritas extricatas dedisset in usu eaque invito vel inscio viro perforasset, ut pertusis in linea uteretur, teneri eam lege Aquilia, sive divertit sive nupta est adhuc. 31. Si quis aedificii mei fores confregerit vel refregerit aut si ipsum aedificium diruit, lege Aquilia tenetur. 32. Si quis aquae ductum meum diruerit, licet cementa mea sunt, quae diruta sunt, tamen quia terra mea non sit, qua aquam duco, melius est dicere actionem utilem dandam. 33. Si ex plostro lapis ceciderit et quid ruperit vel fregerit, Aquiliae actione plostrarium teneri placet, si male composuit lapides et ideo lapsi sunt. 34. Si quis servum conductum ad mulum regendum commendaverit ei, mulum ille ad pollicem suum eum alligaverit de loro et mulus eruperit sic, ut et pollicem avelleret servo et se praecipitaret, Mela scribit, si pro perito imperitus locatus sit, ex conducto agendum cum domino ob mulum ruptum vel debilitatum, sed si ictu aut terrore mulus turbatus sit, tum dominum eius, id est muli, et servi cum eo qui turbavit habiturum legis Aquiliae actionem. mihi autem videtur et eo casu, quo ex locato actio est, competere etiam Aquiliae. 35. Item si tectori locaveris laccum vino plenum curandum et ille eum pertudit, ut vinum sit effusum, Labeo scribit in factum agendum.

28. Paulus *libro decimo ad Sabinum* Qui foveas ursorum cervorumque capiendorum causa faciunt, si in itineribus fecerunt eoque aliquid decidit factumque deterius est, lege Aquilia obligati sunt: at si in aliis locis, ubi fieri solent, fecerunt, nihil tenentur. 1. Haec tamen actio ex causa danda est, id est si neque denuntiatum est neque scierit aut providere potuerit: et multa huiusmodi deprehenduntur, quibus summovetur petitor, si evitare periculum poterit:

age; but if he breaks it not from lack of skill but because it was badly cracked, he may have a defense. Hence most artisans who receive things of this kind stipulate that they will not do the task at their risk, which prevents either an action on the contract or under this statute.

30. If a husband gives his wife unset pearls to use and she, without the knowledge or consent of her husband, perforates them in order to string them and wear them, she is liable under the *Lex Aquilia*, whether divorced or not when the action is brought.

31. If one breaks or shatters the doors of my house or destroys the house itself he is held by this statute.

32. If one tears up my aqueduct, although the materials are mine, nevertheless, since I do not own the land through which I bring the water, it is more correct to grant an *actio utilis*.

33. If a stone falls off a cart and bursts or breaks anything, the carter should be liable to an Aquilian action if the stones fell because he had piled them badly.

34. If one who has hired a slave to drive a mule entrusts him with the mule, and the slave ties the mule to his thumb by its halter, and the mule breaks away, tearing off the slave's thumb, and dashes itself over a cliff; here Mela says, if an unskilful slave was let out as an experienced driver, an action on the contract lies for the mule which was destroyed or injured against the owner of the slave; but if the mule was disturbed, by a blow or by terror, then his, that is the mule's, owner, as well as the owner of the slave, may bring the Aquilian action against the man who disturbed the mule. In the case where the action on the contract was permitted I should say that the Aquilian action also applied.

35. Likewise if you hire a plasterer to repair a cistern full of wine and he makes a hole in it so that the wine escapes, Labeo says that an action *in factum* must be allowed.

28. Those who make pits to catch bears or deer are liable to an Aquilian action if they dig them on pathways and anything falls in and is injured; but if they make them in other places, where this is customary, they are not held.

1. Nevertheless this action will be allowed only for cause shown, as where there was no warning and the plaintiff ignored and could not foresee the danger; for there are many examples of such cases to be found where the plaintiff is refused relief if he could have avoided the danger,

29. Ulpianus *libro octavo decimo ad edictum* quemadmodum si laqueos eo loci posuisses, quo ius ponendi non haberes, et pecus vicini in eos laqueos incidisset. 1. Si protectum meum, quod supra domum tuam nullo iure habebam, reccidisses, posse me tecum damni iniuria agere Proculus scribit: debuisti enim mecum ius mihi non esse protectum habere agere: nec esse aequum damnum me pati reccisis a te meis tignis. aliud est dicendum ex rescripto imperatoris Severi, qui ei, per cuius domum traiectus erat aquae ductus citra servitutem, rescripsit iure suo posse eum intercidere, et merito, interest enim, quod hic in suo protexit, ille in alieno fecit. 2. Si navis tua inpacta in meam scapham damnum mihi dedit, quaesitum est, quae actio mihi competeret. et ait Proculus, si in potestate nautarum fuit, ne id accideret, et culpa eorum factum sit, lege Aquilia cum nautis agendum, quia parvi refert navem immittendo aut serraculum ad navem ducendo an tua manu damnum dederis, quia omnibus his modis per te damno adficior: sed si fune rupto aut cum a nullo regeretur navis incurrisset, cum domino agendum non esse. 3. Item Labeo scribit, si, cum vi ventorum navis impulsa esset in funes anchorarum alterius et nautae funes praecidissent, si nullo alio modo nisi praecisis funibus explicare se potuit, nullam actionem dandam. idemque Labeo et Proculus et circa retia piscatorum, in quae navis piscatorum inciderat, aestimarunt. plane si culpa nautarum id factum esset, lege Aquilia agendum. sed ubi damni iniuria agitur ob retia, non piscium, qui ideo capti non sunt, fieri aestimationem, cum incertum fuerit, an caperentur. idemque et in venatoribus et in aucupibus probandum. 4. Si navis alteram contra se venientem obruisset, aut in gubernatorem aut in ducatorem actionem competere damni iniuriae Alfenus ait: sed si tanta vis navi facta sit, quae temperari non potuit, nullam in dominum dandam actionem: sin autem culpa nautarum id factum sit, puto Aquiliae sufficere. 5. Si funem quis, quo religata navis erat,

29. as where you put traps in a place where you had no right to do so and a neighbor's cattle are thereby caught.

1. If you cut off part of my roof which extends without right over your land, Proculus writes that I can bring the Aquilian action against you; for you ought to have litigated with me the question of the right of projection; and it is inequitable that I should have to endure your cutting off my beams. A rescript of the Emperor Serverus gives a different decision: in a case where a water pipe was laid over another's land without a servitude, he responded that it could be rightfully interrupted; which is correct, the difference being that the former plaintiff built on his own land, the latter on another's.

2. If your ship collides with my rowboat and causes me damage, it is a question what action I have. Proculus says that if it was in the power of the sailors to avoid the collision which occurred through their negligence, the Aquilian action may be brought against the sailors, for it makes little difference whether you do the damage by intentionally directing your ship at the boat, or by negligent manipulation of the rudder, or with your own hands, since in all these cases I suffer damage directly caused by you; but if a rope broke, or the ship collided when it was under nobody's control, there is no action against the owner.

3. Labeo likewise writes that if a ship is driven by the force of the wind against the anchor-ropes of another, and the sailors cut the ropes because they could disentangle themselves in no other manner than by so doing, no action will be allowed. Labeo and Proculus give the same opinion regarding fishermen's nets in which another's fishing vessel had become caught. Clearly the Aquilian action will lie if the sailors have done this culpably. But where the action is brought for wrongful damage to nets, there is no valuation of the fish which have not been caught in consequence of the injury, because it is uncertain whether they would have been caught, and the same should be said of hunters or fowlers.

4. If one ship sinks another coming in the opposite direction, Alfenus says that there will be an action for wrongful damage either against the steersman or the captain, but if the ship was being impelled with such force that control was impossible, no action lies against the owner; if however, the event was due to the fault of the sailors, I should say that the Aquilian action was available.

praeciderit, de nave quae periit in factum agendum. 6. Hac actione ex hoc legis capite de omnibus animalibus laesis, quae pecudes non sunt, agendum est, ut puta de cane: sed et de apro et leone ceterisque feris et avibus idem erit dicendum. 7. Magistratus municipales, si damnum iniuria dederint, posse Aquilia teneri. nam et cum pecudes aliquis pignori cepisset et fame eas necavisset, dum non patitur te eis cibaria adferre, in factum actio danda est. item si dum putat se ex lege capere pignus, non ex lege ceperit et res tritas corruptasque reddat, dicitur legem Aquiliam locum habere: quod dicendum est et si ex lege pignus cepit. si quid tamen magistratus adversus resistentem violentius fecerit, non tenebitur Aquilia: nam et cum pignori servum cepisset et ille se suspenderit, nulla datur actio. 8. Haec verba: 'quanti in triginta diebus proximis fuit,' etsi non habent 'plurimi,' sic tamen esse accipienda constat.

30. PAULUS *libro vicensimo secundo ad edictum* Qui occidit adulterum deprehensum servum alienum, hac lege non tenebitur. 1. Pignori datus servus si occisus sit, debitori actio competit. sed an et creditori danda sit utilis, quia potest interesse eius, quod debitor solvendo non sit aut quod litem tempore amisit, quaeritur. sed hic iniquum est et domino et creditori eum teneri. nisi si quis putaverit nullam in ea re debitorem iniuriam passurum, cum prosit ei ad debiti quantitatem, et quod sit amplius consecuturus sit ab eo, vel ab initio in id, quod amplius sit quam in debito, debitori dandam actionem: et ideo in his casibus, in quibus creditori danda est actio propter inopiam debitoris vel quod litem amisit, creditor quidem usque ad modum debiti habebit Aquiliae actionem, ut prosit hoc debitori, ipsi autem debitori in id quod debitum excedit competit Aquiliae actio. 2. Si quis alienum vinum vel frumentum consumpserit, non videtur damnum iniuria dare

5. If one cuts the rope by which a ship is moored, an action *in factum* may be brought if the ship is destroyed.

6. The action based on this chapter of the law may be brought for injury to all animals except "cattle," for instance a dog, but the same is true of boars, lions, or other wild birds and beasts

7. Municipal magistrates may be held to an Aquilian action if they do wrongful damage. Also an action *in factum* will be allowed, where such a person levies upon cattle and kills them by starvation, refusing to let the owner feed them. Likewise when the official thinks that he is lawfully levying execution, but it is unlawful, and he returns the goods in a worn or spoiled condition, it is held that the Aquilian action is applicable; and the same must be said even if the execution is legal. But if a magistrate is guilty of a slight excess of violence towards one who resists, he will not be liable to an Aquilian action; for even when a slave who had been taken in execution hanged himself, no action was permitted.

8. It is settled that the words "the value in the last thirty days," although they lack the word "highest," are to be understood as if they did not.

30. One who kills another's slave whom he catches in the act of adultery is not held under this statute.

1. If a pledged slave is killed, the debtor has the action. But it is a question whether an *actio utilis* should be granted to the creditor, because he may have an interest, as where the debtor is insolvent or the action barred by lapse of time. But this is inequitable, if it means subjecting the wrongdoer to actions both by the owner and the creditor, unless one should consider that the debtor will suffer no injury in the affair since he will be credited upon the debt for the amount recovered by the pledgee, and can sue the wrongdoer for the rest, or perhaps the debtor will be given an absolute right to sue for the amount by which the damage exceeds the debt; hence, in these cases where the creditor is allowed an action because of the insolvency of the debtor or prescription of the action, he will exercise the Aquilian action to the amount of the debt, crediting the recovery to the debtor; moreover, even the debtor has the Aquilian action for the remaining damages.

2. If one consumes the wine or corn of another, he does not appear to have done wrongful damage, hence the *actio utilis* should be granted.

ideoque utilis danda est actio. 3. In hac quoque actione, quae ex hoc capitulo oritur, dolus et culpa punitur: ideoque si quis in stipulam suam vel spinam comburendae eius causa ignem immiserit et ulterius evagatus et progressus ignis alienam segetem vel vineam laeserit, requiramus, num imperitia eius aut neglegentia id accidit. nam si die ventoso id fecit, culpae reus est (nam et qui occasionem praestat, damnum fecisse videtur): in eodem crimine est et qui non observavit, ne ignis longius procederet. at si omnia quae oportuit observavit vel subita vis venti longius ignem produxit, caret culpa. 4. Si vulneratus fuerit servus non mortifere, neglegentia autem perierit, de vulnerato actio erit, non de occiso.

31. Idem *libro decimo ad Sabinum* Si putator ex arbore ramum cum deiceret vel machinarius hominem praetereuntem occidit, ita tenetur, si is in publicum decidat nec ille proclamavit, ut casus eius evitari possit. sed Mucius dixit, etiam si in privato idem accidisset, posse de culpa agi: culpam autem esse, quod cum a diligente provideri poterit, non esset provisum aut tum denuntiatum esset, cum periculum evitari non possit. secundum quam rationem non multum refert, per publicum an per privatum iter fieret, cum plerumque per privata loca vulgo iter fiat. quod si nullum iter erit, dolum dumtaxat praestare debet, ne immittat in eum, quem viderit transeuntem: nam culpa ab eo exigenda non est, cum divinare non potuerit, an per eum locum aliquis transiturus sit.

32. Gaius *libro septimo ad edictum provinciale* Illud quaesitum est, an quod proconsul in furto observat quod a familia factum sit (id est ut non in singulos detur poenae persecutio, sed sufficeret id praestari, quod praestandum foret, si id furtum unus liber fecisset), debeat et in actione damni iniuriae observari. sed magis visum est idem esse observandum, et merito: cum enim circa furti actionem haec ratio sit, ne ex uno delicto tota familia dominus careat eaque ratio similiter et in actionem damni iniuriae interveniat, sequitur, ut idem debeat aestimari, praesertim cum interdum levior sit haec causa delicti, veluti si culpa et non dolo damnum daretur.

3. In the action arising from this chapter like the first, only malice and negligence are punished; therefore if one sets fire to his straw or brambles in order to burn them up, and the fire escapes and spreads, injuring another's cornfield or vineyard, our question is whether it occurred through lack of skill or care. For if the defendant did it on a windy day, he is at fault, as one who furnishes its cause is held to have committed the damage, and he is open to the same charge who did not watch the fire to keep it from spreading. But if he took all the necessary precautions, or a sudden gust of wind caused the fire to spread, he is not at fault.

4. If a slave is wounded, but not mortally, and dies from neglect, the action will be for wounding, not for killing.

31. If a pruner throws a branch down from a tree, or a laborer throws something from a scaffolding, killing a passing slave, they are held if they threw the thing on to a public place without shouting so that the victim might avoid the accident. Mucius even holds that there may be an action for negligence if the same thing happens on private property, as it is negligent not to foresee what could have been forseen by a careful person, or to give warning when it was too late to avoid the danger. On this view it makes little difference whether the victim was crossing public or private land, as there is often a public way over private property. But if there was no path, there will be liability only for malice, so that one may not aim at one whom he sees crossing; for no care should be required from one who could not foresee that anyone would pass his way.

32. It has been asked whether the practice should be applied to the action of wrongful damage which the proconsul observes in the case of theft by a number of one's slaves, i. e. that an action for the penalty is not allowed in regard to each slave, but it is enough to pay what it would have cost if one freeman had committed the theft. And the better view is that the same rule should be observed, and justly so; for, respecting the action for theft, the reason of the rule is that an owner may not lose all his slaves for one delict, which reason equally applies to the action for wrongful damage; it follows that the same method of computing damage ought to be adopted, especially since the gist of our delict is often less serious, as when the damage is committed culpably but not intentionally.

1. Si idem eundem servum vulneraverit, postea deinde etiam occiderit, tenebitur et de vulnerato et de occiso: duo enim sunt delicta. aliter atque si quis uno impetu pluribus vulneribus aliquem occiderit: tunc enim una erit actio de occiso.

33. PAULUS *libro secundo ad Plautium* Si servum meum occidisti, non affectiones aestimandas esse puto, veluti si filium tuum naturalem quis occiderit quem tu magno emptum velles, sed quanti omnibus valeret. Sextus quoque Pedius ait pretia rerum non ex affectione nec utilitate singulorum, sed communiter fungi: itaque eum, qui filium naturalem possidet, non eo locupletiorem esse, quod eum plurimo, si alius possideret, redempturus fuit, nec illum, qui filium alienum possideat, tantum habere, quanti eum patri vendere posset. in lege enim Aquilia damnum consequimur: et amisisse dicemur, quod aut consequi potuimus aut erogare cogimur. 1. In damnis, quae lege Aquilia non tenentur, in factum datur actio.

34. MARCELLUS *libro vicensimo primo digestorum* Titio et Seio Stichum legavit: deliberante Seio, cum Titius vindicasset legatum, Stichus occisus est: deinde Seius repudiavit legatum. perinde Titius agere possit, ac si soli legatus esset,

35. ULPIANUS *libro octavo decimo ad edictum* quia retro adcrevisse dominium ei videtur:

36. MARCELLUS *libro vicensimo primo digestorum* nam sicut repudiante legatario legatum heredis est actio perinde ac si legatus non esset, ita huius actio est ac si soli legatus esset. 1. Si dominus servum, quem Titius mortifere vulneraverat, liberum et heredem esse iusserit eique postea Maevius extiterit heres, non habebit Maevius cum Titio legis Aquiliae actionem, scilicet secundum Sabini opinionem, qui putabat ad heredem actionem non transmitti, quae defuncto competere non potuit: nam sane absurdum accidet, ut heres pretium quasi occisi consequatur eius, cuius heres exstitit. quod si ex parte eum dominus heredem cum libertate esse iusserit, coheres eius mortuo eo aget lege Aquilia.

37. IAVOLENUS *libro quarto decimo ex Cassio* Liber homo si iussu alterius manu iniuriam dedit, actio legis Aquiliae cum

1. If the same person wounds a slave and later kills him, he will be held both for wounding and killing; for these are separate delicts. It is otherwise where in one attack a person kills another with several wounds; here there will be one action for killing.

33. If you kill my slave, I am of the opinion that my sentiments are not to be taken into account (as for example if one kills your natural son for whom you would willingly pay a high price) but only the market value. Sextus Pedius agrees that the value of property is to be reckoned not by the sentiment or interest of individuals but by the average view; hence he who possesses his natural son is none the richer because he would buy him for a large price if another possessed him, nor does he who possesses another's son own as much as he could sell him for to his father. In short under the *Lex Aquilia* we recover our damages; and we are held to have lost what we could have gained or what we were forced to expend.

1. For the damage which is not included in the *Lex Aquilia* an action *in factum* is allowed.

34. A legacy of Stichus to Titius and Seius: Stichus is killed while Seius is deliberating but after Titius has vindicated the legacy; then Seius refuses it. Here Titius may sue the wrongdoer as if he were sole legatee,

35. because his ownership by accrual is held to relate back,

36. for just as the heir has the action, as if there had been no legacy, where the legatee refused it, so Titius has the action as if he were sole legatee.

1. If the owner orders a slave mortally wounded by Titius to be free and heir, and later Maevius succeeds the slave as heir, Maevius will not have the Aquilian action against Titius, at least according to the view of Sabinus, who thought that an action would not be transferred to the heir which could not have been exercised by the deceased; and indeed it would be absurd if the heir could recover damages for the death of the person to whom he succeeded. But if the owner had ordered the slave to be free and part-heir, the latter's co-heir may bring the Aquilian action for his death.

37. If a free man has committed direct injury by the order of another, an Aquilian action will lie against the one who

eo est qui iussit, si modo ius imperandi habuit: quod si non habuit, cum eo agendum est qui fecit. 1. Si quadrupes, cuius nomine actio esset cum domino, quod pauperiem fecisset, ab alio occisa est et cum eo lege Aquilia agitur, aestimatio non ad corpus quadrupedis, sed ad causam eius (in quo de pauperie actio est) referri debet et tanti damnandus est is qui occidit iudicio legis Aquiliae, quanti actoris interest noxae potius deditione defungi quam litis aestimatione.

38. Idem *libro nono epistularum* Si eo tempore, quo tibi meus servus quem bona fide emisti serviebat, ipse a servo tuo vulneratus est, placuit omnimodo me tecum recte lege Aquilia experiri.

39. Pomponius *libro septimo decimo ad Quintum Mucium* Quintus Mucius scribit: equa cum in alieno pasceretur, in cogendo quod praegnas erat eiecit: quaerebatur, dominus eius possetne cum eo qui coegisset lege Aquilia agere, quia equam in iciendo ruperat. si percussisset aut consulto vehementius egisset, visum est agere posse. 1. Pomponius. Quamvis alienum pecus in agro suo quis deprehendit, sic illud expellere debet, quomodo si suum deprehendisset, quoniam si quid ex ea re damnum cepit, habet proprias actiones. itaque qui pecus alienum in agro suo deprehenderit, non iure id includit, nec agere illud aliter debet quam ut supra diximus quasi suum: sed vel abigere debet sine damno vel admonere dominum, ut suum recipiat.

40. Paulus *libro tertio ad edictum* In lege Aquilia, si deletum chirographum mihi esse dicam, in quo sub condicione mihi pecunia debita fuerit, et interim testibus quoque id probare possim, qui testes possunt non esse eo tempore, quo condicio extitit, et si summatim re exposita ad suspicionem iudicem adducam, debeam vincere: sed tunc condemnationis exactio competit, cum debiti condicio extiterit: quod si defecerit, condemnatio nullas vires habebit.

41. Ulpianus *libro quadragensimo primo ad Sabinum* Si quis testamentum deleverit, an damni iniuriae actio com-

gave the order if he had a right to command, if not, the action may be brought against the doer.

1. If a quadruped for which an action *de pauperie* lies against the owner is killed by another, the latter is liable to an Aquilian action in which the damages should be computed not merely with respect to the animal's market value but also to its accessory value, representing the liability in the action *de pauperie;* thus the defendant in the Aquilian action for killing should be condemned in the amount by which it would have benefited the owner to have made noxal surrender rather than pay the damages.

38. If my slave, bought by you in good faith and while in your service, is wounded by your slave, it has finally been settled that I have a good right of action against you under the *Lex Aquilia.*

39. Quintus Mucius writes: A mare was grazing in another's field, and being pregnant, miscarried while being driven off; it was asked if her owner could bring an Aquilian action against the man who drove her away for damage caused thereby. It was held that an action would lie if he struck her or intentionally drove her too violently.

1. Pomponius: Although one surprise another's cattle on his land, he must drive them off as if they were his own that he had surprised, because if he has suffered any damage in the affair, he has the proper actions. Hence he who catches another's cattle on his land may not lawfully impound them, nor, as said above, should he drive them off otherwise than as if they belonged to him; he must either lead them away without harming them or notify their owner to come and get them.

40. Under the *Lex Aquilia,* if I claim that my chirograph has been destroyed which stated that money was owed me under a condition, and if at the time I can prove this by witnesses who may not be available when the condition is satisfied, and if after a brief exposition I can convince the judge of these facts, I ought to win; however, the execution of the judgment will be permitted when the condition of the debt is satisfied, so that if it fails the judgment will have no effect.

41. If one destroys a will, let us see whether there is an action for wrongful damage. And Marcellus in the fifth book

petat, videamus. et Marcellus libro quinto digestorum dubitans negat competere: quemadmodum enim, inquit, aestimatio inibitur? ego apud eum notavi in testatore quidem hoc esse verum, quia quod interest eius aestimari non potest, verum tamen in herede vel legatariis diversum, quibus testamenta paene chirographa sunt. ibidem Marcellus scribit chirographo deleto competere legis Aquiliae actionem. sed et si quis tabulas testamenti apud se depositas deleverit vel pluribus praesentibus legerit, utilius est in factum et iniuriarum agi, si iniuriae faciendae causa secreta iudiciorum publicavit. 1. Interdum evenire Pomponius eleganter ait, ut quis tabulas delendo furti non teneatur, sed tantum damni iniuriae, ut puta si non animo furti faciendi, sed tantum damni dandi delevit: nam furti non tenebitur: cum facto enim etiam animum furis furtum exigit.

42. IULIANUS *libro quadragensimo octavo digestorum* Qui tabulas testamenti depositas aut alicuius rei instrumentum ita delevit, ut legi non possit, depositi actione et ad exhibendum tenetur, quia corruptam rem restituerit aut exhibuerit. legis quoque Aquiliae actio ex eadem causa competit: corrupisse enim tabulas recte dicitur et qui eas interleverit.

43. POMPONIUS *libro nono decimo ad Sabinum* Ob id, quod ante quam hereditatem adires damnum admissum in res hereditarias est, legis Aquiliae actionem habes, quod post mortem eius, cui heres sis, acciderit: dominum enim lex Aquilia appellat non utique eum, qui tunc fuerit, cum damnum daretur: nam isto modo ne ab eo quidem, cui heres quis erit, transire ad eum ea actio poterit: neque ob id, quod tum commissum fuerit, cum in hostium potestate esses, agere postliminio reversus poteris: et hoc aliter constitui sine magna captione postumorum liberorum, qui parentibus heredes erunt, non poterit. eadem dicemus et de arboribus eodem tempore furtim caesis. puto eadem dici posse etiam de hac actione quod vi aut clam, si modo quis aut prohibitus fecerit, aut apparuerit eum intellegere debuisse ab eis, ad quos ea hereditas pertineret, si rescissent, prohibitum iri.

of his Digest after hesitation refuses the action, asking upon what grounds the damage can be computed. In a note to the passage I remarked that this was true of the testator, because his interest could not be computed, otherwise, however, for the heir or legatee, for whom the will is almost like a chirograph; and in that very place Marcellus writes that the Aquilian action lies for destruction of a chirograph. And if a depositary of a will destroys it or reads it in the presence of others, it is more advisable to bring an action *in factum*, or for insult, if the secrets of one's last will have been published with the intention to insult him.

1. Pomponius neatly remarks that it may often happen that the destroyer of a will is not held for theft but only for wrongful damage, as in the case where he destroyed without any intention of profiting but merely to injure, where he could not be held for theft, which requires not only the act but the intention of stealing.

42. The depositary of a will or any other valuable document who so injures it as to render it illegible is liable in the action of deposit and that *ad exhibendum* for restoring or exhibiting an object so badly injured. For these facts an Aquilian action will also lie, for one is rightly held to have spoiled a will if he has erased part of it.

43. You have an Aquilian action for damage done to the inheritance before your entry, although it occurred after the death of him to whom you are heir; for by "owner" the *Lex Aquilia* does not necessarily mean the owner at the time the damage was done; for if that were true the action could not even pass from the deceased to his heir, nor could you bring it after your return with *postliminium* for damage committed while you were a prisoner of the enemy, nor could a different rule be observed without great injustice to posthumous children who are taken to be heirs to their parents. The same is to be said for trees secretly cut during this period, and I am of the opinion that the rule may be applied to the interdict "*quod vi aut clam*" if the act has been done after prohibition or it appears that the defendant ought to have known that it would have been prohibited by those who would succeed to the inheritance if they had found out in time.

44. ULPIANUS *libro quadragensimo secundo ad Sabinum* In lege Aquilia et levissima culpa venit. 1. Quotiens sciente domino servus vulnerat vel occidit, Aquilia dominum teneri dubium non est.

45. PAULUS *libro decimo ad Sabinum* Scientiam hic pro patientia accipimus, ut qui prohibere potuit teneatur, si non fecerit. 1. Lege Aquilia agi potest et sanato vulnerato servo. 2. Si meum servum, cum liberum putares, occideris, lege Aquilia teneberis. 3. Cum stramenta ardentia transilirent duo, concurrerunt amboque ceciderunt et alter flamma consumptus est: nihil eo nomine agi, si non intellegitur, uter ab utro eversus sit. 4. Qui, cum aliter tueri se non possent, damni culpam dederint, innoxii sunt: vim enim vi defendere omnes leges omniaque iura permittunt. sed si defendendi mei causa lapidem in adversarium misero, sed non eum, sed praetereuntem percussero, tenebor lege Aquilia: illum enim solum qui vim infert ferire conceditur, et hoc, si tuendi dumtaxat, non etiam ulciscendi causa factum sit. 5. Qui idoneum parietem sustulit, damni iniuria domino eius tenetur.

46. ULPIANUS *libro quinquagensimo ad Sabinum* Si vulnerato servo lege Aquilia actum sit, postea mortuo ex eo vulnere agi lege Aquilia nihilo minus potest.

47. IULIANUS *libro octagensimo sexto digestorum* Sed si priore iudicio aestimatione facta, postea mortuo servo, de occiso agere dominus instituerit, exceptione doli mali opposita compelletur, ut ex utroque iudicio nihil amplius consequatur, quam consequi deberet, si initio de occiso homine egisset.

48. PAULUS *libro trigensimo nono ad edictum* Si servus ante aditam hereditatem damnum in re hereditaria dederit et liber factus in ea re damnum det, utraque actione tenebitur, quia alterius et alterius facti hae res sunt.

49. ULPIANUS *libro nono disputationum* Si quis fumo facto apes alienas fugaverit vel etiam necaverit, magis causam mortis praestitisse videtur quam occidisse, et ideo in factum ac-

44. The slightest negligence founds an Aquilian action.

1. Whenever a slave wounds or kills with the knowledge of his owner, there is no doubt that the owner is liable to an Aquilian action.

45. We understand knowledge to include tolerance, so that one is held if he could have forbidden the act but did not.

1. An action on the *Lex Aquilia* may be brought even after the wounded slave has been cured.

2. If you kill my slave whom you believe to be a freeman, you will be liable to an Aquilian action.

3. As two slaves were jumping over a heap of burning straw, they collided, both fell down, and one was burned to death; no action can be brought for him unless it can be proved which knocked over the other.

4. They are innocent who do what would otherwise be wrongful damage when they can protect themselves in no other way; all statutes and systems of law allow force to repel force. But if in defending myself I throw a stone at my adversary, and hit not him but a passerby, I shall be liable under the *Lex Aquilia*, for it is permissible to strike only the agressor, and even him where it is done solely in defense, not for revenge.

5. One who removes a good wall is liable to its owner for wrongful damage.

46. If an Aquilian action has been brought for a wounded slave, this is no bar to another Aquilian action after he has died from the wound.

47. But if damages were given in the former action and after the slave's death his owner brings an action for killing, by the *exceptio doli* his recovery in both actions will be limited to no more that he would have had if he had first brought the action for the death of the slave.

48. If a slave does damage to the inheritance before entry thereon, and after becoming free again damages the estate, he will be liable to both actions because the delicts result from two separate acts.

49. If one by making a smudge drives away or even kills another's bees, he seems rather to have furnished the cause of death than to have killed, so that he will be liable to an action *in factum*.

tione tenebitur. 1. Quod dicitur damnum iniuria datum Aquilia persequi, sic erit accipiendum, ut videatur damnum iniuria datum, quod cum damno iniuriam attulerit: nisi magna vi cogente fuerit factum, ut Celsus scribit circa eum, qui incendii arcendi gratia vicinas aedes intercidit: nam hic scribit cessare legis Aquiliae actionem: iusto enim metu ductus, ne ad se ignis perveniret, vicinas aedes intercidit: et sive pervenit ignis sive ante extinctus est, existimat legis Aquiliae actionem cessare.

50. ULPIANUS *libro sexto opinionum* Qui domum alienam invito domino demolit et eo loco balneas exstruxit, praeter naturale ius, quod superficies ad dominum soli pertinet, etiam damni dati nomine actioni subicitur.

51. IULIANUS *libro octagensimo sexto digestorum* Ita vulneratus est servus, ut eo ictu certum esset moriturum: medio deinde tempore heres institutus est et postea ab alio ictus decessit: quaero, an cum utroque de occiso lege Aquilia agi possit. respondit: occidisse dicitur vulgo quidem, qui mortis causam quolibet modo praebuit: sed lege Aquilia is demum teneri visus est, qui adhibita vi et quasi manu causam mortis praebuisset, tracta videlicet interpretatione vocis a caedendo et a caede. rursus Aquilia lege teneri existimati sunt non solum qui ita vulnerassent, ut confestim vita privarent, sed etiam hi, quorum ex vulnere certum esset aliquem vita excessurum. igitur si quis servo mortiferum vulnus inflixerit eundemque alius ex intervallo ita percusserit, ut maturius interficeretur, quam ex priore vulnere moriturus fuerat, statuendum est utrumque eorum lege Aquilia teneri. 1. Idque est consequens auctoritati veterum, qui, cum a pluribus idem servus ita vulneratus esset, ut non appareret, cuius ictu perisset, omnes lege Aquilia teneri iudicaverunt. 2. Aestimatio autem perempti non eadem in utriusque persona fiet: nam qui prior vulneravit, tantum praestabit, quanto in anno proximo homo plurimi fuerit repetitis ex die vulneris trecentum sexaginta quinque diebus, posterior in id tenebitur,

1. When it is said that the Aquilian action lies for wrongful damage, it must be understood that wrongful damage exists only when there is a wrong in addition to damage, the former element being absent when the act is done under the influence of *vis major*, as in the case reported by Celsus of a man who destroyed a neighboring house to prevent the spread of a fire; here he writes that there is no Aquilian action because the neighboring house was destroyed under the reasonable fear that the fire would spread to that of the defendant; he is also of the opinion that there is no Aquilian action whether the fire reached the defendant's house or was put out before doing so.

50. If one demolishes another's house without his consent and builds baths there, in addition to the rule of natural law that fixtures belong to the owner of the land, he will also be liable to an action for wrongful damage.

51. A slave was so wounded that it was certain that he would die of the blow; in the meantime, he was instituted heir and then died from another blow; my question is whether an Aquilian action for killing can be brought against both wrongdoers. The answer was that one is ordinarily said to have killed who furnishes the cause of death in any way, but under the *Lex Aquilia* the only one who is held to be liable is he who has furnished the cause of death by direct violence, so to speak by his own hand, because the interpretation of the word "kill" is made with reference to the words "slaying" or "slaughter." Moreover, not only those are held liable under the *Lex Aquilia* who have dealt such a wound that death follows immediately, but also those who have wounded a man so that he is certain to die. Hence if one has inflicted a mortal wound on a slave and another later gives the same slave a blow from which he dies before he would have died from the former wound, the better view holds both under the *Lex Aquilia*.

1. And this is in accord with the authority of the ancients who, when a slave was wounded by several so that it did not appear which wound caused his death, decided that all are liable under the *Lex Aquilia*.

2. The damages for the dead slave will not be the same for both wrongdoers, for he who first wounded the slave will pay his highest value in the last year, reckoning back 365 days from the wound, but the second defendant will be liable for

quanti homo plurimi venire poterit in anno proximo, quo vita excessit, in quo pretium quoque hereditatis erit. eiusdem ergo servi occisi nomine alius maiorem, alius minorem aestimationem praestabit, nec mirum, cum uterque eorum ex diversa causa et diversis temporibus occidisse hominem intellegatur. quod si quis absurde a nobis haec constitui putaverit, cogitet longe absurdius constitui neutrum lege Aquilia teneri aut alterum potius, cum neque impunita maleficia esse oporteat nec facile constitui possit, uter potius lege teneatur. multa autem iure civili contra rationem disputandi pro utilitate communi recepta esse innumerabilibus rebus probari potest: unum interim posuisse contentus ero. cum plures trabem alienam furandi causa sustulerint, quam singuli ferre non possent, furti actione omnes teneri existimantur, quamvis subtili ratione dici possit neminem eorum teneri, quia neminem verum sit eam sustulisse.

52. ALFENUS *libro secundo digestorum* Si ex plagis servus mortuus esset neque id medici inscientia aut domini neglegentia accidisset, recte de iniuria occiso eo agitur. 1. Tabernarius in semita noctu supra lapidem lucernam posuerat: quidam praeteriens eam sustulerat: tabernarius eum consecutus lucernam reposcebat et fugientem retinebat: ille flagello, quod in manu habebat, in quo dolor inerat, verberare tabernarium coeperat, ut se mitteret: ex eo maiore rixa facta tabernarius ei, qui lucernam sustulerat, oculum effoderat: consulebat, num damnum iniuria non videtur dedisse, quoniam prior flagello percussus esset. respondi, nisi data opera effodisset oculum, non videri damnum iniuria fecisse, culpam enim penes eum, qui prior flagello percussit, residere: sed si ab eo non prior vapulasset, sed cum ei lucernam eripere vellet, rixatus esset, tabernarii culpa factum videri. 2. In clivo Capitolino duo plostra onusta mulae ducebant: prioris plostri muliones conversum plostrum sublevabant, quo facile mulae ducerent: inter superius plostrum cessim ire coepit et cum muliones, qui inter duo plostra fuerunt, e medio exissent, posterius plostrum a priore percussum retro redierat et puerum

the highest value of the slave in the year preceding his death, which will include the value of the inheritance. Thus for killing the same slave one will pay more, the other less, which is not surprising since each has obviously killed the slave for a different reason and at a different time. And if anyone thinks that we have reached an absurd result, let him consider that it would be far more absurd that neither should be liable under the *Lex Aquilia*, or one rather than the other, since on the one hand misdeeds ought not to go unpunished, yet on the other it cannot easily be decided which wrongdoer more clearly comes within the terms of the statute. Indeed it can be shown by countless examples that many rules have been adopted in the strict law contrary to academic logic on account of common convenience; I shall content myself here with but one: when, with intent to steal, several carry away another's beam which none by himself could have carried, all are held liable to the action for theft, although it might strictly be claimed that nobody should be liable because no one of them really carried it away.

52. If a slave dies from blows and this occurred neither by the ignorance of the doctor nor the negligence of the owner, an action may properly be brought for wrongfully killing him.

1. An innkeeper had placed his lantern at night on a stone by the road, and a passerby had carried it off; the innkeeper followed him demanding the lantern and held him back when he attempted to escape; whereupon the other, to make him let go, began beating the innkeeper with a whip which he had in his hand in which there was a spike. A fierce fight ensued in which the innkeeper put out the eye of the man who had carried off the lantern; the former then consulted me as to whether he might not be held guiltless of wrongful damage because he had first been struck with the whip. I replied that unless he had intentionally put out the eye, he would not be held to have committed wrongful damage, for the fault seems to lie in him who first struck with the whip; if, however, the innkeeper had not first been beaten by the other, but the fight had resulted from his attempt to snatch away the lantern, the act seemed to be his fault.

2. Mules were dragging two loaded carts up the Capitoline hill; the drivers of the front cart, which had got tilted back, were holding it up to make it easier for the mules; meanwhile the team began to move backward so that when the drivers, who were between the two carts, jumped out from their posi-

cuiusdam obtriverat: dominus pueri consulebat, cum quo se agere oporteret. respondi in causa ius esse positum: nam si muliones, qui superius plostrum sustinuissent, sua sponte se subduxissent et ideo factum esset, ut mulae plostrum retinere non possint atque onere ipso retraherentur, cum domino mularum nullam esse actionem, cum hominibus, qui conversum plostrum sustinuissent, lege Aquilia agi posse: nam nihilo minus eum damnum dare, qui quod sustineret mitteret sua voluntate, ut id aliquem feriret: veluti si quis asellum cum agitasset non retinuisset, aeque si quis ex manu telum aut aliud quid immisisset, damnum iniuria daret. sed si mulae, quia aliquid reformidassent et muliones timore permoti, ne opprimerentur, plostrum reliquissent, cum hominibus actionem nullam esse, cum domino mularum esse. quod si neque mulae neque homines in causa essent, sed mulae retinere onus nequissent aut cum coniterentur lapsae concidissent et ideo plostrum cessim redisset atque hi quo conversum fuisset onus sustinere nequissent, neque cum domino mularum neque cum hominibus esse actionem. illud quidem certe, quoquo modo res se haberet, cum domino posteriorum mularum agi non posse, quoniam non sua sponte, sed percussae retro redissent. 3. Quidam boves vendidit ea lege, uti daret experiundos: postea dedit experiundos: emptoris servus in experiundo percussus ab altero bove cornu est: quaerebatur, num venditor emptori damnum praestare deberet. respondi, si emptor boves emptos haberet, non debere praestare: sed si non haberet emptos, tum, si culpa hominis factum esset, ut a bove feriretur, non debere praestari, si vitio bovis, debere. 4. Cum pila complures luderent, quidam ex his servulum, cum pilam percipere conaretur, impulit, servus cecidit et crus fregit: quaerebatur, an dominus servuli lege Aquilia cum eo, cuius impulsu ceciderat, agere potest. respondi non posse, cum casu magis quam culpa videretur factum.

53. Neratius *libro primo membranarum* Boves alienos in angustum locum coegisti eoque effectum est, ut deicerentur: datur in te ad exemplum legis Aquiliae in factum actio.

tion, the rear cart was hit by the other and rolled down and ran over someone's slave boy. The boy's owner consulted me against whom to bring action. I answered that the rule of law depended upon the facts; assuming that the drivers who were holding up the front cart got out of the way of their own accord, thus rendering the mules unable to support the cart, which dragged them back by its own weight, then there would be no action against the owner of the mules, but an Aquilian action could be brought against those who were upholding the tilted cart, for one has none the less inflicted direct damage who voluntarily lets go something which he is supporting so that it strikes another, as where one does not hold in an ass which one is driving, just as one commits wrongful damage who allows a weapon or anything else to escape him. Assuming, however, that the mules shied at something and the drivers, fearing to be crushed, left the cart, there would be no action against the men, but one against the owner of the mules. But if neither the mules nor the men were responsible, but the mules could not sustain the weight or in straining slipped and fell, whereupon the cart began to go back, and because it was tilted the drivers could not sustain its weight, then there could be an action neither against the owner of the mules nor the men. At least it was certain, whatever the facts, that there could be no action against the owner of the other mules, who had gone backward involuntarily because they were hit.

3. Oxen were sold on approval and later delivered for trial, during which a slave of the buyer was struck by the horn of one of them; the question was whether the seller ought to indemnify the buyer. I answered that if the buyer had bought the oxen, no recovery could be had: if not, then if it was by the slave's fault that he had been hit by the ox, there should be no recovery; otherwise, if by a vice in the ox.

4. Several people were playing ball, one of whom pushed a youthful slave who was trying to get the ball; the slave fell and broke his leg. It was asked whether the owner of the child might bring an Aquilian action against the one whose push had caused the fall. I answered, No, since it seems to have occurred rather by accident than by negligence.

53. You drove another's oxen into a ravine with the result that they fell off a precipice; an action *in factum* will be granted against you upon the analogy of the *Lex Aquilia*.

54. Papinianus *libro trigensimo septimo quaestionum* Legis Aquiliae debitori competit actio, cum reus stipulandi ante moram promissum animal vulneravit: idem est et si occiderit animal. quod si post moram promissoris qui stipulatus fuerat occidit, debitor quidem liberatur, lege autem Aquilia hoc casu non recte experietur: nam creditor ipse sibi potius quam alii iniuriam fecisse videtur.

55. Paulus *libro vicensimo secundo quaestionum* Stichum aut Pamphilum promisi Titio, cum Stichus esset decem milium Pamphilus viginti: stipulator Stichum ante moram occidit: quaesitum est de actione legis Aquiliae. respondi: cum viliorem occidisse proponitur, in hunc tractatum nihilum differt ab extraneo creditor. quanti igitur fiet aestimatio, utrum decem milium, quanti fuit occisus, an quanti est, quem necesse habeo dare, id est quanti mea interest? et quid dicemus, si et Pamphilus decesserit sine mora? iam pretium Stichi minuetur, quoniam liberatus est promissor? et sufficiet fuisse pluris cum occideretur vel intra annum. hac quidem ratione, etiamsi post mortem Pamphili intra annum occidatur, pluris videbitur fuisse.

56. Idem *libro secundo sententiarum* Mulier si in rem viri damnum dederit, pro tenore legis Aquiliae convenitur.

57. Iavolenus *libro sexto ex posterioribus Labeonis* Equum tibi commodavi: in eo tu cum equitares et una complures equitarent, unus ex his irruit in equum teque deiecit et eo casu crura equi fracta sunt. Labeo negat tecum ullam actionem esse, sed si equitis culpa factum esset, cum equite: sane non cum equi domino agi posse. verum puto.

54. The debtor has the Aquilian action if the stipulator wounds the promised animal before default in delivery, and it is the same if he kills it. But if the stipulator kills it after the promisor has defaulted, the debtor is discharged; but here there is no right to bring the Aquilian action, for the creditor seems to have wronged himself rather than anyone else.

55. I promised to Titius either Stichus or Pamphilus, at a time when Stichus was worth ten, Pamphilus twenty, thousand; the stipulator killed Stichus before default, the question was as to the action of the *Lex Aquilia*. I answered: since the cheaper slave is assumed to have been killed, the creditor in this matter differs in no way from a third person. What then will be the damages? Ten thousand, the value of the slave who was killed, or the value of the one whom I have to deliver, that is, the amount by which I am impoverished? And what shall we say if Pamphilus dies before default? Will the value of Stichus be diminished because the promisor is discharged? In fact it is enough if Stichus was more valuable when he was killed or within the year. For this reason, even if he is killed within a year after the death of Pamphilus, he will be held to be of the greater value.

56. If a woman damages her husband's property, she will be liable under the provisions of the *Lex Aquilia*.

57. I lent you a horse, and as you were riding it in the company of several others, one of them struck against your horse, throwing you off and at the same time breaking the horse's legs. Labeo refuses any action against you, but permits one against the rider if the accident was due to his fault; clearly there can be none against the owner of the horse. I agree.

COMMENTARY

1. pr. *Derogavit:* cf. 50. 16. 102. Regarding the provisions for corporeal damage to property in the XII Tables, the only earlier statute of which we know, little but conjecture is possible.

I. The delict of *injuria* included breaking a slave's bones, G. 3. 223.

II. In 47. 9. 9 Gaius in his commentary on the XII Tables says that intentionally burning a house is a crime, accidental or negligent burning requires reparation, the ancient formula *noxiam sarcire* being used, or on insolvency slight punishment; the last provision very probably was not in the original statute, cf. C. 6. 1. 4. 2; Coll. 1. 11. 2; Pernice, 2. 38 n. 3. It is generally agreed that the words *n. s.* mean, as they seem to do, that a civil as well as criminal remedy was available, cf. the double liability for destruction of crops, Mommsen, Strafrecht, 773; Huvelin, Furtum, 61 ff.; Fliniaux, Mél. Cornil, 1. 283 n. 3; even our statute may at first have had a criminal aspect, Pernice, S., 102; *contra* Mommsen, *op. cit.*, 826 n. 4; Strachan-Davidson, R. Crim. L., 1. 150 n. 1. There is a dispute whether the liability was absolute; Kunkel, Z., 1925, 331 ff., seems right in maintaining the affirmative, cf. esp. Paul, 5. 20. 3, *contra* Mommsen, *id.*, 837, n. 1, who gives no reason for his scepticism as to the presence of *casus* in the XII Tables, see Pernice, *loc. cit.* Mommsen, *id.*, 841 n. 6 also maintains that this action did not persist, so that all references to the civil remedy for burning, except presumably that of Gaius, should be understood as meaning the Aquilian action. From the texts this is extremely improbable; they never mention the *Lex Aquilia;* the old word *sarcire* is continually used, and in 2. 14. 7. 13, overlooked by Mommsen, an *actio aedium incensarum* is mentioned, the attempts to torture which away are hardly worthy of consideration, see Rudorff, Z. G. R., 14. 364; regarding Lenel's fanciful conjecture, Pal., 2. 433 n. 3, the fact may be remarked that the reading is known to Cyril, Bas. 1. 572, the first of the Beyroot "heroes," who flourished probably 125 years before the compilation and was a recognized authority on the subject of pacts, Collinet, École de Beyrouth, 162, 276; cf. Z., 1887, 224. This was in *duplum*, Paul, 5, 3, 6 (which Huschke emends, Mommsen regards as a case of *turba*, 47. 8. 4. 4, and others refer to our action, Rein, Criminalrecht, 773 n. 1), perhaps *duplum infitiando*, Bull., 16. 128. Kunkel's thesis that the liability was absolute in classical law derives support from Paul, 5. 20. 3, but there are too many contrary texts, nor in spite of recent efforts, has it yet been shown that liability without fault was agreeable to the spirit of that age, cf. 49.

III. As for the action *de pastu pecoris*, Fliniaux's conclusions, Mél. Cornil, 1. 247 ff., are acceptable that it lay for feeding one's livestock on another's natural, not cultivated, land, cf. 19. 5. 14. 3; Cuq, Manuel, 1917, 568 n. 3; Girard, 405 n. 1; Lenel, 3 ed., 198. Our action did not directly apply, cf. 30. 2.

IV. Cutting down trees was also wrongful, G. 4. 11, but the penalty was increased by the *praetor*, Lenel, 139. Notwithstanding Lenel, it seems that there is no possibility of distinguishing the actions, 12. 2. 28. 6; 19. 2. 25. 5; 47. 7. 1; his attempt to establish an interpolation is well refuted in St. Senesi, 24. 370; the texts support Mommsen's view, *id.*, 835, *contra*, Levy, § 117; Naber, 53. 39. For later legislation on fruit trees, 47. 7. 2; Paul, 5. 20. 6, where the word *sarcire* evidently recalls the XII Tables though the action is praetorian. Various attempts have been made to blend these four cases into a principle. The view is widely maintained that any damage was actionable, see Esp., § 200. There are obvious gaps: killing a slave could hardly fail to be an *injuria* if such was the case for breaking his bones. The conception of *injuria* is obscure: cutting down trees or burning houses have been thought mere examples of it, cf. Girard, 409 N. 2; Z. 1915. 434.

V. The noxal action for *pauperies*, *infra* 37. 1, the early history of which is also obscure, may have applied to all wrongs committed by one *alieni juris*, Mommsen, *id.*, 834 n. 4. The most that can be said is that, though our statute practically tended to supersede the XII Tables, we know of nothing which it specifically repealed, cf. 44. 7. 41. pr.; Levy, 2. 203 n. 5.

1. 1. As to the date of the statute the question is as to the credibility of a scholiast, who indicates 287 B.C., cf. Esp., 202; Rotondi, Leges Publicae, 241; Brini, Mem. R. Acc. Bologna, 5. 155, who upholds Theophilus, citing opportunely Nov. 18, ch. 8.

2. pr. *Damnas* is supposed to be a contraction of *damnatus*, cf. Corssen, Kr. Nachtrage, 257, citing *locuples*, *mansues*, *sanas* (Festus, *vo. sanates*). The parallel is inexact in that our word is indeclinable, 30. 122. 1, cf. Erman, Quittungen, 38 n. 2; Beseler, 4. 101 ff.

2. 1. Because of the juxtaposition of *damnatus* with *judicatus* in G. 4. 21, and the fact that two of the actions *dupli infitiando* certainly enjoyed the privilege of the procedure *per manus injectionem*, it is usually held that the latter remedy always applied where the defendant was *damnas*, see Girard, 100 n. 2, 1038 n. 1; *contra* Wenger, Inst. Röm. Zivilpros., 216 n. 12, 218 n. 18; and see *infra* in our text. It is certainly safe to explain the peculiar institution of "*Litiscrescenz*" as a survival of the *legis actio per m. i.*, see Betti, Effetto della Conf., extr. Atti R. Acc. Torino, 50. 712 ff. The fact noticed by him, *op. cit.*, 721, that our claim is not liquid, should have prevented his remarkable assertion, St. sulla litis Aest., 2. 7, that the Aquilian *formula confessoria* is "doubtless a recent praetorian creation," cf. 26, however plausible it may be in other cases, cf., however, Lenel, Ed., 3 ed., 368 n. 3. Hardly more fanciful is his theory that the third chapter had no penalty for denial, see G. 3. 216; Rotondi, 965 n. 3. The former misconception resembles that of the Goths and Byzantines traced by Rotondi, S. G., 413–433.

2. 2. This passage is noteworthy in that it is the only one in the Digest where the word *exaequare* is not suspected by Beseler, Z., 1922, 535. The remainder of the text from *pantherae* is held interpolated by Eisele, Z., 1897, 17. *Mixtus* is a favorite expression of Justinian, cf. 10. 1. 1 with J. 4. 6. 20 (whence it is strange that the former text should be held interpolated by Biondi, A. N., 30 n.); Z., 1915, 217 ff., but in view of G. 2. 16, it seems probable that the mention of elephants and camels is genuine; furthermore, Gaius' decision was probably the same, they being gregarious draught animals. The ingenious reflection of Stella Maranca, Bull., 35. 26 n. 1, on the utility of pigs suggests a difficulty as to the interest. Both Labeo and Gaius seem to forget the fact, implied by the feminine gender of *oves* and *caprae*, that no damage may result from merely killing an animal bred only for food. The rules for wounding, cf. 24, should apply in these cases, cf. 27. 25. The logical error is not so much that of the jurisconsults as of the statute itself, which in assimilating oxen and slaves overlooked the very considerable value of the former's corpses. This may have contributed to the uncertainty manifested in our subject as to *compensatio lucri cum damno*, cf. 29. 1; 50, with 27. 25; 36. 1; the plaintiff was not so well treated in the *condictio furtiva*, cf. 13. 1. 14. 2; Levy, § 99.

3. The obscurity of the ancient idea of *injuria* is hardly relieved for our purposes by Huvelin's definition thereof as "material violence," Furtum, 69 n. 1; Mél. Appleton, 371 ff. It is clear that in classical times the word was used either, as here, to characterize the wrongfulness of an act, or, as in 30. 1, to mean mere damage. In the former sense it covers both *dolus* and *culpa*, cf. 5. 1. Although there is nothing to show what the framer of the law meant by the requirement, *i. e.*, when it was interpreted to cover acts where harm was unintended, the fact that the concept of fault certainly became wider shows that Jhering's generalization does not hold in our field.

4. pr. cf. 45. 4; 43. 16. 1. 27; 48. 8. 9. *Injuria* is now discussed till 7. 1.

4. 1. It is usually held that the requirement of shouting at night is later than the XII Tables, cf. Schöll, Legis D. T. Rel., 144 ff. His authorities seem inconclusive, *contra* Voigt, XII Tafeln, 1. 715. Riccobono, Essays in Legal History, 74 goes further, alleging an interpolation; see Huvelin, Furtum, 33 ff. The old dispute whether this privilege was at first purely punitive is better solved in the affirmative, Pernice, 1.78 n. 2; *aliter* in England, 2 Pollock and Maitland, 2 ed. 479 n. 2. Cujas, Obs., 14. 15, cites C. 3. 27. 1, as a later limitation on the rule.

5. pr. Karlowa, Röm. R. 2. 776 n. 2 notes that *metu mortis* is interpolated, cf. Coll. 7. 3. 3; *acc.* Pernice, 1. 81 ff., Riccobono, *op. cit.*, n. 2, sceptical as to the value of the Coll., holds the passage interpolated from *sin*, disregarding the problem which preoccupied Pomponius.

5. 1. It has been suggested by Beseler, 3. 59, 105, that the last sentence as well as *circa injuriarum* is unnecessary and interpolated, *acc.* Levy, 2. 193. The passage raises the question of the concurrence of the Aquilian action with another private delict, see Savigny, System, 5, § 234; E. G. I., § 45; Levy, §§ 119–123; Naber, 52. 250, 53. 10, 225. The texts state three views: first, as here, that one action has no effect on the other, 44.7.32 pr.; *id.*, 60; 50. 17. 130; second, that only the surplus can be obtained in the second action, 44. 7. 41. 1; third, that one extinguished the other, 44. 7. 53. pr. In spite of the improbability of systematic interpolation in view of the fact that every view is represented in the same title of the Digest, Levy's theory is here briefly given because his work constitutes the most profound and complete treatment of this vexed subject. At civil law neither action had any effect on the other, hence the first statement, but by praetorian or judicial practice the plaintiff was confined to either, hence the last statement. The second view is a Byzantine innovation made possible by the change in pleading and con-

sequent unimportance of *litis contestatio*, but cf. 47; Levy, 2. 8 n. 3, 116, 181, 187, 200. By the varying attribution of interpolations the texts can be made to support any hypothesis, and Levy's work has provoked an attack from Naber, who also combats Beseler, Z. 1924. 365 ff., and supports Savigny (whose theory remains the most appealing) except that he regards our action as reipersecutory not "mixed" for purposes of concurrence, but see 53. 38 where the exceptions outnumber the normal cases and cf. G. 4. 9. Regarding the action for insult it appears improbable that Paul's view, 44. 7. 34. pr., cf. Arch., 79. 337 ff., prevailed in classical law as Levy holds, 2. 192; cf. 47. 10. 15. 46; such, however, according to the scholiast appears to have been Justinian's practice. The theory mentioned by Paul that one might bring the Aquilian action after that for insult but not *vice versa* is explained by 50. 17. 104. The common law in general forbids any second recovery by the doctrine of merger, or "election," Goodrich *v.* Yale, 97 Mass. 15; Dawson *v.* Baum, 3 Wash. T. 464; Porter *v.* Mack, 50 W. Va. 581; but cf. Woody *v.* Jordan, 69 N. C. 189; Barth *v.* Loeffelholtz, 108 Wis. 562. However, the same doubt arises as to *eadem res;* for different views see Hudson *v.* Lee, 4 Coke 43a; Guest *v.* Warren, 9 Exch. 379; Sheldon *v.* Carpenter, 4 N. Y. 579; Morgan *v.* Waters, 122 App. Div. 340; Cook *v.* Cook, 2 Brev. (S. C.) 349.

5. 2. Contrary to the rule of English law, but cf. Bohlen, 23 Mich. L. Rev. 9, the Roman law imposed no liability where there was no "will," *i. e.*, for acts of a lunatic or child under seven. Such events were regarded as *casus*, cf. Rotondi, 956; Huvelin, Furtum, 405.

5. 3. Cf. 19. 2. 13. 4. The last clause, *sed lege* ff., is held by De Medio, 51, to be interpolated on the ground that in his day Ulpian could not have expressed himself so strongly, *acc.* Rotondi, 958 n. 2; Schulz, 56, but that Julian did not think "even faintly" of our action, as De Medio asserts, is shown to be incorrect by the position of the text, Lenel, Pal., Jul., 822. By those who hold it genuine the passage is thought to raise the much-discussed question whether the degree of Aquilian care was affected by a contract relation like deposit, cf. Vangerow, 3. 592; *contra* Ferrini, E. G. I., § 217. The difference between Julian and Ulpian was perhaps not upon this point but on the question of fact as to the defendant's intent; if the moderate injury permitted by the privilege was intended, the problem of negligence is presented, *i. e.*, whether the actual harm was foreseeable; but if more than moderate injury was intended, there is no more to be said (*non dubito*), lack of foreseeability of the actual injury, cf. 7. 5, or *bona fides* of the conviction that such force was permitted are both irrelevant. The commonsense view that the standard of Aquilian care varied with the circumstances is, however, supported by 31; 39; cf. *infra* 38; Esp., §§ 214–217.

6. Cf. 10. The correctness of the word *culpa*, though harm was intended, may be seen by comparing cases 1 and 2, *infra* 9. 4; the cruelty is only objective since the purpose was to "correct and instruct." This is a case of what might have been called *culpa lata*, by Paul, if any distinction had been necessary, by the Byzantines, if they had applied themselves to the question of Aquilian *culpa*. The confusion in this vexed subject (see De Medio, Bull., 17. 5, 18. 260; St. Fadda, 2. 221; Lenel, Z., 1917, 263), may be due to the fact that there are so many different situations, *infra* 9. 4, which were lumped together by the Byzantines in their attempt to treat *culpa lata* like *dolus*. Due to the confusion of the sources regarding contractual *culpa* a doctrine has been recently growing that there was a post-classical change in the idea of Aquilian fault which necessitated extensive interpolation in our statute. It is not easy to discover from these authors exactly what occurred, cf. the efforts of Betti, A. G., 93. 300 ff., 318 n. 1, to expound and distinguish the theories. It is meaningless to assert that the classical law was interested only in the "objective imputability," or causal connection, Rotondi, 954 ff., because in all the texts except 30. 3 the question is not as to the causality but whether and why the act was wrongful, cf. also 5. 2. However, given Rotondi's remarks upon 7. 2, it may be that his idea is that the classical liability was based upon performance of an always dangerous act, not a usually proper act negligently carried out where the fault consists only of an omission. Though everything may be said against this distinction, in view of our difficulties with nonfeasance it is not for a common lawyer to call it historically impossible. Yet upon this hypothesis, not to mention the very text cited, it is impossible to explain the result in 27. 9, or 8. pr., fortified by Coll. 12. 7. 7. Another version of the theory is that the Byzantines developed a generalized, moralistic conception of *culpa*, whereas the classical jurists had operated without a criterion of due care. The author appears to admit that the change required alteration of none of the decisions, Z., 1925, 300, 337 ff. As applied to 31 this theory involves the absurdity of supposing that the consideration of foreseeability was too scholastic for Ulpian and Paul although our law as well as "Oriental justice" has been unable to dispense with it, see Alabaster, Notes on Chinese Crim. Law, 261, 276, 278, 281, 282; v. d. Berg, Minhadj at-Talibin, 3. 172, 177–178. The final touch has been added by Albertario, R. D. Comm., 1923, 1. 506, who apparently for the first time impugns the mention of *culpa* in this text, and 5. 1, 2; 10; 52. 4, leaving the term only in 32. 1, 44. pr.; 45. 4; 57, the last surely by inadvertence. Since he permits the word "negligence" in 7. 2; 30. 4; 52. pr.; cf. 50. 16. 226; and *imperite* in 7. 8; cf. 50. 17. 132, such a thesis is justifiable only on the basis that the ancients had a superstitious terror of a word which, as in our language, would appear more popular and less technical than "negligence," cf. K. V. I., 50. 418, 436. For the opposite extreme see Radin, 12 Cal. L. Rev. 487, who thinks the statute was passed primarily to cover "cases of negligence." The surest proof that the Byzantines left our field untouched is in the fact that there is no attempt to erect a *bonus paterfamilias* therein, and above all that in the texts like this and 10 they never thought of mentioning their favorite *culpa lata*. The question of Aquilian *culpa* was always decided as one of fact, 52. 2, the test of foreseeability, from the point of view of the b. p. f. being adopted if necessary, 31; but the need of a legal principle of due care was rightly not felt, covering as it does any and all cases of liability imposed by the law.

7. pr. De Medio, 58 n. 1, believes this passage and 9. 1. 3; 9. 3. 7, to be interpolated, basing his view on Coll. 2.4. 1; cf. *infra* 27. 17; Pernice, 2.40 n. 1. v. Tuhr, 10, considers this the only case where the interest is independent of the value because there is no value. This is doubtful; though not owner of his son's eye, the father has a legal and marketable right to acquisitions resulting from the former's services, hence the direct action. As for the point that the law mentioned only a slave, Desserteaux, Cap. Dem., 1. 306 (whose view allows the transferee greater rights than the transferor), at the time of its passage interpretation may well have included the son as *loco servi* and the recovery have been later diminished rather than extended, for the form of the action is never qualified. It is hard to see why this action should not survive though the son dies of the wound, and logic, as the glossators saw, requires this result though the death be immediate, *acc.* Van Wetter, Obl., 3. 407 n. 7; cf. Osborne *v.* Gillett, 8 Exch. Div. 88. As for the extraordinary procedure, cf. Coll. 1. 11; Beseler, 4. 244. Our text implies that the son did not have a concurrent action *in factum* for permanent injury, cf. Mandry, Familiengüterrecht, § 27, an omission surprising in Justinian's time.

7. 1. From here to 11.6 the term *occidere* is discussed.

7. 2. The word includes a case where death was unintended, Leone, Riv. D. Comm. 7. 91, holds that the discussion of *culpa* is interpolated; *contra* Rotondi, 961 n. 1, who regards this as a case of "objective *injuria*," a view which seems to suit *oneraverit* but not *transierit*.

7. 3. The last clause is held interpolated, because of its brusqueness, by Beseler, 3, 156; Rotondi, 949. The direct action was available by interpretation if the damage was *corpori corpore datum.* In other cases where recovery seemed proper an action *in f.* or *utilis* was admitted (or the Byzantine *actio in f. generalis*, a supposed subsumption of many unrelated actions under our law, see Rotondi, S. G., 444 ff.; but cf. Riccobono, Ann. Sem. Giur., 4. 638–652). The Institutes, 4. 3. 16, say that the *a. ut.* lay where the damage was *corpori* not *corpore*, the *a. in f.* in all other cases. As there are many other texts besides this which seem to negative this distinction it is usually held an error of Justinian, which is variously explained, cf. Lenel, 198; Esp. § 232; Rotondi, S. G., 451 n. 1, who attributes the divergence to a dispute of the schools, exactly the reverse of that indicated by 11. 5. Accarias, Précis, 4 ed., 2. 513 n. 2, holds that the term *in factum* may apply to an *a. ut.* thus explaining texts like this, but he challenges the production of a text where the *a. ut.* is given though the damage is not *corpori*. 30. 2 is such a one (cf. also G. 3. 202), an objection which Rotondi, *op. cit.*, 456 is forced to meet by suggesting an interpolation. Such an assertion involves two improbabilities; first, that no relief was given in such a case, so also for cases of mixing, 27. 14, 20; second, that the Byzantines, perhaps the very men who wrote J. 4.3. 16, should have forgotten a distinction dear to them and dating, according to Rotondi, from the earliest times. His theory that the *a. in f.* for damage not *corpori* was not assimilated to our remedy till long after the classical age, but rather to those for theft (or *dolus*) has its support in the fact that beyond exceptional cases like 30. 2 or perhaps frightening something to death, cf. Quintilian, De Inst. Or., 7. 3, damage without spoiling can consist only in loss of possession. However, if these actions were modelled on any others, which he seems to admit, the contrary view is upheld, besides 30. 2, by the testimony of Sabinus, 27. 21, as well as by the fact that in these cases of loss not only was no specific intent required but *culpa*, almost certainly Aquilian, was the standard; in fact a comparison of G. 3. 202 with 47. 2. 50. 4 appears conclusive upon an impartial perusal, *contra*, apparently, Pomponius, 19. 5.

14. 2. As regards the nature of the damage, G. 4. 37, there is then, surely no distinction between the subsidiary actions, nor between them and the direct action as to the *duplum*, *contra* Z., 1887, 225 ff., or the back reckoning, cf. 12; C. 3. 35. 5; Naber, 26. 273; Rotondi, S. G. 460 ff. In fact there are many passages which do not make a distinction between the direct and indirect remedies, cf. this text with 11. 5, 37. pr.; also 28. pr., etc.; and our difference between trespass and case, which continued long after its practical importance had vanished, Bacon, Abridg. 6 ed., 6. 588; 1 Chitty, Pleading, 6 ed., 128.

7. 4. De Medio, 57, believes the reference to the *filius* to be interpolated; Albertario, Costruzione *Nisi . . . tunc enim*, 14, says the same of *aut si rell.*, but cf. K. V. I., 50. 419 n. 24. *Occiderit* may refer to the action of 7 pr., but cf. Pampaloni, *infra* 13. pr. There is nothing wrongful in the game, 11. 5. 2. 1, nor any *culpa* if the ordinary methods are pursued, unless the privilege conferred by the consent of the other is exceeded, cf. Reg. *v.* Bradshaw, 14 Cox C. C. 83. If it were not for the context it would be preferable to refer *procedit* to an injury by the slave, for the freeman not only may be ignorant of the *status* but also is less clearly at fault in condescending than the slave in presuming; but cf. 11. 3. 4; *infra* 37. pr. If the freeman knew that his opponent was a slave, consent would bar his recovery contrary to our rule, cf. Lembo *v.* Donnell, 117 Me. 143; Bohlen, 24 Col. L. Rev. 819; Szadiwicz *v.* Cantor, 154 N. E. 251, 49 A. L. R. 958. Much unnecessary confusion has been introduced into this subject by the use of the term *culpa* compensation. Although contributory negligence as such usually depends merely on causation, 28. 1, but cf. 9. 4, the expression objected to includes at least three other kinds of cases, cf. Pernice, 1. 89 ff. First, those like ours where the defendant's *culpa* is irrelevant because the plaintiff has given permission (uninspired by defendant, cf. Arch. P., 349 ff.) for the act causing the injury, 52. 4; 13. 6. 23. Similar to these situations are those where what would otherwise be wrong is justified by the analogy of self-defense, 4. 3. 1. 3, cf. Bekker, Aktionen, 1. 172. Second, there are cases of real compensation of contractual claims based on fault, 16. 2. 10. pr., where the balance may surely be recovered if the claims are unequal, see *infra* 52. 1. Third, there are cases resembling contributory negligence in that there is only one claim wholly barred because of the plaintiff's culpable conduct, but differing in that the fault is causally immaterial; *i. e.*, the injury would have happened had the act been proper, cf. 31, or a negligently driven locomotive striking one approaching a grade-crossing with dynamite to blow up a train.

7. 5. *Culpa* in giving the blow must be assumed, the liability follows, as with us, from the fact of direct cause. The text is a great stumbling block to the adherents of the German theory of "adequate," *i. e.*, objectively foreseeable, cause.

7. 6. As to the existence of a school dispute on this point, see Esp., § 233. The poison was not directly administered, cf. 9. 1.

7. 7. An extension of the direct action, the object producing the harm being in no connection with the defendant.

7. 8. Cf. 50. 17. 132. Many difficulties are raised by 50. 13. 1. 1, cf. Hefke, Arch. P., 45–69, 113–130; Löwenfeld, Festg. Planck, 420–441; Z., 1888, 267 n. 6. It is probable that they are all in the contractual sphere. As for Aquilian liability any distinction between doctors of high or low degree is made improbable by the similar treatment of the midwife, 9 pr.; 50. 13. 1. 2, 9. By 8 pr. it appears that no difference can be taken between a surgeon and a doctor; nor is 1. 18. 6. 7. of any significance in view of *id.* 10, if indeed it is not with Löwenfeld, 428, to be taken as a case of criminal liability. The status of a freeborn professor of medicine who prescribes poison is just as irrelevant for Aquilian liability as it would be in case of theft. The only question would be as to the standard of care if the services were gratuitous.

8. pr. This decision has been suspected only by Biondi, Jud. B. F., 139 n. 2, on the authority of Grupe, who objected merely to the grammatical form of the verbs. The last clause is held interpolated by Beseler, 2. 85; Rotondi, 957 n. 4, whose thesis is not much aided by the more exact restriction in Coll. 12. 7. 7 to the indirect action, *acc.* 30. 3; cf. K. V. I. 50. 436 ff. The only culpable factor here is an omission and it probably was not until the idea of *culpa* was developed that the Romans perceived that this is usually the case in a fault of negligence as distinguished from "objective *injuria*," *supra* 6, cf. Pernice, 2. 62 ff.; Rev. Gén., 46. 266, 47. 96. As for liability for omissions in non-contractual relations the rules of the classical Roman law seem to have largely coincided with ours: There is a duty to act with due care and hence a disability or liability for omissions, always when the damage to be avoided is to oneself; if to others, when their injury is caused by a rightful act of one's own or an object of which one has assumed control; for the former duty see 9. 4; 28. 1; 30. 4; 52. pr.; *contra* Brinz, Pand., 2 ed., § 281b n. 13, 14, and our theory of contributory negligence; for the latter see 27. 9; 30. 3; Black *v.* R. R., 193 Mass. 448; R. R. *v.* Grizzle, 124 Ga. 735; Kelly *v.* R. R. (1895), 1 Q. B. 944. The assumption of control may consist merely in the acquisition of possession; according to the nature of the object the duty may be absolute: noxal liability; J. 4. 9. 1; Filburn *v.* People's Palace Company, 25 Q. B. D. 258; Rylands *v.* Fletcher, 3 H. L. 330; or relative: cf. 45. 1 with the duty to licensees; for its limit cf. 7. 1. 13. 2; 39. 2. 24. 2 with Giles *v.* Walker, 24 Q. B. D. 656; Hayndon *v.* Schultz, 124 Ia. 724. Except for the disability of contributory negligence neither system usually imposes duties to act unattached to assumption of control or the like. This rule is by no means absolute, as often stated, *e. g.*, Z., 1925, 215: cf. the duty to undergo a search, G. 3. 188, 192; 11. 4. 1. 2; J. 4. 1. 4, the duty to aid a policeman, Regina *v.* Brown, Car. & M. 314, or to prevent certain crimes, 48. 10. 9. 1; C. 9. 24. 1; Mél. Cornil, 2. 447 n. 1; State *v.* Wilson, 80 Vt. 249. In these cases any doubt as to the propriety of an action of trespass on the case, or *ad exemplum* L. A. depends upon the intent of the criminal law, cf. 27. Harv. L. Rev. 317, not upon lack of causality, in view of the undoubted liability in 27. 9 (cf. a chauffeur sitting in a parked car started by another) where reliance by the plaintiff upon the assumption of control is certainly immaterial. It is no less certain that inability to prevent the injury, irrelevant upon an indictment, *supra* Reg. *v.* Brown, would preclude civil liability; the contrary rule in the *actio furti prohibiti*, G., *loc. cit.*, is explained by the fact that the remedy originally fulfilled a criminal function. An attempt has been made, 37 Jhering's Jahrb. 353 n. 1, to rest causation upon an exercise of the will, a doctrine which would not apply to cases where negligent ignorance of the emergency would not excuse the omission, cf. C. 9. 24. 1. 4. Where there is a legal duty to act in favor of another, to give it any meaning the law must treat a breach thereof as capable of effect. It is probable that a necessary fiction is involved, as will appear if the possibility of the causality of a non-action be considered in the absence of a duty to act and knowledge of the emergency.

8. 1. As to interpolation see Beseler, 4. 211; Albertario, *supra* 6. Modern writers believe classical jurists incapable of discussing *culpa* in such a generalized manner.

9. 1. Cf. 7. 6.

9. 2. The case is probably that of 47. 8. 2. 20.

9. 4. It is obviously inadequate with Brinz, *supra* 8. pr.; Beseler, Z., 1922, 540, to impute to the classical lawyers the confusion shown by J. 4. 3. 5. *infra* 31, *i. e.*, to assume that the defendant here and in 11 pr.; 28. 1, was not negligent, which besides being apparently untrue makes discussion of the plaintiff's *culpa* immaterial. It is noticeable that the negligence of the slave is imputed to his master. Contributory negligence or *culpa* compensation, cf. *supra* 7. 4, should be regarded as a question of causality; 50. 17. 203; Windscheid, § 258 n. 17; Buckland, 582. The last sentence is taken as authority for the accepted view that the plaintiff's negligence is disregarded if the defendant was guilty of *dolus*,

Windscheid, § 258 n. 18; Steinmetz *v.* Kelly, 72 Ind. 442. Rabel, 482 n. 3, rightly maintains the contrary if the causal connection has been "broken," citing 19. 1. 45. 1; cf. Bull., 16. 72; in our field this is proved by 30. 4; 52. pr. The use of the words *data opera* is significant, this being a wider term than *dolus*, Z. 1917, 287; cf. Ebrard, Z., 1926, 144 ff., who in spite of G. 3. 202, attempts to deprive the classical lawyers even of this expression. In fact, between Aquilian *dolus*, the intention with a "bad" motive (per Parke, B., in Brook *v.* Rawl, *cit.* Odgers, Libel, 4 ed., 320; cf. 17. 1. 8. 10 with 47. 2. 55. 1) to injure property known to be another's, and negligence, an omission without any such intention but merely such as would not be performed by a prudent man dealing with another's property, there appear to be at least four different grades of acts which should be distinguished for an understanding of Aquilian fault, cf. 38. I. Harm is intended with a bad motive under a belief, reasonable or not, that the requisites do not exist for an Aquilian action, 45. 2. II. Harm is intended, but without a bad motive, involving the unreasonable belief that it is justified, which includes mistakes as to the extent of a privilege, 5. 3; 6; 4. 3. 7. 7; 17. 1. 8. 10; *contra?* 16. 3. 7. pr.; cf. De Medio, Bull., 18. 282. III. Harm is not intended, but the act or omission is analytically *proximus dolo*, a possibility not overlooked by the older scholars. Zasius, cit. Rotondi, S. G., 98 n. 1, as it is to-day by De Medio and Lenel. The clearest example is that of a marksman, even an expert, who shoots at a slave for a heavy bet that he can knock off his hat; in this class come all breaches of the concrete standard, 16. 3. 32; the distinction of Sertorio, *Culpa in Concreto*, 264, is of dubious correctness, cf. 13. 6. 5. 4 with 49. 1; also 16. 3. 11; 36. 1. 22. 3. IV. The act or omission may be so dangerous as to amount to gross negligence but the possibility of harm is not envisaged, cf. Paul's epigrammatic definition in 50. 16. 213. 2; *id.* 223. pr. Examples are: going to sleep at the switch, forgetting the slave's presence the instant after seeing him, cf. 10; 47. 2. 50. 4; Coll. 1. 11, which shows how the distinction may be proved. One might be driving at a gallop through the forum to reach one's wife's bedside, cf. Weare *v.* Fitchburg, 110 Mass. 334. Sometimes the motive may even justify the act, *e. g.*, firemen, soldiers, J. 4. 3. 4, cf. our cases of so-called liability without fault. The act or omission may only be so dangerous that it would not be performed by a careful man, the case of "objective *injuria*." This differs practically from ordinary negligence only in being "antecedent," *i. e.*, the liability cannot be evaded no matter what care is later shown in avoiding the accident, a fact which has confused some commentators, *e. g.*, Leone, *cit.* 7. 2; Rotondi, *cit.* 6. *Data opera* applies to the first three cases, G. 3. 202, so that the plaintiff is not barred even if with due care after the defendant's act he could have avoided the damage, otherwise in the last case unless his lack of care was not causal, *i. e.*, the injury would have happened even if he had not been negligent, *acc.* Burkhardt, Sinn und Umfang, 108 ff.; British Col. R. R. *v.* Loach (1916), 1 A. C. 719, is wrong, Bohlen, St. in Torts, 536; see further Pernice, 1. 92 ff.; Aiken *v.* R. R., 184 Mass. 269.

11. pr. Reading *radebat* for *habebat.* See Beseler, 3. 114, who was doubtful; Rotondi, 959, who is sure of interpolation. There is no reason not to include the ball players in *eorum*, cf. v. Leyden, Culpa Comp., 28 ff. This is a case of what we call assumption of risk, and what as applied to the defendant the civilians term "objective *injuria*." It differs from 7. 4 in that the defendant is clearly guilty of *culpa*, cf. Thomas *v.* Quartermaine, 18 Q. B. D. 685. The text shows that the Romans were never misled by the doctrine of "last clear chance," which would allow recovery from the ball players, cf. 3 Harv. L. Rev. 263. From a note in the Basilica it appears that the defense of contributory negligence was as much in disfavor in the later Greek Empire as in modern times. Hagiotheodoret allows a freeman to recover as the "lesser injustice," and refuses to impute the negligence of the slave to the master, thus unconsciously restoring the classical law recently discovered by Beseler, Z., 1922, 540. To a common lawyer this seems a reversal of the probable order; and from other texts it seems clear that Beseler is attributing modern refinements to the common sense of the classical law, 16. 2. 9. pr., 44. 4. 4. 17; *id.* 5. 3; before claiming that the second text is interpolated, Schulz, Z., 1912, 74 ff., should have considered the others (otherwise, however, in 52. pr.).

11. 2. Beseler, 4. 300, holds the clause following *nam* to be interpolated, *contra* Levy, 1. 486. Each is held by the interpretation of *occidere* unless he can offer evidence that his blow did not cause the death, cf. Territory *v.* Yarberry, 2. N. M. 391; Northrup *v.* Eakes, 72 Okla. 66; 33 Harv. Law Rev. 639; 39 *id.* 153; Wharton Crim. Law, 10 ed., 174; but see the opposite result in Cook *v.* R. R., 98 Wis. 624; cf. Miller *v.* R. R., 24 Ida. 567, where one cause was natural, *i. e.*, it was not certain that *somebody* was liable. It appears sounder with this text to explain these cases as a matter of "public policy" than to erect a fiction of causality. As to the penal nature of the action see Levy, Privatstrafe, § 10. There was theoretically (cf. *supra* 2. 2) nothing penal in the damages under the first chapter; v. Tuhr, 1. 9 (inexplicably ignored by Levy, *op. cit.* 148) has shown that the function of the back reckoning was to avoid the difficult questions of damages which have so vexed our law, cf. 39 Harv. L. Rev. 760. G. 4. 9 is correct, if at all, only for purposes of concurrence, cf. Beseler, Z., 1927, 65; Betti, *cit. supra*, 2. 1, 713 n. 1, 714 ff.; the *duplum* was not a substantive penalty, it applied to a legacy, but see Levy, *op. cit.*, 147. The mention of the value as opposed to the interest is explained by the fact that the statute contemplated only an owner's suit. Our action is thus unique, being for a delict of the *ius civile* with purely reparatory damages. In the former character it is penal; being noxal, passively intransmissible, and cumulative as here stated, *contra* Naber, 53. 27, citing 2. 1. 9, which, however, is widely thought interpolated, Levy, 1. 478 n. 4; cf. Freeman, Judgments, 5 ed., §§ 573–578. In the latter character it is sometimes treated as not penal,

27. 30; 17. 2. 50; 47. 10. 7. 1, as Monro says it is delictal rather than penal, cf., however, the obscure remarks of Levy, *op. cit.*, 136 n. 1. Since the nature of the damages was misunderstood by Gaius, it is no disgrace to Justinian that he calls the action "mixed" like that for theft, J. 4. 6. 19; cf. De Francisci, 68 ff.; Rotondi, 967 n. 3.

11. 3. Cf. 15. 1; 51 pr.; State *v.* Scates, 5 Jones L. 420; Walker *v.* State, 116 Ga. 537. As in 49 the back reckoning prevents difficulties of valuation, cf. Mommsen, 2. 155 n. 16; 39 Harv. L. Rev. 154.

11. 4. For interpolation see Beseler, 4. 194.

11. 5. Cf. Dilts *v.* Kinney, 15 N. J. L. 130. This is the chief support for Pernice's suggestion that the Proculians were more willing than the Sabinians to grant the direct action, *supra* 7. 6.

11. 6. Until 2 pr. the "active legitimation" is discussed in relation to the word *erus*, on which term cf. Kooiman, Frag. J. Q., 144.

11. 7. In *b.f.* transactions if an object was to be transferred, all actions in connection with it belonged to the person who bore the risk, cf. 19. 1. 13. 12; Mommsen, 1. 294 ff. In our law the *status quo* having changed, redelivery would probably be disallowed, cf. Williston, Sales, 2 ed., § 610, unless there had been fraud, in which case a difficulty would be presented where actions of tort are unassignable, Defries *v.* Milne (1913), 1 Ch. 98; Prouty *v.* R. R., 174 Ala. 404; R. R. *v.* Shutt, 24 Okla. 96; Murray *v.* Buell, 76 Wis. 657.

11. 8. Cf. 4. 2. 21. 2; Bruns, Besitzklagen, § 17; Mommsen, 2. 244 ff.; Jeffries *v.* R. R., 5 E. & B. 802. The subject of the b. f. p.'s interest with its many complications has been carefully discussed by Eisele, Arch., 67. 41, whose results seem somewhat vitiated by the assumption that the Roman rules of interpleader correspond to those of the German Code. There is nowhere a hint that the holder of a real right had to give the security which fulfilled the function of interpleader, 3. 5. 30. 1; 5. 3. 57; 31. 8. 3; cf. *infra* 27. 14. Hence it is very doubtful whether a usucapting b. f. p. may recover in full; but more plausible that a m. f. p. with a lien for expenses, C. 3. 32. 5, may use our action. Buckland, 583 n. 11, 13, thinks that in classical law the b. f. p. gave up all that he recovered to the owner, 5. 3. 55, which text is not an analogy for several reasons. First, there were differences between the b. f. p. of an inheritance and the ordinary case, especially with regard to the fruits, cf. Buckland's earlier remarks, Slavery, 336; N. R. H., 1910, 763 ff.; Beseler, 4. 21. Second, it deals only with enrichment; otherwise if the *duplum* had been obtained in the action *in factum?* Third, the b. f. p. there appears to have recovered as owner, cf. Esp., § 243. In fact since suit must always have so been brought in the absence of supervening knowledge, in which case there would be a claim only on the basis of the lien, 41. 1. 48. 1 (but cf. 22. 1. 25. 2, and 55 as to the influence of the back reckoning), it is probable that Ulpian was thinking of a bonitary owner, cf. 17; De Medio, 68 n., who maintains an interpolation. In the rare case when suit had to be brought *qua* b. f. p. if the tort had been committed one moment before usucaption, the defendant might have to pay full damages twice. These considerations make it probable that the chance of usucaption either was not regarded, cf. Arch., 51. 261, 52. 15 n. 110 (the contrary view of Bonfante, Scritti, 3. 564 ff., rests on texts which probably referred to the "bonitary" owner, cf. 50. 16. 49), or was wholly a matter of discretion for the *judex*. In other respects the b. f. p.'s action would be much like that urged in 8 Exch. Div. 88, any lack of good faith caused by the defendant's dispute of title probably not being material. If there were recovery as owner, in a later suit by the real owner the b. f. p. could retain the amount which he would have had in this action; but a very difficult situation would be presented if the owner sued the wrongdoer. The value of the lien against the owner should be recovered either by a b. or m. f. p. If the slave is merely injured, the b. f. p.'s action is like that in 7. pr., and either type of possessor would have a claim for the amount by which the lien exceeds the present value of the slave. The whole subject is affected by the obscurity of the rules as to burden of proof of ownership and interest, cf. Jhering, trad. Meulenaare, Fondement des Interdits, 48.

11. 9. This passage is an authority for the usual view that our action was given only to one with a real right, cf. 27. 14; 4. 3. 18. 5; some, however, take it as excluding only the direct action, in spite of the preceding text, cf. 9. 1. 2. pr.; Debray, N. R. H. 1909. 664 n. 2; Pampaloni, St. Senesi, 10. 82 n. 27; but cf. 47. 2. 54. 2; Schäfer, Activleg. bei L. A., Diss. Tuttlingen, 16, justifies the result because plaintiff is a donee, 43. 24. 13. 4; 44. 4. 4. 29, forgetting that he might have assumed liability to the owner. Haymann, Z., 1919, 198, tries desperately to prove from the text that the *custodia* obligation included Aquilian damage, cf. however Buckland, 575 n. 3.

11. 10. At the other extreme from those just mentioned who allow our action like that for theft to anyone with an interest, it has been suggested by Baviera, *cit.* De Medio, 65 n. 1, that the classical law did not allow the usufructuary an action *against a third person*, cf. 4. 3. 7. 4, and hence that the words following *ego* are interpolated; see also Arangio Ruiz, A. G., 82. 420 ff. As for 47. 7. 5. 1. cutting down trees would not usually be an injury to the usufruct, 7. 1. 9. 7; *id.* 10, 11; cf. 43. 24. 16. 1. In view of 39. 2. 5. 2; 48. 5. 28. 3 it seems scarcely worth while to doubt that the usufructuary recovered only the value of his interest, but cf. Arch., 75. 303 ff.; Esp., § 245. It is usually assumed that Julian's doubts were as to the existence, not the form, of the action, but without reason, cf. N. R. H., 1909. 660 n. 2.

12. There is no support for the view that *pro portione* refers to a co-owner of the usufruct, or that recovery of a quasi-usufruct in the full value is intended, cf. Glück, It. trans., 9. 71 n. *m*. The assessment of the expectancy, 35. 2. 68. pr., the lower of the two in the case of a slave, should be made as of a year before. Two questions arise: can one go back to a time when one had none or a different interest to value his present interest? and can one go back to a time when one had a different interest and claim that? This text answers the first question, cf. 23. 7. It is however doubtful whether the rule does not depend upon the conception of a usufruct as *pars dominii*, see Buckland, 270 n. 3, just as if an owner had bought the slave within a year; *i. e.*, would it apply to a pledgee of a painter who lost his hand within the year, but before the creation of the pledge by a now insolvent owner? But see 55.

13. pr. De Medio, 61 ff., thinks that Ulpian refused the action. If a free painter's arm were paralyzed and then cut off by defendant all within a month, could the extra amount be recovered? v. Tuhr's view, *supra* 7. pr., would appear to require a negative answer in contradiction to his general thesis, but the *utilis* action treats the limb as if it had a value. Pampaloni, 32 A. G. 392 n. 14, maintains that the heir of a freeman had a *utilis* action for his death, an opinion better confined to the father, 7. pr.; cf. 9. 3. 1. 5. Another question is as to a freeman enslaved between a mortal wound and death, see Z., 1925, 437; Buckland, Slavery, 413, 435.

13. 1. See *infra* 38. A more lenient standard of care is here applied, 41. 1. 54. 2; cf. Z., 1918, 12; 40. 12. 13. pr. This fact seems very cogent in proving that contractual relations modify the Aquilian standard; it is hard to see why Vangerow's observations, 3. 590, upon 54. 2 *cit.* do not apply to contracts; on the point, cf. Gooch *v.* Presbyterian Hospital, 239 Fed. 828.

13. 2. The statement that the inheritance will be considered the owner is thought an interpolation by many who believe that the classical lawyers could deal with this subject without unnecessarily committing themselves upon the point whether the testator or the heir was represented, Buckland, Slavery, 252; Rabel, 533 n. 3. The latter author is certainly right in urging us not to take these dogmatic fictions too seriously. We speak of relation, of title in the probate court, or the state, or in abeyance, cf. Brackett *v.* Hoitt, 20 N. H. 257; 2 Bl. Comm., 494 ff.; Smith, Personal Prop., 2 ed., 106 ff.; Litz *v.* Bank, 15 Okla. 564.

13. 3. This text has been called a *lex damnata.* Ferrini, Legati, 394, Esp., § 308, explains the confusion on the assumption that the compilers tried to alter a text dealing with a personal legacy to fit their law, which for this purpose applied the rules of a real legacy. This suggestion is disposed of by the fact that the text would then have been dealing, not with the legatee's right to bring the action, but with the quite different question of 4. 3. 18. 5, cf. *infra* 54. The difficulty remains that the Sabinian view prevailed that acceptance was not necessary for the acquisition of the title to an object left *per vindicationem:* 8. 6. 19. 1; 28. 1. 16. 1; Windscheid, § 643 n. 2; and was applied here by Ulpian, *infra* 35; but cf. 30. 86. 2, where Julian says that acceptance will relate back, see also Thompson *v.* Leach, 2 Vent. 198; Standing *v.* Bowring, 31 Ch. Div. 282; Kingsbury *v.* Burnside, 58 Ill. 310. The attempts at explanation are reviewed by Vanni, St. Serafini, 175, who adopts the scholiast's suggestion that only the direct action is excluded. Many follow the Vulgate's *si modo* or insert a *non,* Glück, Pand., 49. 168 n. 4; or read *repudiavit* for *agnovit.* Others are satisfied with this exception, Castellari, 22 A. G. 401 ff., failing to note that the decision conflicts with 35. Wlassak, Z., 1910, 298 ff., gives it up. From 46. 3. 13 it appears that the legacy was accepted, *agnoscere,* if a reasonable time passed without refusal, which text, also from Julian, lends great support to Von Crailshem's theory, Arch., 47. 389, that *si* should be understood as *etsi,* or that *non* is connected with *agnovit,* not *si.* This, implying that the legatee has the action if he is, for example, still deliberating when the slave dies, satisfactorily explains the next clause, refusal being the only case where he has not the action.

14. For the position of this text see Wlassak, *op. cit.,* 243 n. 1. From the context and in view of 4. 3. 7. 5 it is not unreasonable to assume that the action is Aquilian, cf. 27. 10

with Coll. 12. 7. 8 (*Aquilia lege*), and the killing after entry. The legacy must then have been real as even Ferrini is disposed to admit, Esp., 309. The question is as to the heir's position when he is ignorant of the legacy. If it had been personal there was apparently a very strict liability, the limits of which are much disputed, see Girard, 668 n. 4, 669 n. 1, 4; Salkowski-Glück, Pand., 49. 276–278, 317 ff.; Ferrini, 78 Arch. 321 ff. Just as the heir was treated in that case as harshly as, if not more so than, a promisor who knew of the obligation, so if the legacy were real the heir must have been held not *qua* b. f. possessor, *infra* 38, but like an ordinary heir, for whose liability see 30. 47. 5. Having been put upon inquiry by entry he may well have been under an absolute duty to distinguish what was his. In view, then, of his Aquilian liability, there is no reason in the attempt to apply here the rules of a personal to the case of a real legacy as does Salkowski, *op. cit.*, 323 ff.; *contra* Segrè, St. Scialoja, 1. 244 ff.; Ferrini, *op. cit.*, 322. If the heir's act is committed before entry, the only texts are 4. 3. 7. 5; 34. 3. 24. *Priusquam factus sit* in the former text seems irresistibly to point to the fact that it was written of a real legacy, *contra* Ferrini, Legati, 393. If so, the personal action can be explained only as an interpolation, Segrè, *op. cit.*, 253 n. 1; Wlassak, *op. cit.*, 226, or on the ground that such an action was allowed in classical law for a valid real legacy, Salkowski, *op. cit.*, 258 ff., which seems discordant with principle, Segrè & Ferrini, *cit. supra;* Lenel, 3 ed., 540 n. 5. Hence Wlassak's theory is the most acceptable, the words *priusquam*, etc., as well as the next decision show that the Romans failed to carry the doctrine of *dies cedens* to the logical and desirable conclusion contended for by Ferrini, Legati, 388–395. Although there is room for nothing but conjecture as to the classical method of dealing with this situation for any kind of legacy, the theory adopted points to the *actio doli*, and for Justinian's law to the same standard of care as was applied after entry to an heir personally bound.

15. pr. This decision seems inconsequent, see the confused explanation in Glück, Pand., 49. 171–178. Ferrini and Fadda, E. G. I., § 58 think that the legacy was personal, so that the heir was always released till Justinian, who in fusing legacies, applied the rule of a vindicatory bequest that fruits (an analogy of little value) from *dies cedens* belong to the legatee, Paul, S. R., 3. 6. 46. Although the legatee ought then always to have the action, the change was not carried out "intensely" enough. Wlassak, *op. cit.*, 236 ff., interprets the legacy as real, denies that fruits from *dies cedens* belong to the legatee, 30. 86. 2; *id.* 120. 2; 35. 2. 73; Glück, 49. 479–495, and holds that the legatee never got the action, and that the assignment was hastily interpolated. Another view is that the legacy was *sinendi modo*, cf. Mommsen, 1. 304 n. 30; G. 2. 280; although this is ingenious, cf. Ferrini, Resp. dell' herede, 9 (Estr. R. Ist. Lomb., 1900), *ad* 30. 84. 4, it requires the hypothesis that the heir was at fault in allowing the damage. Buckland, Slavery, 254 n. 11, adopts Voet's explanation, that the action disappeared as an accessory, 33. 8. 2, which imputes to the Romans confusion of thought. Beseler, 2. 77, gave the best interpretation, which he now rejects, 3. 181; *i. e.*, for a deterioration affecting the *corpus* recovery may be had as an incident of the vindication, 6. 1. 13; *id.* 17. 1, but there is no foundation for the vindication if the object has disappeared without fault of the heir; so substantially Faber, Rat., *ad* 4. 3. 18. 5; see further Glück, It. trans., 30 (2) 147 n. *b*. Even this is not satisfactory because there were methods by which the owner could recover the enrichment, cf. 20. 5. 12. 1 (on which see Riccobono, Ann. Sem. Giur., 610 ff.); C. 4. 2. 2, and these though probably not Byzantine in substance, were so agreeable to the compilers' attitude that any suggestion that this text was interpolated so inadequately is very unlikely.

15. 1. Beseler, 3. 9, thinks *haec . . . occisus* an interpolation, *acc.* Levy, 1. 25 n. 4; cf. Z., 1925. 437. For the shipwreck, cf. 11. 3; for the manumission, cf. 44. 7. 56, perhaps otherwise for a *statuliber*, 47. 2. 52. 29; but cf. 40. 7. 29. pr.; Buckland, Slavery, 288. For the last decision three reasons are given, cf. 36. 1. One is that the action was extinguished by merger since the slave died a freeman; this is invalidated by the case of the *manumissus*. Another is that since the slave could not bring an action for his death he could not transmit it. This is thoroughly unsound as it would forbid an action's being brought for injury to a *jacent* inheritance. On the other hand, if the action is held to accrue in the life of the slave, G. 2. 232, only lack of time prevented him from exercising the inherited direct action for his death. The question is often asked: if the wound were not mortal could the freedman bring an *actio utilis* for what first gave rise to a direct action. Although the negative is usually maintained, Esp., §§ 305 ff., it would appear permissible *a fortiori* since the nature of the action may change during trial, 3. 2. 14; cf. 9. 4. 15; 40. 12. 24. 4. In truth the problem cannot arise, as the freedman will sue directly, just like any heir to a testator who has freed a wounded slave. The third and valid reason, directly contrary to v. Tuhr's theory that the interest may not reduce recovery, is that the heir cannot sue in so far as the value of the inheritance is greater than that of the Aquilian action. Oertmann, Vorteilsausgleichung, 89, tries weakly to justify the contrary modern rule, on the ground of lack of causation, which it would be startling to allege in a case like Riggs *v.* Palmer, 115 N. Y. 506. Pampaloni, A. G. 32. 395 ff., holds that the interest can be judged only in relation to the time of the delict, giving the case of an heir presumptive promising under a penalty one of the testator's slaves. It seems from 41 that this difficulty is illusory, cf. also 21. 2. 38; Grünhut's Z., 25. 561 ff.

16. Cf. however 50. 17. 85. 1; J. 2. 20. 14.

17. De Medio, 44, thinks the reference to the pledgee interpolated, saying that the contract action is sufficient, but cf. *infra* 19. On account of doubts as to the age and scope of the latter the converse view is now held, Biondi, Jud. B. F., 99.

For the damages, cf. 20. 1. 27; De Medio, 40 ff. Monro makes an unfortunate citation; 13. 1. 22. pr. was written of *fiducia*, Z., 1882, 108. As to the b. f. p., interpolation is alleged by Buckland, *supra* 11. 8; De Francisci, Synallagma, 2. 84, seems unnecessarily troubled by the form of the action. This text is rightly used as an argument for the fact that the b. f. p. does not recover in full against a third party; see E. G. I., § 59. The recovery here should comprise only the amount of the lien, for the b. f. p.'s claim for services stops the moment the owner asserts his right. The scholiast's suggestion that full damages may be had because of the loss of the claim for eviction seems Pickwickian and refuted by 18. 1. 35. 4. Although it amounts to saying that the defendant is liable to Aquilian damages because the plaintiff has not the Aquilian action, it still finds favor, Pernice, 1. 53 n. 5; Buckland, Slavery, 336; *contra* Eisele, Arch., 67. 88; Mommsen, 1. 299 n. 21. The answer to the question whether the decision is limited to an owner who knows of the possession depends upon one's view of the lien, the "most weakly protected property right," Bull., 28. 57. In view of its function it is reasonable to treat the owner exactly like the b. f. p. in 38; cf. 50. 17. 36. The case suggested by Buckland of one ignorant of his ownership is a further complication, but the author's remarks seem to disregard the rule *plus est in re quam in existimatione*, cf. 47. 2. 43. 5; 47. 19. 6. Longo, Circ. Giur, 19. 273 ff., appears to maintain that if the b. f. p. is usucapting he may base his claim upon the owner's negligence in discovering that fact, which view, strangely enough, has been approved, K. V. I., 33. 60. It is plausibly suggested that this text may have referred to a "bonitary" owner, Brinz, Pand., 2 ed., § 340 n. 23; *acc.* apparently Lenel, 3 ed., 203 n. 4, so that our difficulties are all Byzantine, for similar cases cf. 11. 8; 27. 3.

18. Cf. Levy, §§ 80–90. His view is that where a tort action concurred with a real or contractual claim, the *judex* was able to impose the alternative by reason of his freedom in the latter types, cf. 5. 3. 36. 2; 6. 1. 13; 19. 2. 25. 5; *id.*, 43, and that it was not till Justinian that the surplus was recoverable, 13. 6. 7. 1; 44. 7. 34. 2, a change which v. Tuhr considers to be caused by a misconception of the back reckoning.

19. Cf. Bond *v.* Hilton, Busb. L. (N. C.) 308; Agnew *v.* Johnson, 17 Pa. St. 373; McClellan *v.* Jenness, 43 Vt. 183, which show that our difficulty was possessory. Riccobono, Essays in Legal History, 56, makes the surprising statement that our action did not lie between co-owners till Justinian, *contra* Biondi, Jud. B. F., 107 ff., cf. 17. 2. 47. 1. As neither mentions this text it must be that they disagree with the universal interpretation which supposes the defendant a co-owner.

20. For the origin of this text, cf. Lenel, Pal., Ulp. 2893; Levy 1. 401 n. 5.

21. pr. From here to 27.3 the computation of damages is discussed. A persistent view regards the rule as limited by C. 7. 47. 1; but cf. 23. 3; so recent an enactment could hardly have been forgotten by the compilers, see Vangerow, 3. 46 ff.

21. 1. See v. Tuhr, 1–9, Pampaloni, A. G., 32. 387 ff. As he applied this rule against the plaintiff, 51. 2, Julian, probably correctly, did not regard it as a fiction.

21. 2. In view of Julian's decision in 23. 2 a protest must be registered against the frequent statements that this rule is "very recent" or "late-classical," Grüber, Arch., 75. 305; Levy, Privatstrafe, 149 n. 2; H. Krüger, Z., 1925, 70; while Beseler's affirmations, *infra* 30. 1; 54, would appear to presuppose an interpolation.

22. pr. If the stipulation were gratuitous the damages appear to be either the highest value of the slave within the year, or the penalty, whichever is greater, cf. *infra* 23. 2; if it were in connection with a sale, risk on the seller and a penalty, the price may be added to the second alternative. If a stipulation had been made over a year before to put a horse out of his misery would recovery be reduced? Pampaloni asks whether this decision would apply if the penalty had been paid within a year, cf. 55. The text may be reconciled with

45. 1. 69 either on the hypothesis that that text does not apply if the impossibility supervenes, Studi e Doc., 15. 200 n. 3, or by assuming that the intention was here explicit, Vangerow, 3. 344.

22. 1. This being a case of interest, not value, it is only if 55 is accepted that Monro's distinction holds good as to successive and simultaneous killing. The *quadriga* here must be distinguished from that in 31. 65. 1; the rule would not apply if an accessory member were killed.

23. pr. The damages here are purely a question of value, not interest, Monro correctly remarking that the rule applies if the inheritance were refused; so equally if it were accepted. Pampaloni, A. G., 32. 414; Windscheid, § 258, n. 12, would have avoided the error of citing this as a case of interest by consulting Pedius, 35. 2. 63. pr. The only difference between this extra value and that in the case of a painter who has lost his hand is that here it may be realized instantaneously without loss of the object.

23. 1. The case is like 15. 1 except that the reference to the substituted heir shows that the slave died in the testator's lifetime. This makes the decision hard to support because the death of the slave is not a cause *sine qua non* of enrichment; this might equally have been obtained by revocation of the will, the ambulatory nature of which and the fact that the inheritance depended on the testator's intent after the slave's death being forgotten. Ulpian has been rightly reproached for this slip, Circ. Giur, 19. 254 ff. His statement that the slave would have been free if he were heir is simply untrue, G. 2. 188; Buckland, 308 n. 11, which disposes of Pampaloni's attempt to excuse him, A. G., 32. 401 ff. The chance that the testator would not revoke the will might increase the *pretium* of his own slave and it is hard to find a reason for refusing to include this extra amount, although of course neither the testator nor the heir can claim all the inheritance as the death of the slave could never have caused them to lose it.

23. 2. On the irreconcilable conflict on this decision with 30. 54. 2. see Windscheid, § 92 n. 8; Bufnoir, Condition, 91 ff.; Ferrini, Legati, 366 ff.; Bull., 27. 194 n. The difficulty is not with our passage, which is supported by many others, *cit.* Brinz, Pand., 2 ed., 4. 157 n. 18.

See Buckland, 33 Yale L. J. 363; Beseler, 4. 124, a freshman in whose class appears to have been the first to see that the value of the slave cannot be recovered if the inheritance is included in the claim; cf. Julian's error in 19. 1. 23; Mommsen, 2. 140. "Also" the value of the services till the last moment when manumission would have fulfilled the condition should be allowed, and in later law probably that of the patronal rights, see 19. 1. 45. 2; Z., 1889, 310. Here it is to the wrongdoer's disadvantage for the *judex* to attempt the valuation, otherwise in 19. 5. 5. 5; cf. 12. 6. 65. 8; 24. 3. 64. 5. The correctness of Buckland's remark, that any advantage in the back reckoning may be included, is to be doubted That is inseparable from a claim of the slave; it cannot be considered in damages which depend on the assertion that the slave would have been lost. In fact, a claim ought not to be allowed which depends upon proof that the value of the slave for Aquilian purposes is not the real value, cf. 37. 1; if an animal worth 20 within the year is sued noxally for damage of 15 when its value is 10, Buckland's principle would allow Aquilian damages of 25. If the slave predeceases the testator a better reason why there are no damages is because they are too conjectural, *i. e.*, the slave was never a medium of inheritance, cf. 38 L. Q. R. 228 ff. The reasoning of the text would lead to the application of the rule of 21. 1 against the plaintiff if the testator's death intervened before death from the mortal wound; such, indeed, seems to have been Julian's view, 51. 2.

23. 4. For interpolation, Beseler, Z., 1922, 540. Even if it were "common experience that a bad slave always confessed," which it seems was not the case, 48. 18. 1. 23, there is nothing to show that there was anything to confess. Yet this seems to have been the regular practice, cf. 43. 16. 6, justifiable only by supposing that the existence but not the identity of accomplices was known, cf. 41. pr.

23. 6. This passage literally covers all the cases suggested *infra* 55, and Savigny so understood it, Esp., § 230; A. G., 32. 414 n. 20.

23. 8. *Ceterisque successoribus* is rightly held interpolated by Longo, Bull., 14. 156; it does not even express Justinian's law, 44. 7. 56; v. Tuhr, 16 n. 16. The last clause following *nisi* is held by De Francisci, 70, to be interpolated; cf. Levy, Privatstrafe, 112 n. 6. This is plausible, as the need for the action is very slight, the *condictio furtiva* usually sufficing, 13. 1. 14. 2. The case is not "inconceivable" as Albertario, Bull., 26. 283, unimaginatively asserts, cf. 30. 2; 41. 1, or Monro's case of killing a slave to whom one is substituted heir, cf. 24. 1. 5. 14. On the form of this action see Girard, 407 n. 3; 4. 2. 17. Levy, *op. cit.*, 96, is misleading; our action was probably not *ad exemplum* L. A., the back reckoning could not apply, cf. J. 4. 3. 9, and it would be unjust to impose the *duplum*, cf. Wenger, Actio Judicati, 68. For a convincing refutation of the theories which hold the development largely Byzantine cf. Levy, *op. cit.*, 108 ff.

23. 9. The difficulties of this text are caused by the statement in 47. 8. 2. 1; 48. 1. 4 that our action as well as the purely penal remedies for theft and robbery "sometimes were *praejudicia*," and by the ambiguity of this word, which allows our passage to be interpreted as meaning: 1, that the criminal action is not lost by the judgment in the civil suit; 2, that the civil judgment should not influence the trial for the crime; 3, that the former should be postponed till completion of the latter. The first view, upheld by Francke, Commentar über H. P., 68; Ferrini, Diritto Penale Rom., 1899, 238; Naber, 27. 266, depends upon the untenable doctrine that there ever was a doubt as to the unrestricted cumulation of a public delict with a private action like ours; Naber, 53. 19 ff., cites a number of late texts giving the plaintiff an election which may equally refer to the order of bringing suit. Indeed, it is incredible that the bringing of an action for reparation such as the *actio locati*, or a penal but reipersecutory remedy such as ours, can on any theory prevent another from bringing an accusation. The only hesitation (quite differently expressed, cf. G. 3. 213; 19. 5. 14. 1) was as to the right of the same person to do both, which was forbidden where the right of accusation was not public, 47. 2. 93; 47. 10. 6; 48. 5. 1. 3; cf. 47. 1. 3; 47. 2. 57. 1; incorrect, Pernice, 2. 1. 45; and there may have developed a view that the offense of insult was merged in the crime of murder, 47. 10. 7. 1, which is, however, often explained as referring merely to the order of suit; Accarias, Précis, 4 ed., 2. 494 n. 5. These exceptions may serve to explain the language of C. Th. 9. 20; C. 9. 31, if it is not an example of didactic pleasure in stating the obvious. The second view, maintained by Mommsen, Strafrecht, 892 n. 3, following Cujas, imputes to Ulpian perhaps an even greater platitude. Since, aside from *res judicata*, there is no possibility of one decision's having any legal effect upon another, Ulpian would be making a banal direction to the *judex* not to allow himself to be improperly influenced. The last interpretation, Savigny, Verm. Schr., 4. 133; Planck, Mehrheit, 231 n. 1, accords best with Cicero and texts such as 43. 5. 5; 48. 6. 5. 1, which, in conjunction with 43. 5. 3. 6; C. 9. 22. 24; cf. C. 3. 8. 4, show that there was a rule by which the criminal issue had first to be decided (the procedural mechanics are not important for our purpose), but which, being discretionary, was "sometimes" infringed in the classical period (as where the defendant's property was in danger of disappearance), finally to disappear under Justinian, C. 9. 31. The language of these texts is unfavorable to the theory that the doctrine was restricted to cases of pendency of the criminal suit; 40. 12. 24. 2 is not conclusive for a case in which the public interest is at stake, but cf. Bülow, Processeinrede, 194 n. 1. There is more plausibility in Lenel's contention, 136 n. 6, that the rule applied only to capital crimes, cf. C. 9. 20. 2 (213 A.D.). The common law seems to have undergone much the same hesitant development on this point, cf. Midland Ins. Co. *v.* Smith, 6 Q. B. D. 568 ff.; 1 Bishop. Crim. L., 8 ed., §§ 267–278.

23. 10. The nature of this *actio confessoria* (as to the name cf. Mél. Girard, 2. 551 ff.) is involved in the obscurity attached to *confessio in jure*, cf. Rotondi, S. G., 428 n. 1. According to Demelius, Confessio, 181, 192; Thomas, N. R. H., 1903, 594, the institutions are quite different, ours more nearly resembling an action upon an interrogation *in jure*, a view which has been attacked by Püschel, Confessus, 184 ff.; *acc.* Z., 1925, 544. Pleading a dilatory exception amounted to a confession, 44. 1. 2. 4.

23. 11. For interpolation, Beseler, 3. 138; Z., 1925, 544 n. 5; Lenel, 3 ed., 201. From 25 pr.; 42. 2. 4, the rule emerges that the confession was not binding if the slave had not been killed or wounded, or had been killed or wounded by no human being. This cannot be explained by any doctrine of impossibility, cf. Monro, 86 ff. But *occidere* means damage *corpore corpori datum;* in this sense, and perhaps in any sense, a slave is not killed who dies of pneumonia. The rubric of Coll. 12. 7 states the confession as "wrongfully killed," cf. Mél. Girard, 2. 512 ff. The terms must have been stereotyped or the effect of a dilatory exception would have been doubtful, and the Coll. is to be preferred to 42. 2. 4, where the content of the confession is not dealt with *ex professo*. Thus it is possible that the defendant is interpreted merely to confess that if anyone is liable, he is the man, so that he will get off if another had killed the slave in self-defense. As to the effect of confession upon the real wrongdoer, see 11. 1. 20. pr.; Püschel, 215 ff.

24. This text is grateful as showing that a sensible method of computing damages was used, a fact not otherwise obvious, cf. 27. 5. The difficulty as to the date is equally applicable to killing, which might have excited suspicion in recent times.

25. 1. Solazzi, Minore Età, 209, thinks that the passage spoke only of the *procurator*. This rule is not applied to *con-*

fessio in jure, 42. 2. 6. 4., cf. 3. 3. 39. pr., but see Püschel, 212 ff.

25. 2. Beseler, 1. 54, regards this whole text as a gloss; it is indeed rendered almost meaningless by the pr. and 23. 11, if those are not to be explained with Püschel as cases of *restitutio*, cf. Lenel, 3 ed., 201 n. 4.

27. pr. It is not technically concurrence if there are separate acts, and cumulation is proper, cf. Levy, § 57; 47. 1. 2. 1. If the damage occurred first, the reduced value of the slave would represent the interest in the *actio furti*, 47. 2. 50. pr. For the *condictio furtiva* in our case, cf. 47. 1. 2. 3; Levy, § 82; it was not passively cumulative, C. 4. 8. 1.

27. 1. If the slave damages another's property with his master's consent, the latter is of course liable. As for the noxal action, G. 4. 76, the co-owner plaintiff is just as liable for the delict of the common slave as the defendant. Hence, as Professor Pound suggests, there is no liability because "the slave cannot serve you," *i. e.*, the defendant, "alone," cf. the Gloss *ad h l.*; Steinlechner, Juris Communio, 2. 158. This clause has now been supposed interpolated by Riccobono, Essays in Legal History, 56 n. 2, on the ground that the direct action did not lie in such a case, and by Biondi, Jud. B. F., 109, for exactly the opposite reason. He fails to note the difference explicitly drawn in our text between actions for the wrong of the defendant, and those *servi nomine;* see his attack, *op. cit.*, 113, on 9. 4. 41 with reference to 17. 2. 47. 1, and his belief, A. N., 117, that 4. 9. 6. 1 supports his theory. Beseler, Z., 1926, 105 ff., 108, maintains the surprising thesis that a noxal action was proper with surrender of the undivided share. Neither Beseler nor Biondi seems to be able to find even a hint in the sources to show that this text does not represent genuine doctrine, cf. the opening sentence of 9. 4. 41; none of the many probable interpolations in this subject touches our point, cf. 9. 4. 8; *id.* 9; *id.* 17. pr.; 47. 2. 62. pr. The disability to claim noxally, though quite logical in a suit which depends upon the nature of the right, of course does not exist in one where the amount is in question. The necessity of a noxal basis for the claim of contribution may be seen in the case where the *socii* own two slaves in different proportions; there will be a claim if one slave kills the other out of spite, but none if it is done in a fit of madness. In such a situation Beseler's view entails not only procedural circuity but substantial arbitrariness; if the object destroyed is of greater value than the wrongdoing slave, two noxal actions are needed, resulting merely in an exchange of the shares in a perhaps worthless thing, the interest in the other thing owned in common being quite disregarded, cf. 39. 2. 27.

27. 2. See 9. 4. 19. pr.; Biondi, A. N., 233; Beseler, *op. cit.*, 108, 112, who applies his theory of part surrender.

27. 3. As to Marcellus see Roby, Introduction, clxxxv. For other delicts noxal liability depended on *potestas*, Buckland, Slavery, 101 n. 11, so that a b. f. p. was noxally liable, and an owner was not if the slave were in flight, 9. 4. 11; *id.* 21. 3; 47. 2. 17. 3, Paul, S. R., 2. 31. 37; in view of the treatment of pledgee and usufructuary in comparison with 9. 4. 13, Beseler, *op. cit.*, 105, is certainly right in holding that the former rule is true in classical law only of a "bonitary" owner. For Girard's explanation, cf. Buckland, *op. cit.*, 130; see Lenel, 154 n. 13, citing 9. 4. 19. 2 and cf. Buckland, *op. cit.*, 248 n. 7, who anticipated Beseler, 3. 9. Biondi, A. N., 288 ff., considers this another case where our action is treated as not penal but "patrimonial." It may have been that the owner was protected by a *taxatio* much as in 32. pr. For a fanciful and complicated theory of interpolation, see Beseler, *loc. cit.*, 108, who does not make clear the reason for the compiler's inconsistency, cf. Lenel, 3 ed., 159 n. 14.

27. 4. See G. 3. 215, 216; Kooiman, Frag. J. Q., 140 ff. It does not appear so sure as Kr. thinks that this text is interpolated, cf. Lenel, Ulp. 622. Bonfante, Lezioni di Storia, 100, certainly does not hit the point by remarking that adstipulations were still important in Ulpian's day; for in order that the charge of fraud should be grounded, an understanding must have existed giving rise to the action of mandate. Indeed everything goes to prove the genuineness of the statement. The surprising significance of such a conception of *damnum* in primitive times has been noticed by nobody but Brini, Mem. R. Acc. Bologna, 5. 152. It seems very clear that chapter 2 must have been obsolete by the time of Augustus, otherwise it would have been an inexcusable defect of the jurists to reason from chapter 1 in their hesitating efforts to extend the active legitimation, and incredible that they should have refused, in principle if not absolutely, our action to one with a personal right. In connection with the principle of 4. 3. 6, the case reported by Wenger, Arch. R. und W. Phil., 6. 172 (preventing a judgment from being paid), would have been far less of an extension of Aquilian liability in the days of Brutus than in Byzantine or even modern times. It would be interesting to know whether the back reckoning applied, which would have been useful if the debtor were insolvent. The problem of the next passage perhaps did not arise because of the impossibility of a partial release, G. 3. 172.

27. 5. See Monro; A. G., 32. 402; 38 L. Q. R. 220; Z., 1922, 577. For those dissatisfied with the form of the ancient law as here given, Lenel's suggestion that *ceterarum . . . occisos* is of later origin, as it involves the most radical change, is the one leaving the fewest difficulties, *contra* Stella Maranca, Bull., 35. 26. n. 1 *i. f.*, who seems to confuse Lenel's view with that of Jolowicz. It is usually assumed that the statute required payment of the full value for the slightest injury. Jolowicz's theory that only cases of complete destruction were contemplated is not plausible, for it neglects injuries to slaves which were very important in the old law, G. 3. 223, and includes cases which were arrived at only after doubt, 27. 7, 31. The dominant view regards the provision as a penalty, a theory which derives support from 2. 3. 1. 4; 43. 17. 3. 11; cf. Mommsen, 2, § 6. It seems so unreasonable that a penalty should be attached to the less serious delict, especially as the shorter time limit appears to show a desire for milder treatment, that Monro's doctrine seems preferable that *quanti ea res*, the stock expression in the formula for the damage as opposed to the value (cf. *id.* in 2. pr.), was used in that sense here. Although it is undoubtedly illogical to mention the time limit in connection with anything but the value, the fact that this appears never to have been perceived by the Romans, *supra* 2. 2; *infra* 55, is better explained by assuming that the difficulty was inherent in the words of the statute than by supposing that the jurisconsults created the problem without noticing its implications. The popularity of the other doctrine may be due to the modern historical point of view, which always welcomes a theory showing a change or development of any sort no matter what is thereby imputed to the earlier experts. There is no support for Pernice's suggestion that the object was surrendered in return for full payment, which would be open to the abuse of "expropriation," and would be particularly inapplicable to land, which of course may not have been included till after the rejection of the supposed penalty. As for the omission of *plurimi*, see G. 3. 218; Karlowa, Röm. R. 2. 801, whose theory seems to attribute strange confusion to the framer of the law.

27. 7. From here to 27. 12 the Coll. 12. 7 should be consulted for a less abridged version. This and 27. 31 probably show traces of an old doubt whether immovables were included in the third chapter, Karlowa, *op. cit.*, 797.

27. 8. This is a direct injury like throwing a torch or shooting. It is regrettable that a case of *dolus* is chosen, but even so the text shows that lack of foreseeability is no excuse, cf. Hoyt *v.* Jeffers, 30 Mich. 181.

27. 9. See Beseler, 4. 232. The liability here depends upon a pure omission, a fact which is faced by few, but cf. Crouzel, Rev. Gén., 46. 177, who regards the decision as therefore wrong. For a similarly mistaken view in our law, now properly discredited, see 20 A. L. R. 97 ff. Grueber makes a specious attempt to erect a causative act out of the inducement of the first slave to desist, but the liability of the second would seem equally clear if the first had suffered a stroke shortly before relief was due. Likewise Ferrini's explanation, Esp., § 209, fails to cover the case where the servant is sent to watch a fire started by natural causes. It is the assumption of control that creates the duty, whether of one's own or another's force, cf. Osborne *v.* Morgan, 137 Mass. 1, 5. There is probably no liability to third persons where there is failure to assume control in breach of contract. It is true that the Aquilian action did not lie, although and because other remedies did, 39. 2. 24. 2, for damage resulting from inactive property, where the cause may be thought of as external. This is the explanation of 7. 1. 13. 2; although our remedy was proper if there were an act, 8. 2. 18, *contra* Rotondi, S. G., 457 n. 3, there was no occasion for extending it to omissions already covered by the *cautio;* to which instead of to our action any subsidiary remedies were assimilated, cf. Lenel, Ed., 3 ed., 369 nn. 1, 2.

27. 10. Beseler, 3. 83; Schulz, 22; Riccobono, *cit. supra* 19, regard this passage as hopelessly glossed; *contra* Rotondi, 949 n. 4. Its interpretation hinges upon whether Proculus allowed an action *in f.*, a fact which is too often assumed without consideration of the *focum* clause. The usual view that his difficulty was merely as to the form of the action, cf. 27. 8; 30. 3, fails to appreciate that the damage is no less direct if done *foco*, than *furno*, and it may be direct or indirect in either case; in fact his statement is too absolute in form to permit the explanation that such a minor distinction was contemplated. It seems more reasonable to assume that Proculus' view was that building the fire was one of the ordinary acts implied in residence, as though the wall had fallen while furniture was moved in the house, *i. e.*, that the damage was imputable rather to the wall than to the defendant. The objection is that in Coll. the same author, not named, who mentioned the hearth seems to have allowed the action *in f.* As, however, all names are omitted in the MSS., it is permissible to assume that *putat* refers to Vivian, whose theory may have been that there was a negligent omission to guard a reasonable fire. This explains the "childish" remarks of Ulpian or his glossator. Regarding this fire, probably for commercial purposes, as analogous to that in 30. 3, he was unable to explain Proculus' refusal of any remedy except upon the gratuitous supposition that the damage had not yet occurred. Upon such a hypothesis the question only too pressingly arose as to the propriety of Vivian's indirect action, "which was perhaps what Proculus felt," *i. e.*, in refusing it. Proculus, unlike his commentators, saw the real difficulty; if it were an ordinary fireplace there would be no liability for lack of *culpa*, *non constat* that the use of the oven was not reasonable, and the fault to be attributed to deterioration of the firebrick, when there might be no recovery, 39. 2. 40. 1. If the wall were owned in severalty, the case is like 30. 3.

27. 11. The text is probably interpolated from *sed haec*, Coll. 12. 7. 9. On the standard of care here see Windscheid, § 401 n. 5; Schultz, Grünhut's Z., 38. 30 ff.; Haymann, Z., 1919, 232 ff.; Levy, § 90. Albertario *et al.*, Riv. D. Comm., 1923, 1. 506 n. 4, to the contrary notwithstanding, it seems certain that in classical law one entrusted with another's property might be held upon contract and delict for fault in choosing guardians thereof, Coll. 12. 7. 7; cf. 13. 6. 11. That one may also by contract expressly assume liability for more than Aquilian care, cf. *infra* 29. 3; 19. 2. 11. 2, 4; *id.* 29, in no sense violates the rule that contractual relations may of themselves decrease the Aquilian standard of care as Levy hints, 2. 76 n. 6, and Biondi explicitly states, A. N., 122 n. 1. The question remains whether such duties were attached by law in the absence of express agreement. Given the recognized defenses involved in the doctrines of *vis major*, *quae custodiri non solent*, Levy, 1. 409 ff., *impetus praedonum*, and burglary in general, it seems analytically true that the only case where harm to the property can occur without fault of the defendant is that in which this is due to the fault of his subordinates, which case is then the only one where there is room for dispute on the unduly vexed problem of *custodia*. With regard to our text Levy shows, by reference to the scholiast, that the noxal election should not be taken to refer to the contract action, such an anomaly being allowed (if at all in classical law) only where the plaintiff temporarily owned the property, on which point cf. Biondi, A. N., 71 ff.; Z., 1926, 426 ff., 437. Thus the contract action was given by Proculus in concurrence with the noxal remedy, the school dispute in the Coll. is one of substance, not form, and it is idle to assume systematic interpolation to explain the divergencies, cf. Krüger, who impugns the characteristically early remark of Alfenus in 18. 6. 12; cf. Filliter *v.* Phippard, 11. Q. B. 347, 354, yet says the same of the exactly opposite limitation in 19. 2. 11. pr.; *contra* Costa, Locazione, 55 ff. Proculus' theory was not known to Alfenus, 19. 2. 30. 4, yet from *id.* 30. 2, it appears that the latter held the lessee liable if the injury was committed by an employee. Thus there is no reason to regard 4. 9. 7. 4 as Byzantine, this distinction being of hoary antiquity. As to the lessor, see Labeo 19. 2. 60. 7; and by a later analogy from the lessee, it may have been the same for all the lessor's subordinates, cf. Levy, 2. 76 n. 3. The Proculian theory thus allowed: liability of the lessee (or lessor?) for *extranei*, presumably because the duty was non-delegable, cf. 17. 2. 23. 1 with the situation of *nautae, etc.* (3. 5. 20. 3 depends on the principle of 19. 5. 17. 1, cf. 3. 5. 10); liability of the lessor on a tacit warranty of fitness, cf. 27. 34; 19. 2. 19. 1; and liability of the lessee for his own slaves, either because of the frequency of the pact in 19. 2. 30. 4 or from the idea that the injury would not have happened but for the contract, cf. 47. 2. 62. 5 (which is not interpolated as Heldrich, Leipz. R. St., 7. 24 ff., thinks, cf. the decision of the same Julian in 17. 2. 52. 4; cf. 17. 2. 61; *contra* Paul, 17. 1. 26. 6, 7, who agreed with Labeo, 17. 2. 60. 1), *acc.* Marcellus, 19. 2. 41; Ulpian, if 19. 2. 11. pr. is interpolated. others accepting Sabinus's requirement of *culpa*, rejected all three results, Neratius, Coll. 12. 7. 7; Julian, 13. 6. 19, 20, whose remark is equally applicable to theft; Paul, 13. 6. 11; 19. 2. 45. The view of the compilers is doubtful, cf. Dorotheus on our text with the suspicious 19. 2. 11. pr. This discovery of Levy's has surprising effects as to the supposed liability of the commodatary and *conductor operis* in G. 3. 205 ff. In regard to the latter contract praetorian aid was needed to arrive at the Proculian rule for the employees even of *nautae*, *etc.*, and the praetor himself never went beyond noxal liability, 4. 9. 7. 6; 47. 5. 1. 5; Biondi, A. N., 145, n. 4, which texts conclusively imply an absence of contract responsibility, and show that Pernice's analogy to the *redhibitor* is incorrect, 2. 2. 257 n. 3. The remarks of Gaius, referring as they do to an ordinary *conductor*, must then be understood, as the context shows, to refer to the contrast with deposit, where there was no obligation to guard another's property differently from one's own, *i. e.*, *culpa in concreto*. As for the case of the *horrearius*, Coll. 10. 9, the rule may have been a compromise to meet the typical case of grain which must usually have involved a "*locatio irregularis*."

27. 12. See Coll. 12. 7. 10; it is a question of the *animus revertendi*, cf. Goff *v.* Kilts, 15 Wend. 550.

27. 13. Appleton's thesis, Mél. Cornil, 1. 61, should be accepted that, as the following *ideo* shows, the text is laying down the requirement of damage *corpori*, not attempting to define *rumpere* in a sense which it already possessed at the passage of the XII Tables; *membrum ruptum* G. 3. 223; cf. 27. 16.

27. 14. Since Pampaloni, Bull., 3. 241 ff., the part of this text relating to the tenant is widely supposed interpolated, *contra* Debray, N. R. H., 1909, 648 ff., who devotes a long article thereto, upholding the older view that the action is given by exception to the tenant with only a personal claim, because of his peculiar inchoate (or already existing, but then why the security?) right to the fruits which are the subject of the action, *acc.* Costa, Storia, 2 ed., 326 n. 4; *contra* Lenel, 3 ed., 542 n. 1. Ferrini, E. G. I., § 63, thinks that the tenant originally had only the interdict and that the security was against repetition thereof. Levy, § 118, maintains that the security was required against the owner's bringing the action after the interdict, by this reconstruction obtaining mention of what he thinks to have been the classical means of avoiding concurrence. Rotondi, 950, declares that even the owner was refused the action, because his doctrine requires that cases of mixture be held Byzantine, *supra* 7. 3, yet he doubts De Medio's thesis that the freeman's action is interpolated. At any rate, unless we are to assume with Levy that the compilers senselessly retained mention of the security, its presence throws light upon the recovery of the holders of a real right. It implies that they sued for a share independently of the owner, whereas the tenant is thought of as exercising the owner's action.

This security has been the object of a study by Debray, N. R. H., 1912, 1, as this is the only example of its use in the legal literature except in connection with that *de rato*, cf. Lenel, 517 n. 3; 36. 3. 2, which proves that it is here not necessarily Byzantine. In function it is, however, indistinguishable from the *cautio defensu iri*, 34. 3. 4, which in turn was interchangeable with the *cautio de indemnitate* (for some of the forms of which see 6. 1. 57; 50. 16. 71. 1), cf. 17. 2. 28 with *id.* 67. pr.; 33. 4. 1. 9 with *id.* 7. pr. Even in their form the institutions seem to have been confounded, 24. 3. 25. 4 (*praestatum iri*); 23. 3. 29 (*indemnem adversus . . . agentem*), where a word from each of the three is used, see further Brisson, De Formulis, 5. ch. 56, 161; 6. chs. 182–186. From the references in Cicero it is probable that ours was the oldest form, borrowed without a change in form from the extrajudicial promise of *transactio*, and used for the *procurator* before the more specialized words of ratification were introduced. The *c. def. iri* may have originated in a situation like that of 5. 3. 57, Neratius being the earliest to mention it, where a *cautio judicatum solvi* had already been given by the defendant, and was assumed by the plaintiff, an *extrinsecus*,

46. 7. 5. 3, merely for purposes of convenience, see Pellat, De Rei Vind., 331. It was later perceived that the clause *ob rem def.* of the latter security, Lenel, xv, was literally applicable to a suit by another plaintiff, exactly the case of the words of compromise. Of course the far more general *c. de ind.* was also suitable in this connection. As far as the classical law is concerned, there seems no justification for Lenel's and Debray's treatment of our *cautio amplius non agi* or *peti* as an independent institution, and Levy's attempt, 1. 36 n. 1, to draw a distinction between the other two seems refuted by 5. 3. 57, cf. 6. 1. 57; Planck, Mehrheit, 171; the *c. def. iri* might equally apply to an *actio judicati*.

27. 16. Cf. 27. 13, which indicates that Celsus confused the statute and its interpretation, an indication in favor of Appleton's view, *supra* 27. 13, that *rumpere* and *corrumpere* were synonymous.

27. 17. The opposite solution being given in Coll. 2. 4. 1, there is doubt as to Ulpian's view, see Buckland, 33 Y. L. J. 352; *contra* Rotondi, 950. From *mihi* it might be deduced that Ulpian disagreed with Paul, 33. pr.; 45. 1.

27. 20. Cf. 27. 14. It is doubtful from *quasi* whether the action is indirect, cf. 15. 1; Rotondi, S. G., 457 n. 3, holds that it marks an interpolation, but cf. K. V. I., 50. 433; Riccobono, An. Sem. Giur, 4. 697 ff.

27. 21. Cf. G. 3. 202; 4. 3. 7. 7; 19. 5. 14. 2, *id.* 23; 41. 1. 55; 47. 2; 50. 4, *id.* 52. 13; J. 4. 1. 11; Monro; Rotondi, S. G., 454. Sabinus could not have allowed either action; Ferrini's interpretation, Esp., 297, is forced. Rotondi has to give up here in maintaining his theory that the action *in factum* for damage not *corpori* was never thought of as Aquilian. Huvelin, Furtum, 343 ff., to whose thesis the text is not favorable, hints at interpolations.

27. 25. Pringsheim, Z., 1921, 321, in the course of a thorough eradication of the idea of intention from the transaction of gift holds this text interpolated. His theory seems to depend on a perversely literal construction of the word *donaverit*, cf. Suman, Saggi Min., 80 n. 3. A tendency is, however, noticed toward the reëstablishment of the genuineness of the indispensable conception of intent, cf. Mél. Cornil, 1. 427–437.

27. 26. Cf. 43. 24. 18. pr.

27. 28. Since the scholiast, the second *aut* has been regarded as an error, omission thereof giving the satisfactory result that there is but one unknown action, see Lenel, 529; better, Karlowa, Röm. R., 2. 1301. For castration as a crime, see 48. 8. 3. 4; *id.* 4. 2, 5, 6. It appears that v. Tuhr's and Karlowa's principles, *supra* 27. 5, would lead to the result that if the slave were worth 50 on May 1, 25 when castrated on May 15, and 40 in consequence thereof, there would be recovery of 10. Although the Aquilian value is the highest within the year, yet damage caused by the act is required, *i. e.*, the interest may decrease recovery.

27. 29. As to interpolation, see Z., 1925, 461, Haymann, *id.*, 1919, 190. The text has figured in the recent discussion of the risks in *locatio operis*, Beseler, 4. 134; Haymann, Z., 1920, 155 ff. The latter maintains the surprising thesis that the classical law placed liability for damage caused by secret defects upon the workman, to support which proposition all the texts must be held interpolated, as indeed they ought to have been. This theory seems especially strange in one who disbelieves in the genuineness of the rule *periculum est emtoris.* In our case, however, the defect may have been so evident that attempting the work would be culpable, and the text is unsatisfactory in that *periculo* does not seem to refer to Aquilian liability. It is hard to use the passage in the dispute about the relation of Aquilian and contractual care, cf. E. G. I., § 23; Vangerow, 3. 592. A pact not to be liable for *culpa* was apparently valid, 50. 17. 23, otherwise for *dolus*, 2. 14. 27. 3. With us "contracting out" of liability for negligence, which is analytically identical with assumption of risk, is forbidden by the weight of modern authority as between master and servant, Roesner *v.* Herman, 8 Fed. 782, or, in their public capacity, by carriers, Williston, Contracts, § 1109, innkeepers, Maxwell *v.* Harper, 138 Tenn. 640, and warehousemen, Pilson *v.* Tip Top Co., 67 Ore. 528; otherwise for the carrier *qua* lessor, 44 L. R. A. (N. S.) 1129, cf. World's Exposition *v.* France, 96 Fed. 687; cf. also Anthony *v.* Syracuse Univ. 130 Misc. 249, 41 Harv. L. Rev. 495.

27. 30. The rule that penal or infaming actions were forbidden between spouses or for acts committed during marriage has been attributed to Justinian by Zanzucchi, Riv. It. per S. G., 42. 1, 47. 1, 238; *acc.* Levy, Privatstrafe, 124 n. 2; cf. 11. 3. 17 with 37. 15. 5, 6. Too much emphasis appears to be placed on 23. 3. 38 in view of the fact that the weight of modern opinion holds the action there mentioned not to be infaming, Rev. Gén., 24. 233 ff.; Pernice, 2. 223 n. 6; Buckland, 515 n. 16; *contra* Biondi, Jud. B. F., 65 ff. The champions of the theory cannot explain 25. 2. 2; cf. 24. 2. 11. 2; Zanzucchi, 42. 67 ff. Though there remains a possibility that the carlier law did not apply the prohibition to actions against the husband, arg. 47. 10. 2; but cf. Lenel, 3 ed., 408 n. 4, this text may still be regarded as an example of the classical tendency in some respects to treat our action as not penal. The scholiast reminds us that the *duplum* is not available; cf. 4. 4. 9. 2; 10. 2. 17; 11. 3. 17.

27. 32. De Medio, 33, doubts the words *melius rell.* The problem is strangely theoretical if the *actio "confessoria,"* Elvers, Servitutenlehre, 805, the interdict *de aqua*, 43. 20. 1. 1; Berger, Z., 1915, 208 ff., or that *quod vi aut clam*, Windscheid, § 465 n. 18 on 8. 5. 6. 1, were adequate remedies; it is like bringing trespass alleging that the pipes are corporeal instead of an action on the case, Washburn, Easements, 570. The text therefore tends to support the thesis of Arangio Ruiz, A. G., 81. 387 ff., that these actions lay only against the servient owner. The ownership of a pipe, not to mention the water, in connection with an easement is doubtful with both us and the Romans; following this text that there is merger, Ubbelohde-Glück, Inderdicte, 4. 331 n. 4*e*; Beale, 4 Harv. L.

Rev. 83; *contra* Biermann, 34 Jhering's Jb. 177 ff.; cf. 39. 2. 30. 1. Whenever the question arises the holder of the easement seems to be preferred. In addition to (1) legal redress for injury by anyone he is (2) always taxed upon the pipe, Ewell, Fixtures, 2 ed. 559 ff. The English decision cited by Professor Beale, if it is to be understood as holding a merger, has in effect been overruled by Queen *v.* Waterworks, 18 Q. B. 705, cf. Metropolitan *v.* Fowler [1893], A. C. 416. (3) His view that the holder of the easement upon abandonment has not the *jus tollendi* was not followed in E. Ohio *v.* Akron, 81 Oh. St. 33 (declared unconstitutional); Clements *v.* Phila. Co., 184 Pa. St. 28; cf. Cleveland R. R. *v.* Cleveland, 204 U. S. 116, 142; Ga. R. R. *v.* Haas, 127 Ga. 187. (4) In Moore *v.* New Orleans Co., 114 Fed. 880, the court assumed it to be axiomatic that the pipes belonged to the holder of the easement upon separation by a third party. (5) Where a house is disposed of the pipes pass with it, an indication that they are not part of the soil, 18. 1. 47–49; 19. 1. 38. 2; Nicholas *v.* Chamberlain, Cro. Jac. 121, which accords with the tax policy of the Iowa court declared by Professor Beale to be contrary to common sense. In view of these five results the question of title seems academic, if not decided, see Taylor *v.* St. Helens, 6 Ch. Div. 264, yet the subject is in a state of confusion, cf. Paris *v.* Norway, 85 Me. 330; Metropolitan *v.* Fowler, *cit.* Though all the cases are concerned with public utilities, they regard the easement as acquired with an intention that it be permanent, so that no distinction can be made regarding a private right, cf. the unconvincing remarks in 32 L. Q. R. 76 n. 1. In Taylor *v.* Oldham, 4 Ch. Div. 395, 402, 411, the court evidently thought that there was merger in the case of an easement, but it is difficult indeed to perceive how the there so-called owner was better off than the holder of an easement, see Att'y Gen'l *v.* Guardians, 20 Ch. Div. 595, 604; West Skokie *v.* Dawson, 243 Ill. 175; Clark *v.* Worcester, 125 Mass. 226.

27. 34. Cf. 19. 2. 60. 7. Although the Aquilian action against the lessor seems to be thought of as direct for *culpa in* *eligendo*, the Gloss takes it as noxal. The action against the third person should be indirect, 9. 1. 1. 7, cf. J. 4. 3. 16. The text, confused in thought and expression, has perhaps been glossed but as the breach of contract is clear, *pro perito, etc.*, it is hard to believe with Haymann, Haftung des Verkäufers, 57 n. 1, that the reference to the contract action is interpolated (the distinction between a *genus* and a *species* in regard to 19. 1. 6. 4; 19. 2. 19. 1, cf. Heldrich, Leipz. R. St., 7. 21 ff., seems unfounded and illogical, cf. Z., 1927, 122 ff.), cf. Pernice, 2, 64, who sees a development of the idea of Aquilian *culpa* because Mela refused the action.

27. 35. If *tector* is a plasterer, the *laccum* cannot be wooden, cf. 47. 2. 21. 5, and the learning in Cujas, Obs., 10. 9.

28. 1. Beseler, 3. 73, thinks this whole passage is a gloss, thus avoiding the difficulty of *ex causa*, cf., however, K. V. I., 50. 418. Without entering on the dispute as to the power of the praetor to refuse an action, see N. R. H., 1925, 457 ff.; it seems clear that the question of contributory negligence could never have been decided *in jure*. As to whether an exception was needed for this defense, *i. e.*, lack of causation, as well as for those of lack of *injuria*, like self-defense or necessity, the only evidence is 43. 24. 7. 4. As the *legis actiones* were then in force, cf. Jobbé-Duval, Mél. Cornil, 1. 536 n. 1 *et pass.*; *supra* 2. 1, in the absence of another hint of the kind it may be assumed that these pleas could be proved *in judicio*, *acc.* Tijdschrift voor Rechtsgeschiedenis, 5. 386. The famous question as to the theory of the exception is best resolved by Bekker, Aktionen, 2. 283, 297; Bozzoni, Eccezioni, 126 ff., to the effect that the necessity therefor gradually declined, and any reasonable distinction was lacking in classical times, cf. 7. 9. 4; 27. 2. 2. 1; 44. 7. 34. 1; 46. 8. 22. 8. Nothing can be said as to the burden of proof. The Roman principles as to delictal *culpa* are so obscure, cf. 22. 3. 18. 1, that the commentators are hopelessly split as to proof of the defendant's fault; Pernice, S., 228 ff.; Ferrini, E. G. I., § 74, place it on the defendant; *contra* Busch., Arch., 45. 148 ff.; Reinhold, Klaggrunde, § 27; cf. Rotondi, 957. 11. 2 is hardly an analogy. By their neglect of the burden of proof as a merely practical matter the Romans here saved themselves much trouble, cf. Beach, Contributory Negl., 2 ed., ch. 15.

29. 1. See Beseler, 2. 38. The passage is important on the question of the limit of ownership, unduly debated by civilians, cf. Bonfante, Corso di D. R., *2a.* 221 ff. On the question of damages it is hard to distinguish the first case from 27. 25, cf. also 43. 8. 2. 15, unless the decree of D. Marcus against self-help was supposed to apply by analogy, cf. v. Tuhr, Nothstand, 71 ff. As for the aqueduct, ownership was lost by merger, C. 3. 34. 2; cf. R. R. *v.* Dunlap, 47 Mich. 456; Greve *v.* R. R., 26 Minn. 66; Justice *v.* R. R., 87 Pa. St. 28.

29. 2. Beseler reconstructs this text in Z., 1922, 540. The last part of the passage may refer to a boat moored without *culpa* and left.

29. 3. Beseler, 4. 242, thinks that the action lay in the first part of this text; he might then have enlightened us as to his view of 49. 1; see also Pernice, 1. 71 n. 2. The damages are held too conjectural; *acc.* Wright *v.* Mulvaney, 78 Wis. 89; *contra* Pacific Co. *v.* Alaska Assn., 138 Cal. 632. The case is different from an *emptio spei*, 18. 1. 8. 1. Aside from the rules as to gambling, one can buy a chance which would be too conjectural as a basis for damages in tort; the fact that the obligation is valid though nothing is caught shows that the lack of probability of a catch affects only the extent, not, as here, the existence of the damages. It is a mistake often committed, *e. g.*, by Petražycki, Einkommen, 2. 393 ff., to use this text as an analogy for contract cases. As with us, the rules are different; given direct causation, the damages in tort are limited by certainty, in contract by the contemplation of the parties. In this case the contract rule is more lucrative, for the converse situation cf. 7. 5 with 19. 1. 21. 3; see also 18. 6. 20; Sedgwick, Damages, 9 ed., §§ 144 ff.; 13. 4. 2. 8 should be compared with 19. 2. 11. 4, the explicit requirement of payment at Ephesus constituting notice to the borrower, but cf. Beseler, 1. 65.

29. 4. The confused antitheses may be due to abridgment by the compilers, see Rotondi, 960 n. 2; Beseler, Z., 1922, 541.

29. 7. See Beseler, 3. 71. There is nothing unusual about the Aquilian liability of officials, although difficulty occurs in other connections, Z., 1918, 210 ff. *Bona fide* wrong execution is not a theft nor a spoiling, see 47. 8. 2. 20. Magistrates with the *imperium*, Girard, Org. Jud., 228 n. 1, could not be sued while they held the office, 2. 4. 2; 47. 10. 13. 1; cf. Mechem, Public Officers, § 648.

30. pr. Cf. 48. 5. 21 ff. It is to be presumed that in Texas, Vern. Cr. Code, 1916, § 1102, there would be no liability under Lord Campbell's Act, cf. March *v.* Walker, 48 Tex. 372.

30. 1. For the older theories of this, the most-discussed text in our title, see Arch., 75. 312 ff. Ever since Gradenwitz, Interp., 89 it has been thought interpolated, see De Medio, 35 ff.; Esp., § 313; Levy, 1. 411; Z., 1925, 35; the finishing touch having been lately added by Beseler, Z., 1926, 270; *contra* Manigk, Pfandr. Unters., 1. 124; Debray, N. R. H., 1909, 662 n 1. Beseler holds that the pledgee's damage is "subjective," which affirmation is not reconciled with the decisions in 21. 2; 22. pr., 1; 23. 2, 4; 37. 1, *etc.* Gradenwitz's material objections are strangely weak: the argument that the owner's suit for the whole cannot be opposed without use of an *exceptio ex jure tertii*, Windscheid, § 186 n. 16, would allow full damages to a "naked" owner who had parted with "bonitary" title, cf. 11. 8; Circ. Giur., 19. 269. Of course the plaintiff fails to prove his interest, even assuming that an exception is necessary, as in 47. The argument that there is no danger of double recovery because the pledgee must furnish the security mentioned in 27. 14 is a *petitio principii*, because there is no record of its application to one with a real right, cf. 47. 2. 15. pr. The text is reasonable enough, even though in some cases of insolvency cession in the pledge action might have been adequate protection. However, as the sentence following *et ideo* is suspicious on linguistic grounds, it may be that the compilers preferred Paul's reasoning, but Ulpian's conclusion, the former giving the action for the full amount, arg. 47. 2. 15. pr.; *id.* 88, while the latter split the action, arg. 47. 2. 12. 2. In view of the confusion as to the action of theft and the complicating influence of *fiducia*, there is room for nothing but conjecture as to the classical law, cf. N. R. H., 1917, 44 ff. This solution follows from a desire to reconcile the principle of interest with a reluctance to value a contingent claim, cf. 35. 2. 22. 3; *id.* 63. 1; Bull., 26. 76 ff.

30. 2. See *supra* 7. 3. Is not this a case where the heir might be unjustly enriched if a saving in the grocer's bill could be proved? Cf. Windscheid, § 421 n. 13; Phillips *v.* Homfray, 24 Ch. Div. 439. In view of the recent theories about theft, Huvelin, N. R. H., 1918, 73; Bull., 33. 263, this text is interesting, referring as it may to one conscious of his wrong. If the *condictio furtiva* is not allowed, and such is the implication of the text in spite of Monro, it must be because merely eating another's corn was not thought of as an assumption of possession. This is an important limitation of the conception of contrectation; moving another's property would not be theft unless a change of possession were involved, 41. 2. 3. 18; 47. 2. 68. pr.; see Huvelin, Furtum, 370 ff.; 47. 2. 37; *id.* 48. 4; *id.* 55. 1; *id.* 67. 2; cf. *supra* 27. 21. If the decisions in 38; 45. 2 be considered, it seems that our action might fill a considerable gap in the law of the *condictio*, cf. Windscheid, § 422 n. 8.

30. 3. As to the procedural difficulty, see Coll. 12. 7. 4, 6; Jordan *v.* Wyatt, 4 Grat. 151. The text is thought interpolated for the same reason as 31 *q. v.*; cf. *supra* 6. From the exactly similar decision of Tubervil *v.* Stamp, 1 Salk. 13, Ld. Ray. 264, cf. Querry, Droit Musulman, 2. 629, our jurists have felt forced to erect a special category for cases of fire, where not mere lack of negligence but only an "act of God" will excuse, Wigmore, 7 Harv. L. Rev. 449; Bohlen, Cas. on Torts, 2 ed., 619. Their mistake is disclosed by this passage, so thoroughly founded on negligence that its genuineness is doubted. There is nothing special about the case except that it is very difficult (but cf. the facts in Haverly *v.* R. R., 135 Pa. 50) to imagine a cause of the fire's escape, not an "act of God," which would not involve ordinary negligence, cf. 18. 6. 12; Riv. Dir. Civ., 5. 579; otherwise, if plaintiff is a co-owner, cf. 27. 10.

30. 4. In accordance with the violent struggle to avoid the doctrine of contributory negligence, it is often maintained that this text shows no duty to mitigate delictal damages because the death happens to be included in the first chapter, on which artificial principle the passage would apply to a cow but not a dog. Those who disbelieve in liability for omissions sometimes apply this text only where the plaintiff did something to make the property worse or perhaps when the act did not improve it, but not if nothing was done (this point is missed by Ferrini, E. G. I., § 33, who is troubled by *mortifere* in view of 11. 3, though it is correct if, as he thinks, omissions are disregarded). From the lack of logic in these distinctions as well as from 21. 1. 31. 12; cf. 28. 1, they may be rejected, cf. *supra* 8. pr.; 27. 9. In our law the duty to mitigate is not imposed if the defendant intended to injure, Heaney *v.* Heeney, 2 Den. 625; cf. Smelting Co. *v.* Dairy Co., 236 Fed. 510; Shannon *v.* McNab, 29 Okla. 829; 22 L. R. A. N. S. 684, which courts might have difficulty with (19. 1. 45. 1). From 9. 4 it may be deduced that the plaintiff's negligence would not bar him if this slight wound had been inflicted in an unsuccessful attempt to kill, *contra* Ferrini, *loc. cit.*

31. pr. Because it describes *culpa* in general terms, *supra* 6, this text is held interpolated by Beseler, 3. 156; Rotondi, 959 n. 4; Kunkel, Z., 1925, 299, who at least perceives that the distinctions are necessary. It may be remarked that the clauses containing *culpa* are rejected because unnecessary reasons are given, by the same authors who impeach other texts, esp. 30. 2, because no reasons are given, *itaque*, *ideoque*, cf. Rotondi, S. G., 457 nn. 1, 2. The interesting case in which plaintiff is a trespasser upon a private way is omitted. It appears from J. 4. 3. 5 that this way was *vicinalis*, which usually connoted a public easement by long use, 43. 7. 3; 43. 8. 2. 22; cf. Savigny, System, 4. §§ 195, 196. In discussing the case where there is no road the Institutes say that there is no liability because the plaintiff is a trespasser. This is a poor reason, as the defendant would usually be free from *culpa* and it does not apply to an "invitee," but it indicates that the Romans did not impose the ordinary duty of care toward trespassers, cf. R. R. *v.* Barnett [1911], A. C. 361; Maynard *v.* R. R., 115 Mass. 458; *contra* Schmidt *v.* Mich. Co., 159 Mich. 308. This is a case of real *culpa* compensation because the injury would have happened had the plaintiff acted rightly, *i. e.*, had permission; for the standard applied to the defendant see 39.

32. pr. See Beseler, 3. 45; Kniep, Gaius, 178; E. G. I., § 71. Although the edict is here extended in general terms, in 47. 6. 1. 2 Ulpian mentions damage done *culpa*, but cf. 6; 10, and in 2. 1. 9 Paul refused the extension altogether. The last text on account of its lack of logic is usually supposed interpolated, see Levy, 1. 478 n. 4, though the reason for this is obscure. Beseler, 4. 299, sees numerous largely undefined interpolations in all three texts and decides that Paul's view, cf. Naber, *supra* 11. 2, represents classical law for the strange reason that the penal damages of the third chapter show that our action is like that for insult, cf. Levy, 2. 30 n. 5. The damages at most merely show that there was a penalty in very early times, and it is hard to see why the same was not true of theft with its double or quadruple penalty.

32. 1. Regarding *uno impetu*, cf. Hite *v.* Long, 6 Rand. (Va.) 457. In spite of the resemblance to 27. pr., Levy, § 60, thinks that cumulation was avoided here for the same reasons as in 47, a theory which is of doubtful correctness, treating, as it does, our action as analogous to the *condictio furtiva*, cf. 11. 2 with C. 4. 8. 1.

33. pr. If the father is plaintiff the text shows that, as with us, sentimental damages cannot be recovered. These are sometimes hard to distinguish from the interest, cf. family heirlooms, Baker *v.* Lewis, 78 Conn. 198; Green *v.* R. R., 128 Mass. 221; 27 Col. L. Rev. 850. The damages should be the cost of replacement as far as this is possible, what is excluded is computation of the non-replaceable residuum, which cannot be supposed impossible to calculate in money since it is allowed in other cases, cf. Bull., 16. 219 ff., 279. In systems like ours where such damages are given for injury to the person the only difference as regards property is in the foreseeability, yet the cause is direct, and it would be hard to justify this rule if the paternal sorrow had been desired. It is difficult to see what damages can be recovered for wrongful destruction of pre- or post-prohibition liquor, cf. Burleson *v.* Bundy, 206 App. Div. 644; 10. 2. 4. 1. As for the owner of another's natural son, in the absence of a contract by the father, 22 pr., what he might have paid is too conjectural, but any increased market value should be allowed as in 23. 1. Paul here makes an unhappy citation. Pedius was discussing the *Lex Falcidia*, where not even the market but the "ordinary" value was the standard, 35. 2. 63. pr.; Matthews, 34 Harv. L. Rev. 229.

33. 1. This may have been torn from its context to represent the Byzantine "general" indirect action, cf. Rotondi, 951.

34, 35, 36. pr. Cf. 40. 2. 3; Lenel, Pal., 2. 525 n. 1; Z., 1910, 272 ff. The rule follows from the fact of accrual, G. 2. 199. Ulpian's remark can have followed only 13. 3, not 15. pr. as Lenel proposes.

36. 1. Beseler, 3. 27, regards *nam . . . exstitit* as interpolated, the words which give the only tenable reason for the decision. As to the last sentence, in spite of its unrestricted language, ever since the scholiast it has been disputed whether the coheir's action is for the whole, see A. G., 32. 398 ff.; Esp., § 241; Circ. Giur., 19. 259 ff. If the interpretation of the case in 15. 1 is correct, it is only because there is no accrual of the inheritance that the co-heir may have even his share of the action, the other share of which goes to the slave's heir in so far as it is greater than the value of his share of the inheritance; as it usually would not be, it accrues to the co-heir only if the slave never got it, which is perhaps the better view, but cf. G. 2. 232; *supra* 15. 1.

37. pr. It is usually held that if there is a right to command, the *iussus* will escape if the act was not atrocious, 50. 17. 157; *id.* 169. pr. Levy, 1. 289 n. 6, thinks that the rule applied only to the interdict *quod vi aut clam*, 43. 24. 11. 7, and that the doctrine was elsewhere unsettled, cf. 44. 7. 20; 47. 10. 17. 7. From the texts the distinction seems rather to have been whether the act was a crime, cf. Buckland, Slavery, 680; theft by a slave was criminal in the XII Tables, so that 44. 7. 20 need not be interpolated. The *iussor* without authority is sometimes held as a joint wrongdoer, 39. 2. 18. 14; 39. 3. 5; 47. 7. 7. 4; 47. 10. 11. 4. Aquilian liability is disputed: for it, Windscheid, § 455 n. 27; *contra* Hefke, Arch. P. 344 ff.; Levy, 1. 295, should be estopped from using an argument *a contrario* here in view of his interpretation of 32. 1. It is hard to see why 11. 3. 4 is not conclusive; *dolus* is required because, if the *iussus* is normal, cf. 7. 6, the cause is too remote, *infra* 52. pr., in consequence of the requirement of damage *c. c. d.*

37. 1. Cf. 22. pr. The nature and development of the action *de pauperie* are the subject of much controversy, see Z., 1921, 357 ff.; Levy, § 121; Biondi, A. N., 1–41, who attempts to maintain the scarcely plausible hypothesis that it was not noxal till Justinian, *contra* Lenel, Z., 1927, 2 ff. The killing must be after *l. c.* in the action *de p.*, 9. 1. 1. 13. The law was later changed 9. 1. 1. 16 (not necessarily by Justinian, Beseler, 3. 181, as Ulpian wrote a century after Javolenus), to allow the owner to cede the Aquilian action to the plaintiff *de p.*, a doctrine which Buckland, Slavery, 112 n. 2, fails to notice to be inconsistent with our text, cf. 55.

38. If the action is direct, there is a difficulty about the *culpa*. *Omnimodo* may show that in Javolenus' time the

Roman law was the same as ours in that absence of fault was no excuse, given the intention to produce the damage complained of, cf. Pernice, 2. 86. But from 5. 3. 31. 3; 6. 1. 45 it appears that when Ulpian wrote the b. f. p. before *l. c.* was liable only for *dolus*. Because of a feeling that this expression is inapplicable to a b. f. p. these texts are either ignored, Girard, 352 n. 1, or artificially explained, Pfersche, Priv. Abh., 210 ff.; Pernice, 2. 87 ff. Whatever be thought of their suggestions, in view of our text and of common sense they have no relation to Aquilian liability, where the solution is given by Faber, see Pellat, De Rei Vind., 292 ff. First, it is obvious that for our purposes supervening bad faith is fatal to the b. f. p. status, cf. 41. 1. 48. 1; Buckland, 227. As for the b. f. p. there cannot be *dolus* in the technical sense, *supra* 9. 4, but its meaning is shown by 45. 2, where, if the mistake is reasonable, there is no negligence, only *dolus*. So here if the b. f. p. kills the slave from spite, the act is a crime; and a mistake as to civil liability, however reasonable, is irrelevant. The criminal liability is not necessary, as our texts deal with deterioration, cf. 11. 3. 5. 1, *infra* 45. 2. *Dolus* is thus used to cover case 1 and probably 3, and to exclude cases 2 and 4, *supra* 9. 4. Perhaps the reason why the b. f. p. was not liable to the action for corrupting a slave 11. 3. 1. 1, is because of its praetorian origin and the lack of a criminal element. In our law a purchaser in good faith from an infant owner is in much the same situation. If the action here is noxal, the difficulties are not removed, as is usually thought, for such liability of course depended on the delict of the slave who must be guilty of *culpa*. If one *in loco servi* is liable only for "gross" negligence (not concrete care because he had no affairs of his own) because he reasonably thought he was a slave, 41. 1. 54. 2, *a fortiori* must this be the case if he was a slave. The lower standard of care includes all four cases in 9. 4; in so far is the duty of an owner to his supposed property less rigorous than the converse duty. As for the interpolation widely alleged in 41. 1. 54. 2, the fact seems highly improbable, both because of the exactness of the description *gravior culpa*, in a case where, though *culpa in concreto* is demanded because of the "enduring relation," it cannot be applied, and because the term is so out of line with the Byzantine tendency to regard any kind of serious fault as equivalent to *dolus;* but see Riccobono, Ann. Sem. Giur., 4. 686, who terms the decision "absurd" after holding that practically no contract could arise in these circumstances.

39. Cf. Harris *v.* Brummell, 74 Mo. App. 435, Gilson *v.* Fisk, 8 N. H. 404; Tobin *v.* Deal, 60 Wis. 87. *Proprias actiones* are probably those for *pauperies* and *pastus pecoris.* Monro properly questions the value of a distinction between striking and purposely overdriving; the latter is no less without the privilege because proper driving would be within it. The privilege is not defined with regard to the nature of the act but also the intent, the same act may be within or without it according to the state of mind, cf. Lodge Holes Co. *v.* Wednesbury [1908], A. C. 323. Recently the clause *si percussisset . . . posse* has been supposed interpolated because the direct action would not lie for too violent driving, *i. e.*, not *corpore*, Fliniaux, Mél. Cornil, 1. 261. In spite of G. 3. 219, nothing could be a weaker test than an inobservance of an academic distinction of which there are so many in our title; there is also the possibility that Scaevola agreed with Proculus, 11. 5; or that the driving was done with a stick rather than the voice, in which case *percussere* means that the pain of the blow caused the damage while *agere* refers to exhaustion, cf. also 8. 1. Since the Aquilian standard of care is objective, the subjective test here creates difficulty not removed by Ferrini's explanation, Esp., § 259, that this refers only to the "objective tort," for mention of the concrete standard is irrelevant if liability may occur even though it is observed. The problem has lately been laid to interpolation, Z., 1921, 370 n. 3, by scholars who dispute whether the innovation is a sign of Greek love of animals or Christian love for one's neighbor, *contra* Fliniaux, *op. cit.*, 262 n. 1, a more plausible example of which latter tendency

might be suggested in 41. 4. 8; cf. Pernice, 2. 1. 474 n. 3; but see Riccobono himself in Bull., 7. 259 ff. The text clearly lays down a concrete test of care (for the classical origin of which, besides 16. 3. 32, see the arguments in Sertorio, Culpa in Concreto, 72 ff., 186 ff.) which is justified by the fact that the cattle are trespassing, cf. 31 whence it appears that this is a case of *culpa* compensation; all violations of this standard involve an act *proximus dolo* which justifies the expression *culpa latior* in 16. 3. 32 as distinguished from *culpa lata* in case 4, *supra* 9. 4; neither this nor any other standard of care can be applied if the injury is intended, from a bad motive, 23. 4. 23. 5; one could not excuse keeping an object attractive to trespassing children by the plea that one wished thus to get rid of some of one's own offspring. It is not obvious why distinctions should be termed "scholastic," cf. Rotondi, S. G., 102, the purpose of which is to prevent persons being held liable for *dolus* when their act has none of the characteristics thereof.

40. A conditional judgment must have been, if not impossible, far more objectionable under the formulary than under the extraordinary procedure, indeed in 49. 4. 1. 5 relating to appeals in the latter system, Girard, 1068 n. 3, it is clear that it was, though undesirable, not invalid, see Vassalli, Sentenza Condizionale. Hence our text is thought interpolated by Beseler, 1. 79; *acc.* Schulz, Z., 1912, 65 n. 3; Vassalli, Bull., 27. 261; H. Krüger, Z., 1925, 68 ff., who cites 43. 5. 3. 14 for the classical practice. It cannot be maintained that only the damages, not the judgment, are conditional, as the former apparently had to be equally certain, 42. 1. 59. pr., 1, 2. The Romans developed no proceeding to perpetuate testimony, cf. Bank *v.* Widmer, 2 Up. Can. Jur. 256, where the condition seems to have been fulfilled before suit. If the defendant here were not the obligor, there is danger of the latter's unjust enrichment. Hence Biondi, Bull., 30. 243, assumes that the text originally referred to the contract claim. Such a view seems unlikely in view of the mention of the Aquilian action in a parallel passage of Gaius, 2. 13. 10. 3; Lenel, Pal., 1. 970 n. 2,

and of the fact that from *interdum* in 41. 1 it seems that a debtor-destroyer is to be presupposed; finally, even were this not the case the praetor could compel assignment in the *actio judicati*, cf. 4. 9. 6. 4. Whenever a third person converts evidence of a debt the damages should never be the value of the debt unless the defendant may collect on the instrument, there being no subrogation for a thief. This rule is not sufficiently generalized in Sedgwick, Damages, 9 ed., §§ 256 ff.; cf. Daggett *v.* Davis, 53 Mich. 35; Moury *v.* Wood, 12 Wis. 413; Evans *v.* Kymer, 1 B. & Ad. 528; the English practice exactly corresponds to a Roman vindication and appears to have been unfortunately neglected in Stafford *v.* Lang, 25 R. I. 488. If the instrument is destroyed, the cost of reëstablishment in chancery is all that should be paid by the wrongdoer.

41. pr. The action *in f.* at the end of the text may be the *actio depositi*, 16. 3. 1. 38, which was often so drawn up in classical law, G. 4. 47, and would be in this case because of the peculiar nature of the damage. As for the former decision it is noticeable that it is not required that the will be destroyed after the death of the testator; if not, the plaintiff is including this interest in an action belonging to another, *supra* 15. 1. In 4. 3. 35 Ulpian gives a *scriptus heres* or legatee the *actio doli*, which must be because a copy has been found after failure in the *hereditatis petitio*. As Ferrini, Esp., § 248, ingeniously saw, the *scriptus* gives a clue to our text, where if the heir or legatee had to enter on intestacy for a lesser share and the will contained a condition no longer observable, the Aquilian would lie for the difference. Beseler, Z., 1922, 541, apparently overlooks this possibility in suggesting that the reference to the legatee is interpolated. It might also happen that a *scriptus heres* had entered by proof *aliunde*, 28. 4. 4; 29. 3. 10. 2; 48. 10. 26 (cf. 37. 11. 1. 7, which may explain the *post mortem* in 4. 3. 35, see 29. 4. 6. 3); when he might bring our action for the extra expense incurred, as in Taylor *v.* Bennett, 1 Oh. Circ. Dec. 57. The Romans avoided the logical impasse created by allowing suit for damages against one not the debtor where the realization of the debt is uncertain, cf. 2. 13. 10. 3; 47. 2. 27, 32; yet the decision in Dulin *v.* Bailey, 172 N. C. 608, is approved in L. R. A., 1917 B, 558. The strange doctrine is maintained by Rotondi, 951 n. 1; Vassalli, Bull., 27. 262, that more than the value of the material could not be recovered in a classical Aquilian action. They both entirely neglect 10.3 *cit.*, and cite Riccobono, Z., 1913, 235, as stating that such was Paul's view in 47. 2. 32. 1. Not only can no trace of such a thesis be found in the passage but the opposite view is stated, *i. e.*, that Aquilian recovery may be had if the contract action is unavailable. In holding 47. 2. 27. 3 interpolated, Riccobono, 237 n. 3, seems to forget that the damage may be committed by the debtor, cf. Levy, 1. 463 n. 3. Nevertheless, because it requires the hypothesis that there was a desire to die intestate, the statement that the testator has no action may indicate a possibility that some of the difficulties of this passage are due to Tribonian. The problem as to damages is not without difficulty where the object has no market value and replacement is specifically not desired, cf. *supra* 33. pr.

41. 1. It may be remarked that destruction of a document by the debtor is the only case of real concurrence of the Aquilian action and that for theft, cf. Levy, § 57. This statement and our text appear to be merely Byzantine, if Albertario is to be believed, Bull., 33. 263, who would say that Aquilian *dolus* is always theft. Although it is not impossible that the stupid repetition of the *nam* clause represents an interpolation, it is difficult to agree to Berger's attack, Bull., 32. 183 n., on the *animus furti faciendi*, without which the elegance of the remark would be extremely obscure.

42. Beseler, 1. 23, regards the reference to the action *ad. exh.* as interpolated; Riccobono, Z., 1913, 238, says the same of *aut instrumentum*. The text shows that the testator has the Aquilian for the value of the old tablets and the cost of making another will. No question of inheritance is involved but only the interpretation of *corrumpere.*

43. Beseler, Z., 1925, 197, in accordance with a theory that relation in *postliminium* is Byzantine, regards the text as interpolated, the original calling for an *actio utilis;* Buckland, Slavery, 254 n. 9, prefers an action *in factum;* Albertario, Riv. It. Per. S. G, 52. 51, objects to the last sentence because the interdict is styled an action (*acc.* Scaduto Ann. Sem. Giur., 8. 19 ff., 22), which last criterion of interpolation has been thoroughly overthrown by Lenel, Ed., 3 ed., 477, who cites G. 4. 155. Here is another fiction to achieve the same purpose as in 13. 2; all these expedients are applied only as far as convenient, Rex. *v.* Horsley, 8 East 405; 1. 5. 7 (cf. Bull., 33. 20), which has formed the English Law, Blasson *v.* Blasson, 2 De G., J. & S. 665; Villar *v.* Gilbey [1907], A. C. 139.

44. pr. This is a just description of the abstract standard of care, which has been described as "nothing but shamefaced liability without fault," Radbruch, *cit.* Exner, Fahrlässigkeit, 10; *contra* Rotondi, 955, who sees the classical idea of "objective imputability" portrayed; Arangio-Ruiz, Corso, 1. 272, who hints at an interpolation. The Romans often used the superlative; their standard, the same as ours in effect, was couched more strictly, cf. Sertorio, Culpa in Concreto, 115 ff.; for a sophistical proof of the inefficacy of the superlative in this connection, see Doneau, *cit.* Hasse, Culpa, 2 ed., 144 n. 1, who shows what can be done with the concept of due care *in the circumstances.*

44. 1. 45. pr. Cf. 9. 4. 2. 1; *id.* 4. 2, 3; Levy, § 16; Biondi, A. N., 335 ff.; Moreland *v.* State, 139 S. E. 77, 41 Harv. L. Rev. 398. The noxal action is preferable in case of insolvency. The liability here rests on a pure omission.

45. 1. See 27. 17; De Medio's suggestion, 50 n. 1, that a final diminution of value is presupposed needs no refutation. To support his theory that the interest was never separated from the value, v. Tuhr, 12, explains the recovery as necessary expenses charged upon the value, which, as Jolowicz remarks, 38 L. Q. R. 226, is "really no explanation at all." The action is unusual in that an *ex post facto* view is taken, the decrease

of value in the meantime not being considered, also the back reckoning cannot be applied, cf. 7. pr., unless the view suggested in 27. 28 be adopted.

45. 2. This text is of great help in discovering the liability of the b. f. p., *supra* 38; cf. 11. 3. 5. 1, Beseler's view, 4. 244 n., is too simple; it seems that Binding, Normen, 2. 2. 709 n. 87, like Monro, supposes that the mistake must be unreasonable, but cf. 13. 1.

45. 4. This decision seems inexplicable in view of 49. 1, unless it be assumed that *culpa* is implicit in the means of defense adopted, Pernice, S., 74 n. 23; cf. Morris *v.* Platt, 32 Conn. 75; Shaw *v.* Lord, 41 Okla. 347 with Vincent *v.* Lake Erie Co., 109 Minn. 456, but the same error is repeated in modern times by Demogue, Obligations, 3. 401 n. 3, cf. 411 n. 2. It is a mistake to argue from cases of unintentional injury in deciding liability for intended harm under a reasonable mistake, Paxton *v.* Boyer, 67 Ill. 132; Courvoisier *v.* Raymond, 23 Col. 113; Crabtree *v.* Dawson, 119 Ky. 148, cf. 49. 1 (*iusto*); *contra* Chapman *v.* Hargrove, 204 S. W. (Tex. Civ. A.) 379. These situations illuminate the weakness of the foundations of the doctrine of negligence.

45. 5. v. Tuhr, Z., 1887, 164, is certainly right in connecting this passage with 39. 2. 36. Strangely enough he assumes the facts to be different: whereas a common wall is there mentioned, he understands this to be the case of another's wall. Following the scholiast he then draws an inference *a contrario* that there is no action for demolishing a defective wall, 27. 25–28. Aside from the fact that a defective wall may well have some value, especially upon reckoning back, Grueber's explanation that the question was whether the consequential damage to the house supported by the common wall was direct or not, cf. 27. 8, 30. 3, has the merit of using *idoneus* in the sense of 36 *cit.*

46, 47. The surplus only is here recoverable, see *supra* 5. 1; Levy, § 114, who agrees to Krüger's suggestion of interpolation. The principal reason for this view seems to be the conviction that the text states the supposedly unclassical possibility that the *exceptio* may reduce recovery, which, however, does not seem even implied; Pernice, 1. 298 n. 2, with equal reason cites the passage as embodying just the opposite rule, cf. Girard, 1050 n. 2. The opposite problem has greatly vexed our courts, cf. Perry *v.* R. R., 199 Ky. 396; Freeman, Judgments, 5 ed., §§ 553, 554, 599; 2 A. L. R. 530.

48. The other action is that of 47. 4, Lenel, 322; for the standard of care see De Medio, Bull., 17. 15; *supra* 9. 4. The case is like 32. 1, unless as Levy, 1. 472, ingeniously suggests, all the damage is done *uno impetu* in the course of which the heir enters, when the action *in factum* would not lie on account of its subsidiary character, 47. 4. 1. 16.

49. pr. Cf. 27. 12. Grueber, cf. Cujas, Obs., 15. 26, suggests that the bees here flew into the fire built to keep them off. Pernice, S., 154, adduces these passages as evidence of the school dispute mentioned *supra* 7. 6.

49. 1. This shows the Roman rule that intentional aggressions on an innocent person's property were excused if committed under the stress of necessity; nothing could more clearly prove how thoroughly the classical theory of *culpa* had developed and how the necessity therefor obsessed the jurists, cf. 29. 3; 47. 9. 3. 7; 19. 5. 14. pr. (where the general average may be excluded because the damage was done by a passenger, Pernice, 1. 72, a possibility overlooked by De Francisci, Synallagma, 1. 334, cf. Palazzo, Lex Rhodia, 36 ff., 46, 86, who appears confused; Kreller, Z. f. Handelsrecht, 85. 327, who avoids the problem by interpreting *actio* as *ex delicto*), see also 29. 5. 1. 28 discovered by Leone, Riv. Dir. Civ., 7. 87 n. 6. Traces of an older doctrine may be seen in 43. 24. 7. 4, a better explanation of which is given by v. Tuhr, Nothstand, 63 n. 2, than by Windscheid, § 258 n. 15; cf. 39 Harv. L. Rev. 154 ff. Although we, like Servius Sulpicius, admit the privilege if the action is done under public authority or for the public safety, even, it seems, if there was a reasonable mistake as to the danger, Conwell *v.* Emrie, 2 Ind. 35; Cope *v.* Sharpe,

[1912] 1 K. B. 496; cf. *iusto* in our text, yet there is doubt if the action is purely for a private interest, see Newcomb *v.* Tisdale, 62 Cal. 575, 579; Vincent *v.* Lake Erie, *supra* 45. 4.

50. The owner may not always retain the property in fixtures; for the *ius tollendi* see Girard, 338 ff.; Riccobono, Ann. Sem. Giur., 4. 445 ff. Since, as Ulpian assumes, there is here no such right, the value of the baths ought to go in mitigation of damages, cf. 17. 1. 16; Oertmann, Vorteilsausgleichung, 29; Leone, Filangieri, 1916, 196.

51. A reconciliation of this text with Julian's statement in 15. 1, cf. 11. 3, has been attempted in many ways. Windscheid, § 258 n. 15; Pernice, S., 179 ff., regard it as impossible. Brinz, Pand., 2 ed., § 281*b*, nn. 6, 15, remarks that Julian wished to punish the attempt, on which theory, after a slave's natural death, actions on the first chapter might be brought against all who had ever tried to kill him. Pacchioni, 4 L. Q. R. 178, thinks that Julian allowed an action for killing before the death. Recently the difficulty has been laid to interpolation; Beseler, 4. 194, would never permit as classical such a digression as that of § 2 (cf. the earlier remarks of Pampaloni, A. G., 55. 515; Segrè, Mél. Girard, 2. 557 n. 1); encouraged by this discovery and apparently for no other reason he decides that the pr. is changed; Levy, 1. 25, discards 15. 1 holding that Julian disagreed. If the compilers had applied themselves to the texts the result obviously should have been a suppression, not an aggravation, of any inconsistency. The theory of Grueber and Vangerow that the second wound here would not alone have been mortal is not refuted by the reckoning back therefor from the death as is thought by Pacchioni and Windscheid; their assumption that the second slight wound could not then have caused immediate death is incorrect, as that fact is quite consistent with the possibility that death occurred sooner than it would from either wound alone, all that is required for each to be a direct contributory cause. Conversely, the Gloss made the inadequate assumption that in 11. 3 the first wound was not mortal. It seems best to accept Julian's own reason and with Ferrini, Esp., § 223, to suppose that this was what must have been the usual case where it was impossible to tell which wound caused the death, cf. 11. 2. This may be Haymann's view, Z., 1919, 219 n. 2, who obscurely remarks that the only doubt was as to the reckoning, not the liability of all. If there had been but one wound here, which caused death before the later accruing inheritance could be accepted, Julian's rule causes hardship by not allowing for damage actually caused by the defendant, cf. *supra* 23. 2.

52. pr. Cf. 8. pr., 30. 4. Alfenus evidently failed to distinguish between the intervention of the doctor and that of the plaintiff or an independent actor, an error often committed by modern scholars, *e. g.*, Pernice, 1. 102; Ferrini, E. G. I., § 33. The defendant's act, however, caused the doctor's intervention and so the death, but not directly, 39 Harv. L. Rev. 169 ff., the only question being as to the remoteness of the cause, cf. Mommsen, 2. 161 ff.; Jhering's Jahrb., 37. 424 ff. Assuming death to have been unforeseeable, as where the wound took a strangely bad turn, cf. 7. 5; 39 *op. cit.* 164 ff., the defendant should be liable for death caused by the wound alone though a doctor not chosen by the plaintiff could by due care have saved the slave, cf. *supra* 8. pr.; 27. 9; Howard *v.* Redden, *cit.* 39, *op. cit.*, 177, for the fiction of causation by an omission should not be applied to release another. Otherwise, the absurd result would follow that the defendant would escape where the doctor did nothing but not where he accelerated the death, in which case the defendant remains a direct contributory cause. In discussing proximate Aquilian cause relating to tangible injury by an *extraneus*, the rules of damages prevailing in contract relations are not helpful, *supra* 29. 3; the distinction is clearly shown by 19. 2. 57. In our field there is no room for the construction of a promise as a guaranty, or the doctrine of estoppel, which may form the basis of the rules of *mora* or deviation, or for considerations of *bona fides* which may prevail in certain confidential relationships, cf. Fottler *v.* Moseley, 39 *op. cit.*, n. 106. As regards tort liability there seems no reason for a distinction between cases where the question is as to the extent from those where it is as to the existence of the damage, though the apparently wrong cases cited *supra* 30. 4 justify Mr. McLaughlin's remark, n. 106 *cit.* If so, it is hard to avoid the conclusion that the Romans drew our difference between direct and indirect causes, for which see 39 *id.* 167 ff.: that is, lack of foreseeability was no excuse in the former case, 7. 5; 22. pr.; 23. pr., 2, 4; 27. 8; 19. 5. 14. 1; otherwise in the latter, as here, where the result is not repugnant to common law theory, 39 *id.* n. 72, cf. the lunatic of 7. 6, 30. 3; 37. pr.; 11. 3. 3. 1; 19. 2. 57; Leone, Riv. Dir. Civ., 7. 89 ff. In the last text by construction of the contract an intent to avoid damage of this kind may have been perceptible, cf. *supra* 29. 3; 13. 4. 2. 8; 19. 2. 11. 1, 4; *id.* 12. In the usual case where the plaintiff chose the doctor, the negligence of his slave would not be imputed to him, *supra* 11. pr., as we do that of the agent to the principal, Salmond, Torts, § 11, for as he is not seeking to claim through this slave, as in 11. pr., the maxim of 50. 17. 133 should apply, and as in the case of an *extraneus* the standard would be *culpa in eligendo*, arg. 21. 1. 31. 12, which we apply to doctors as independent contractors, Pearl *v.* R. R., 176 Mass. 177, so that we do not hold the defendant if he chose a negligent doctor where we would do so if the choice had been made by the plaintiff, see 8 A. L. R. 507 ff.

52. 1. Reading *dolon* for *dolor*, cf. 9. 1. 1. 7. The utmost confusion has been caused by treating this as a case of *culpa* compensation, E. G. I., § 34; Pernice, S., 63, but cf. 1. 98 n. 3. Obviously the innkeeper is either liable for an excess of force, 4. 45; Coll. 7. 3. 3, or his defense is justifiable, which may happen even though there was what might otherwise be negligence if there is a *bona fide* attempt to avoid a crisis intentionally created by the defendant: otherwise if the defendant is merely negligent; given a legal act by the plaintiff, the cases in 1 Shearman & Redfield, Negl., 4 ed., 132 n. 3, are hard to justify if a difference is intended from those in n. 2, cf. *supra* 9. 4. These considerations show the fallacy of the prevailing doctrine that if the same delicts occur on either side in the same transaction neither may recover. The texts cited either present cases where, on account of the delict, no right arose, 43. 8. 2. 15, or no damages 2. 10. 3. 3; cf. 29. 4. 7, or relate to the remedies for *dolus* 4. 3. 36, 44. 4. 4. 13; 50. 17. 154 where a "clean hands" rule applied exceptionally just as in English equity, cf. 24. 3. 39. The rules as to excess of force are conclusive to show the ordinary rule, so if I steal your slave in a fight where you steal mine, cf. 9. 4. 38. 2. The real difficulty here is that Alfenus appears to hold it unlawful for the owner to use reasonable force to recover his property. Huvelin, Mél. Girard, 1. 559 ff., after suggesting much interpolation and supposing that our text refers to the *actio in iuriarum*, solves the problem by assuming that the rule of 4. 1 did not refer to "*soustractions*" but to *furtum improprium*, which includes breaches of confidence, "*détournements*," *etc.*! See Huvelin, Furtum, 272. The problems connected with the punishment of self-help in C. 8. 4. 7 (for the earlier state of the law cf. 4. 2. 12. 1, 2; 43. 16. 3. 9; *id.* 17; 43. 24. 7. 3; Pernice, 1. 53 ff., 95 ff.) do not seem to be here involved, since the question is not as to the fate of the property but as to the *culpa* in giving the blow. The remainder of the text from *sed si* cannot have been written by Alfenus, in whose time the thief might have been killed, Coll. 7. 3. 2; or by any pre-Justinian glossator when killing would be excused if it was required to apprehend the thief, cf. Coll. 7. 3. 3, cf. the interpolated 5. pr.; third, the assumption that it is necessarily wrong *first* to give the blow is not even in accord with Justinian's law, in view of the possibility that possession has not been lost, cf. 3. 9. *cit.*, and that this is a reasonable method of *defending* it, *i. e.*, to prevent escape. For authorities on recaption with us, see Bohlen, Cas. on Torts, 2 ed., 116 ff.

52. 2. Cf. 6 Cal. L. Rev. 295; Z., 1925, 437.

52. 3. Haymann, Z., 1921, 363, regards *si emptor . . . tum* as interpolated, which destroys the point of the text; as for the repetition, whether or not it is a sign of "elegance" as Bonfante holds, Lezioni di Storia, 109 n. 1, it is certainly characteristic of Alfenus, cf. § 2, *plostrum* 11 times, *mulae* 10, not varied by *animalia*. Since the injury took place in *experiundo* the buyer had not made up his mind at the time. Nor is it possible with most commentators, cf. Vernay, Servius, 215 ff., to refer *si haberet emptor* to the nature of the condition, which might be either subsequent or precedent, Buckland, 493. If the buyer later refuses, the seller is liable, whatever the condition, for all are agreed that upon fulfilment of a condition subsequent, as between the parties the transaction is treated as if it had never occurred, Windscheid, § 91 n. 2, 3, although the classical procedural mechanics are doubtful, cf. 21. 1. 23. 8; Z., 1926, 427 ff. If the buyer has accepted, he has no action, whatever the condition, for even if the property has not passed for non-payment of the price, bringing the action is a breach of good faith. The words must refer to the time suit is brought, an action which manifests the refusal, cf. 45. 1. 112. pr.; Rabel, 474 n. 2; Ferrini, Pandette, 532 n. 4.

52. 4. The consent of the plaintiff prevents recovery, *supra* 7. 4.

53. Cf. 47. 2. 51; J. 4. 3. 16; G. 3. 219.

54. Cf. Cujas, Quaest. Pap., *ad h. l.*; Pernice, S., 208 ff.; v. Tuhr, 18; Pampaloni, A. G., 32. 412; Beseler, Z., 1925, 458 ff. This and the next passage raise most of the unanswered questions as to Aquilian liability. A dispute rages as to the amount recoverable by the promisor *ante moram*. Apparently he should receive nothing more than the value of the use before delivery. As to any advantage due to the back reckoning two types must be distinguished: the change in *interesse* due to the stipulation, and the normal change of value. In holding that such enures to the promisor Beseler weakens his argument by mentioning only the first and least defensible case. Except for the thoroughly incorrect decision in 55, radically expunged by Beseler himself, there is no hint that the back reckoning would allow a claim that the stipulation had not been made a year before, which would seem to conflict with 27. 25. Neither should a difference in value be considered, *supra* 23. 2.

If this had been a sale and the property had been destroyed by a third person, the buyer could have required cession of the action as a changed form of the *res*, *supra* 11. 7, a question then arising as to the effect of C. 7. 47. 1, assuming that it applied only to contract obligations, *supra* 21. pr. Hence if the buyer has destroyed the *res* the seller cannot recover its full value; as v. Tuhr says, *dolo facit qui petit quod redditurum est*, 50. 17. 173. 3. Mommsen, 1. 302 ff., holds that the rule did not apply to "strict" obligations such as stipulation, or legacy *per damnationem*. The absence of any hint of limited damages in the text, the decision in 4. 3. 18. 5 and the possibility of reckoning back, seem most strongly to support Mommsen's view, as well as that of Pampaloni and v. Tuhr, that full recovery can be had here. The analogy of a personal legacy is formally but not substantially correct. It is doubtful whether the testator's intent would be construed to allow his heir the action. In 4. 3. 18. 5 an *actio doli* is given to the promisee when the stipulated slave was killed by a third person, thus failing to reach the case of *culpa*, cf. 40 Harv. L. Rev. 304 n. 20; its denial of any action to the owner must be an oversight, or an interpolation (Beseler), because he has at least an interest in the use, overlooked by some commentators, Glück, Pand., 49. 177 n. 23; Levy, 1. 23 ff.; and even the latter's critic, Beseler. Hence, although the principles of cession of actions are obscure and not confined to *bona fide* obligations or vindication, cf. 4. 4. 27. 1 (Beseler 3. 178; but see Last, Jhering's Jahrb., 62. 111 n. 2); 4. 9. 6. 4; 15. 3. 3. 5; 35. 1. 73 (cf. Savigny, System, Beil. 13, ch. 9), it is probable that they did not extend to stipulations of a definite object, cf. 45. 1. 83. 5. The fact that the promisor may recover in full does not support v. Tuhr's thesis that the interest cannot diminish recovery, because a rule of contract law gives the promisor the whole interest in any changed form of the *res*. The distinction made according to the fact of *mora* does not seem "absolutely incomprehensible," as Beseler holds, suggesting the reverse, and the fact that the promisor cannot be released from his obligation by *casus* affords a reason for considering the object as substantially that of the promisee; (the distinction drawn by Cujas as to the fruits is unfounded, 22. 1. 38. 7; cf. *id.* 4. pr.; Mommsen, 3. 229 n. 11). Of the two, Beseler's distinction would appear the more nearly to merit the reproach: first, he does not explain why the promisor *ante moram* has not as much interest if the promisee kills as if this is done by another; second, in refusing the action where the promisee kills before default, he forgets the possibility of subsequent release; third, as to killing *post moram* it is Pickwickian to hold that the promisor has the Aquilian *because* he is not released, as well as an *exceptio doli* to the action *ex stipulatu*, the possibility of which defense justifies the term *liberatur*, 50. 16. 55; 50. 17. 112. Equally fallacious is Faber's distinction, Rat., *ad h. l.*, between wounding and killing, on the ground that in the former case the debtor is not released. In spite of Beseler the decision seems correct if the stipulation is gratuitous, cf. Glück, *op. cit.*, n. 33, but it is in the highest degree inequitable if the promisee has transferred property to the promisor, who is thus allowed a double recovery, for the consideration can scarcely be condicted when counter performance has been prevented by the fault of the would-be plaintiff, on 14. 3. 17. 5 see Riv. It. per. S. G., 49. 58. The text cannot apply to a sale, for 18. 5. 3; 19. 1. 3. 1; *id.* 25 (Lenel, Pal. Jul. 713); 22. 1. 4. 1, show that by whatever means the *bona fide* nature of the transaction will override its apparent formality, cf. Z., 1927, 130 ff., 138 ff. The question remains whether the passage was meant to apply to a stipulation in return for services or property other than money, *i. e.*, to what would without it have been an innominate contract, some of which at least were *bona fide* in Justinian's time, J. 4. 6. 28. In such cases the law seems to have implied a *clausula doli* if none was expressed, 12. 6. 65. 4;

Naber, 24. 55 ff.; cf. 4. 8. 31; 45. 1. 36; C. 2. 56. 3, which clearly would forbid unjust enrichment of this kind. Our text and 4. 3. 18. 5 are, however, not to be restricted to the case of a mere donee, cf. Gradenwitz, Ungültigkeit, 213; full recovery may be had if the act promised or performed in return does not tend to the promisor's enrichment, like manumitting a slave or marrying, where the slave is promised for a dowry, cf. C. 5. 12. 31. 2; Petrażycki, Einkommen, 2. 49. This may be one distinction between a *bona fide* transaction and a stipulation with the *clausula doli*, see Karlowa, Rechtsgeschäft., 228.

55. The promisor has the election in the absence of a special provision, 13. 4. 2. 3, and it used to be thought that he might still tender the value of the cheaper object if it was destroyed without his fault. The contrary view is now prevalent, the texts which caused the difficulty being very probably interpolated, 46. 3. 95. 1; cf. Rabel, 474 n. 1. This passage seems conclusive, but Mommsen, 1. 313, followed by Schulz, 102, ingeniously argues that even though death of S will not prejudice his owner, yet while he is alive his value is greater, *i. e.*, he would not be sold for less than 20, a theory which is disposed of by 21. 2 and which closely approaches admission of a sentimental value, cf. Huber, Alternative Obligationen, Inaug. Diss. Solothurn, 1892, 64 ff., who maintains, 60 n. 4, that the promisee may renounce his right to P instead of paying 20, which is negatived by the comparison of the creditor to a third party, so Faber Rat., *ad h. l.*, if P is killed. Vangerow, 3. 25, following the older theory that recovery was limited in 54, observes that if the creditor kills both at once or S before P, only 20 may be recovered; if P before S, 30, a view which has been both opposed and followed, see Ryck, Schuldverhältnisse, 252 n. 2. De Ruggiero, Obbligazione, § 52, is satisfied with all but the last sentence, which he suggests is an interpolation. Beseler, 3. 62, thinks that nothing after *respondi* is original except *nihilum . . . creditor*. Pampaloni, A. G., 32. 423, wishes to read the sentence beginning *et sufficiet* as a question, to be answered indirectly in the negative by the last sentence, *contra* Esp., 291. His position that nothing extra can be recovered if P dies before delivery, and that the value of P is to be computed as of the date of delivery is logically irrefutable. It is useless to cite 23. 2 with De Ruggiero, because in this case the interest must be calculated *ex post facto* depending as it does upon a subsequent event, cf. 45. 1. The promisor ought to wait until he delivers P unless an attempt be made to value the contingent claim, 35. 2. 45. 1. Reluctance to impute to a classical jurist such reasoning as these decisions involve explains the desperate methods of Beseler, De Ruggiero, and Pampaloni. If the decision here be law, it would follow that if one makes a contract to deliver a slave under a penalty and the contract is rescinded, the value of the penalty may be recovered if the slave is killed within the year, so also if the slave does damage greater than his value and the injured party gratuitously releases the master. Pampaloni mentions the two cases but assumes that the master had already paid the penalty. Other hypotheses may be imagined where the *utilitas* is of the kind to reduce damages: can a pledgee or usufructuary recover in full because he may have been owner within the year? Cf. *supra* 12. It is hard to see why this theory might not be applied to allow recovery for the cutting of ripe olives, 27. 25, because it would have involved liability to cut them within the month. If the Romans had more clearly distinguished the interest from the value, they would have noticed that the *quanti fuit* in 2. pr. ought not, and was not intended, to apply to the former conception.

As for the intervention of *mora*, unless the unfounded principle be adopted that the debtor thereby loses his right of election, cf. Vangerow, 3. 19 ff., it is difficult to grant it much effect where only one slave is killed. Mommsen, 3. 260 n. 7, holds that if S is killed by the promisee after *mora*, the value of P cannot be considered, because if the contract had been properly performed, P and S would have ceased to stand in any relation to each other. While analytically correct, on the reasoning of the text this would be important only if the *mora* had continued for more than a year, and there is no room for the assertion that the creditor has merely injured his own property.

56. Cf. 27. 30.

57. The possibility of the action *de pauperie* is overlooked. Haymann, Z., 1921, 391, attributes abridgment and interpolation to the compilers, following his thesis that their policy was to increase the field of Aquilian liability at the expense of that action. Such cases as these show the difficulty of escaping the supposedly ridiculous application of the standard of care to animals. If the injury were occasioned by the horse's mistaking his master's command, is it a case of the former's "initiative," cf. Haymann, *op. cit.*, 359 n. 1, or the "physical compulsion" of the latter, cf. the *vis absoluta* of the schoolmen? The *actio de pauperie* would obviously be allowed, however strictly a pure causation theory were maintained.

DE DONATIONIBUS INTER VIRUM ET UXOREM

ABBREVIATIONS

A. G. . . . . *Archivio Giuridico.*
Accarias . . . . . *Précis de Droit Romain,* 4 ed.
Arch. . . . . *Archiv für die Civilistische Praxis.*
Ascoli . . . . *Trattato delle Donazioni.*

Bechmann . . . *Das Römische Dotalrecht.*
Beseler . . . . . . *Beiträge zur Kritik der Römischen Rechtsquellen.*
Biondi . . . . *Appunti intorno alla Donatio Mortis Causa.*
Bonfante. . . . . *Corso di Diritto Romano,* vol. 1, "Diritto di Famiglia."
Bonfante, S. G. *Scritti Giuridici.*
Brinz . . . . *Lehrbuch der Pandekten,* 2 ed.
Buckland . . . . *The Roman Law of Slavery.*
Buckland, T. . *A Textbook of Roman Law.*
Bull. . . . . *Bullettino dell' Istituto di Diritto Romano.*
Burckhard . . . *Schenkungsannahme.*

Cugia . . . . *L'Espressione* "Mortis Causa."
Cuq. . . . . *Manuel des Institutions Juridiques des Romans.*
Czyhlarz . . . . . *Das Römische Dotalrecht.*

De Medio . . . . "Per la Storia," *etc.*, in *R. I. S. G.*, 33. 361 ff. (His Nullitá was inaccessible.)
De Retes. . . . . *De Don. int. V. et Ux.*, Lib. Sing., Salamanca, also in Meermann, Thes., 6. 663.
Desserteaux . . *Études sur la Formation Historique de la Capitis Deminutio.*

Enneccerus . . . *Rechtsgeschäft, Bedingung und Anfangstermin.*

Gentilis . . . . . . Scipio Gentilis, *De Don. int. V. et Ux.*, Hanover, 1604.
Girard . . . . *Manuel Élémentaire de Droit Romain,* 6 ed.
Glück . . . . *Ausführliche Erläuterung der Pandekten,* vol. 26.
Gotofredus . . . *Corpus Juris Civilis cum notis Dionysii Gotofredi.*
Gradenwitz . . *Die Ungültigkeit Obligatorischer Rechtsgeschäfte.*

H. S. . . . . Heumann-Seckel, *Handlexicon,* 9 ed.
Haymann . . . . *Die Schenkung unter einer Auflage.*

J. J. . . . . Jhering's *Jahrbuch für Dogmatik.*

Karlowa..... *Römische Rechtsgeschichte.*
Kr.......... *Corpus Juris Civilis*, 14th stereotyped ed., 1922, by Paul Krüger.

Lammfromm . *Teilung, Darlehen, Auflage und Umsatzvertrag.*
Lenel........ *Palingenesia Juris Civilis.*
Lenel, Ed. ... *Edictum Perpetuum*, 2 ed.
Levy........ *Der Hergang der Römischen Ehescheidung.*

Machelard ... Machelard-Labbé, *Dissertations de Droit Romain.*
Mitteis...... *Römisches Privatrecht bis auf die Zeit Diokletians.*

Pernice...... *Marcus Autistius Labeo.*
Pflüger...... *Condictio und Kein Ende.*
Pothier...... *Pandectae*, trans. Bréard-Neuville, vol. 9.

R. I. S. G..... *Rivista Italiana per le Scienze Giuridiche.*
Rabel....... "Grundzuge des Römischen Privatrechts," Holtzendorff's *Enzyc.*, 7 ed., vol. 1.
Riccobono.... "Dal Diritto Romano Classico al Diritto Moderno," in *Annali del Seminario Giuridico de Palermo*, vols. 3, 4.

Salkowski.... *Zur Lehre vom Sklavenerwerb.*
Savigny...... *Traité de Droit Romain*, trans. Guenoux, vol. 4.
Senn........ *Études sur le Droit des obligations*, vol. 1.

Vangerow.... *Lehrbuch der Pandekten*, 7 ed.

Windscheid... *Lehrbuch der Pandekten*, 8 ed., § 509.

Z........... *Zeitschrift der Savigny Stiftung*, Romanistische Abteilung, 1925.

DE DONATIONIBUS INTER VIRUM ET UXOREM

XXIV. 1.

1. ULPIANUS *libro trigesimo secundo ad Sabinum* Moribus apud nos receptum est, ne inter virum et uxorem donationes valerent. hoc autem receptum est, ne mutuo amore invicem spoliarentur donationibus non temperantes, sed profusa erga se facilitate.

The origin of our prohibition, in common with that of other Roman institutions, is veiled in an obscurity which permits of many conjectures, a number of which are almost equally plausible, since, though each is propounded to avoid a serious improbability inherent in the others, it in turn is subject to some new objection from which they were free. Inasmuch as a choice in such a matter must necessarily be of a largely arbitrary nature and the subject has been fully treated, cf. De Medio, 361 ff.; Nikolsky, Z., 1903, 441, a few considerations only need be added. It is a trite observation that the nullity of the transaction was so extreme and in most cases unnecessary a characteristic that the lawyers made every effort to limit it by honeycombing the rule with exceptions. This phenomenon renders very unlikely any theory which assumes that the existing type of prohibition developed by custom out of a milder form at any comparatively late date. Especially is this true of the hypothesis that the origin is to be sought in the *retentio*, in itself so weak a protection that the greatest difficulty was experienced till very late even in allowing it as the basis for a condiction, cf. Pflüger, 61 ff.; Riccobono, 370 n. 4. The conjecture which at present enjoys the greatest favor, cf. Kipp, Windscheid, n. 1; Bonfante 213 ff., is that of Alibrandi that it was introduced in the marital law of Augustus. If ingenuity were decisive, this supposition could not find an opponent, but aside from the objections excellently retailed by De Medio, and cf. *infra* 7. 6; 51; 64, no reason can be given why the compilers should have omitted the sentence attributing the rule to Augustus, contrary to their practice and their historical sense, cf. Erman, Mél. Appleton, 217. It might seem that all the lawyers, even contemporaries, would not have wasted time trying to find so many different reasons for a rule laid down by imperial statute, cf. 2; 3. pr. Since the institution could not be assigned to any law, there would then be no difficulty in believing this statement that it was due to a custom of ancient times when law might be thus made by the jurisconsults, if it were not for Vat. Fr. 302, where it is stated that H. and W. were excepted persons in the *Lex Cincia* of 550, cf. 48. 11. 1. 1. Savigny supposed that this referred to the exceptional cases where gifts were allowed, as on death or divorce. On account of the obvious truth that a proper law must have been so framed if any such gift were allowed, the usual rejection of this theory seems too hasty; the objections are often frivolous, cf. Francke, Arch., 18. 2, citing *omnibus* in Vat. Fr., 298. It seems, however, far from certain that just marriages without *manus* had been invented in 550. The earliest mention of that institution is found by Karlowa, 2. 168, to be by Ennius, born 35 years before (Accarias, 1. 243 n. 2, wrongly attributes the verse to Pacuvius), but H.'s Greek name would clearly indicate a lack of *conubium*, or a peregrine marriage, the transaction following a well-attested rule of Greek law, cf. Beauchet, Histoire, 1. 389 nn. 1, 2. At any rate the provisions of the *Leges Cincia* and *Julia de repetundis* become much broader if it is remembered what a large number of marriages were possible which were not "just," by Romans to Latins without *conubium* or to peregrines, cf. 48. 5. 14. 1, Girard, 111 n. 5, 162 n. 11; Bonfante, 196. In accord with the view that gifts between H. and W. were never allowed in a just marriage is the fact noted by Karlowa, *loc. cit.*, that the earliest parties to that union were of ill repute. Not only would all the motives of policy mentioned by Francke, *loc. cit.*, be present, but the natural feeling that such women ought not to be allowed advantages denied to more respectable matrons (cf. 3. 1), may be a contribution of the institution of *manus* towards our rule.

---

2. Paulus *libro septimo ad Sabinum* ne cesset eis studium liberos potius educendi. Sextus Caecilius et illam causam adiciebat, quia saepe futurum esset, ut discuterentur matri-

monia, si non donaret is qui posset, atque ea ratione eventurum, ut venalicia essent matrimonia.

The support of this passage for the possibility that S. Caecilius was an early authority in our field seems to have been overlooked by Karlowa, 1. 711, when he suggests reading *Caelius* in 64, cf. Lenel, 1. 35 n. 3; Levy, 87 n. 4.

---

3. Ulpianus *libro trigesimo secundo ad Sabinum* Haec ratio et oratione imperatoris nostri Antonini Augusti electa est: nam ita ait: 'Maiores nostri inter virum et uxorem donationes prohibuerunt, amorem honestum solis animis aestimantes, famae etiam coniunctorum consulentes, ne concordia pretio conciliari viderentur neve melior in paupertatem incideret, deterior ditior fieret.'

In suggesting an interpolation, Beseler 2. 74, apparently overlooked the importance of the word *honestum* brought out by Lenel, Ulp. 2760 = 39. 5. 5. The interpretation of *majores* required by Alibrandi's thesis seems very forced. Caracalla thus named the *Lex Julia* of Augustus because it was voted in the *comitia*. No reason is apparent why Ulpian in 1 should have mentioned Augustus, when to a subsequent emperor his part appeared so unimportant. This is perhaps an unprecedented method of describing an Augustan statute.

---

1. Videamus, inter quos sunt prohibitae donationes. et quidem si matrimonium moribus legibusque nostris constat, donatio non valebit. sed si aliquod impedimentum interveniat, ne sit omnino matrimonium, donatio valebit: ergo si senatoris filia libertino contra senatus consultum nupserit, vel provincialis mulier ei, qui provinciam regit vel qui ibi meret, contra mandata, valebit donatio, quia nuptiae non sunt. sed fas non est eas donationes ratas esse, ne melior sit condicio eorum, qui deliquerunt. divus tamen Severus in liberta Pontii Paulini senatoris contra statuit, quia non erat affectione uxoris habita, sed magis concubinae.

Cf. *infra* 32. 27, 28; 65. The sentence *fas . . . deliquerunt* is held interpolated by Vassalli, Bull., 27. 213 n.; Beseler, Z., 470, on the ground that *fas* was never used except in a religious sense, in spite of the fact that according to H. S. the proper use of the word is quite rare in the Digest, cf. 32. 2. Beseler asserts the very simple conclusion that gifts were always valid if the marriage were not. In so doing he appears to ignore Faber's work in connection with 32. 27, 28. The *Lex Papia Poppaea* punished parties to a marriage forbidden for unequal rank by disallowing either to benefit by the other's will, Ulp. 16. 2; cf. 23. 2. 44. 1; Accarias, 1. 219 n. 3. This rule was extended to marriages which were later forbidden because only one party was at fault, 23. 2. 63; 30. 128; 34. 9. 2. 1, 2. If the disability was there applied by analogy, not statute, the same should be true *a fortiori* in a case where the transaction would have been void had the marriage been valid, so that the guilty person is deriving a benefit made possible solely by his offense. The genuineness of the decision is reinforced by C. 5. 16. 7, for the interpolation of which Beseler refers to Solazzi, Minore Etá, 50 n. 1, who can find no other objection than the hypothetical form, so frequent in the Code. The result is that the gift though valid by the civil law may be recovered *ex injusta causa* from one who cannot take by will.

---

2. Qui in eiusdem potestate sunt, prohibentur sibi donare, ut puta frater mariti, qui est in soceri potestate.

For various criticisms of the arrangement of the following sections, see Kr.; Lenel, Ulp. 2762; Beseler, 3. 159. The subject is well characterized by DeRetes, 3. 1, as "intricate but not difficult," see Windscheid, n. 20; for some of the peculiarities caused by its application, cf. 32. 16 ff.; 58. 2.

---

3. Verbum potestatis non solum ad liberos trahimus, verum etiam ad servos: nam magis est, ut hi quoque, qui aliquo iure subiecti sunt marito, donare non possint. · 4. Secundum haec si mater filio, qui in patris potestate esset, donet, nullius momenti erit donatio, quia patri quaeritur: sed si in castra eunti filio dedit, videtur valere, quia filio quaeritur et est castrensis peculii. quare et si filius vel privignus vel quivis alius potestati mariti subiectus de castrensi suo peculio donavit, non erit irrita donatio.

This rule was of course considerably enlarged in scope with the appearance of the later *peculia: quasi castrense*, cf. 32. 17, and *adventicium irregulare*, see Vangerow, 1. 237. As for the *p. a. regulare* in which the father had a usufruct, Savigny's view, 176 n. *o.* that the donee took it absolutely seems the logical one; to hold that the donor retained it would seem more audacious; Bonfante, 217, seems to think that logic requires that something cannot be given to the son merely because the law forbids its being given to the father. The decision in C. 5. 16. 19 which created in Pothier the mistaken belief that in Justinian's law the father had no right to *bona materna*, cf. C. 6. 61. 6, may be explained with the Gloss as referring to an emancipated donee, or with Gotofredus that the marriage was that of the daughter and donee. For another situation see Machelard, 251 n. 1.

---

5. Prohibetur igitur et uxori et nurui donare etiam is, qui est in soceri potestate, si modo maritus sit in patris potestate. 6. Ab uxoris nurusve parte prohibitum est donari viro vel genero. sed et his, qui sunt in eorum potestate si fuerit donatum, vel in quorum sunt potestate, non valebit donatio, si modo vir et socer in eiusdem sunt potestate vel vir in soceri: ceterum si in alia familia est maritus, neque socero neque ei qui est in eius potestate neque ei in cuius est donatione interdictum est. 7. Socrui a nuru vel contra donari non est prohibitum, quia hic ius potestatis non vertitur. 8. Si servus meus, cuius usus fructus alienus est, donet uxori meae ex eo peculio, quod ad me non pertinebat, vel homo liber bona fide mihi serviens, an valeat donatio, quaeritur. et in libera quidem persona utcumque admitti potest donatio: ceterae enim personae alienationem peculii ut donent non habent.

Beseler's criticism, Z., 443, of this passage is hardly convincing. Mention of the validity of *iussum* by the usufructuary would seem unnecessary, cf. *infra* 3. 11. The case of a freeman serving in *good faith* who knows himself to be free is surely an impossibility. The *peculium* clause refers to the freeman to show that it is his property which is given, cf. G. 2. 92; Ulp. 19. 21. Beseler seems to miss the contrast, that is, that a mistake as to the authority is irrelevant for the slave, but as to the freeman it removes the difficulty which exists in the cases to which he refers, cf. 41. 1. 19; however, even without this belief that he is empowered to transfer his supposed *peculium*, the freeman's gift is *utcumque* valid, cf. J. 2. 20. 11; 40. 2. 4. 1; Windscheid, § 172 n. 9; Buckland, 230 n. 4.

---

9. Non tantum autem per se maritus et uxor ceteraeque personae dare non possunt sed nec per interpositam personam. 10. Sciendum autem est ita interdictam inter virum et uxorem donationem, ut ipso iure nihil valeat quod actum est: proinde si corpus sit quod donatur, nec traditio quicquam valet, et si stipulanti promissum sit vel accepto latum, nihil valet: ipso enim iure quae inter virum et uxorem donationis causa geruntur, nullius momenti sunt.

In view of the repetition and the pedagogic ring of *sciendum*, Beseler's suggestion, 4. 318, that the first sentence is interpolated deserves consideration. This is the first of the texts which De Medio, 383, is forced to discard to maintain his thesis that such gifts were merely voidable till Justinian. The idea that convalescence cannot be otherwise explained is refuted by such cases as 5. 9; 7. 8, which are striking examples of the truism in 50. 17. 1. In spite of the great number of interpolations required by his theory it has been approved by Costa, Storia, 2 ed., 566 n. 1, who stands, however, alone, cf. Rabel, 513 n. 1. It would require some labor to discover all the doubtless numerous texts on other subjects which imply the prevailing doctrine, *e. g.*, 9. 1; 37 (*actio legis Aquiliae*); 41. 7. 5. pr. (on which cf. Bull., 32. 168), with some of which De Medio, 395 n. 1, attempts not very satisfactorily to deal. The nullity need not be taken very seriously; in classical law its chief function was by the vindication to insure to the donor appreciations which, because of the rules of enrichment, he would otherwise have acquired.

---

11. Si quis igitur nummos uxori dederit, non fieri eius apparet, quia nihil corporis eius fieri palam est.

Beseler, *loc. cit.*, considers the last clause too obvious; cf., however, 46. 3. 78, they would soon become hers.

12. Sed si debitorem suum ei solvere iusserit, hic quaeritur, an nummi fiant eius debitorque liberetur. et Celsus libro quinto decimo digestorum scribit videndum esse, ne dici possit et debitorem liberatum et nummos factos mariti, non uxoris: nam et si donatio iure civili non impediretur, eum rei gestae ordinem futurum, ut pecunia ad te a debitore tuo, deinde a te ad mulierem perveniret: nam celeritate coniungendarum inter se actionum unam actionem occultari, ceterum debitorem creditori dare, creditorem uxori. nec novum aut mirum esse, quod per alium accipias, te accipere: nam et si is, qui creditoris tui se procuratorem esse simulaverit, a debitore tuo iubente te pecuniam acceperit, et furti actionem te habere constat et ipsam pecuniam tuam esse.

Cf. Faber, Conj., 3. 19; Gradenwitz, 220 ff.; Riccobono, Bull., 8. 211 ff.; Lenel, J. J., 36. 107 ff.; Last, *id.* 62. 29, 44 ff.; Beseler, *loc. cit.*, whose conjecture is rendered especially improbable by the Celsian fiction in 39. 5. 21. 1. It has been variously maintained that this solution depends upon *traditio brevi*, *longa*, *manu*, or *const. poss.*, cf. Riccobono, 219 n. 1. The confusion may result from the false analogy at the end of the text, the proper case being 21. 2. 61. The difficulty is increased by 46. 3. 38. 1, which makes the same comparison with a different answer to each question, but where, although the W. case is the same, that of the *procurator* is not, delivery occurring against the will of the creditor. Observing this, Gradenwitz ingeniously argues that there is no contradiction as regards W. in that here H. was present (*iubente*) at the delivery, *contra* Riccobono; Eck. K. V. I., 30. 87. This reconciliation, plausible as it is, depends upon what has been termed the false analogy by which our case is compared to that where possession is transferred to A with the intent to benefit B, and the doubts are born of B's lack of control together with an absence of the proper authority or intent in A. There the problem is whether B may acquire through A; but no such question can arise where the intention of all is unanimous that both possession and property shall be absolutely transferred to A. Whether the purpose is thereby to create an obligation from A to B, 12. 1. 9. 8; *id.* 15, or to extinguish one from B to A, 21. 2. 61, there is never a hint of the necessity of B's presence, cf. also 21. 1 *cit.*, the obvious reason for which is that, present or absent, he has no intent to acquire anything. Gradenwitz's reluctance to follow the usual theory that the texts are irreconcilable rests upon two assumptions: the first doubtful, *i. e.*, that Julian is cited in 38. 1, cf. Karlowa, 1. 713 ff.; *infra* 39; the second wrong, *i. e.*, that the next passage shows that he agreed with Celsus. Though there is no reason to suppose that Africanus did not accept the fiction in 21. 2. 61 where there was a valid obligation between A and B, he balked at so doing when the transaction between them was void and adopted a clumsier method of reaching the same result. For the sake of completeness reference may be made to Last, 46 n. 2 for the refutation of another attempt at conciliation, cf. also Gentilis, 75, and the desperate expedient of De Ruggiero, A. G., 63. 443, who holds that 38. 1 *cit.*, with its complicated play of exceptions and assignment as well as the quite different solution of 39 are Byzantine. The feature of this subject which is perhaps the most striking and puzzling is that without any difficulty or self-consciousness so many other decisions were reached which seem to involve the same problem and to require the use of this fiction, *e. g.*, 7. 7; 26. pr.; 50; cf. *infra* 32. 23.

---

13. Huic sententiae consequens est, quod Iulianus libro septimo decimo digestorum scripsit si donaturum mihi iussero uxori meae dare: ait enim Iulianus nullius esse momenti, perinde enim habendum, atque si ego acceptam et rem meam factam uxori meae dedissem: quae sententia vera est.

Upon the usual interpretation followed by Riccobono, *op. cit.*, 218 ff., Julian, though using Celsus' fiction, reached the opposite result that all the acts were void. The fact seems to be the contrary, cf. De Ruggiero, *cit.* 438 ff.; no reason can be discovered why the "acceptance" should not be valid, and the next text strongly implies that H. benefits if death ensues. It is thought, however, that this solution entails a contradiction of Julian with himself in 38. 1 *cit.* More important for us, it seems to conflict with 5. 13, 14; 31. 7, the later efforts to explain which antinomy have been conspicuously unsuccessful, see Pothier; Glück, 26. 7. In view, however, of 56 the distinction might be held to rest upon the delivery by the *donaturus*. But if H. asked his rich uncle to make W. a present, cf. 31. 7, and the uncle spent 100 with which he intended to buy a slave for H.'s birthday or a jewel for W., can it be said that there was a fictitious delivery of the jewel to one who had no use for it? Besides the difficulties as to defining the *habiturum* the decisions here and in the next passage are wrong for lack of impoverishment. As all the older writers saw, cf. DeRetes, 4. 9, every difficulty disappears if we here adopt Gradenwitz's view and assume a tender or whatever was necessary for a *const. poss.* between H. and the *donaturus*, cf. Buckland, N. R. H., 1925, 355. Only then is the former impoverished and any problem possible, for as in the first case the gift was void although the *tradens* owned the property, so here it must be valid unless H. owned it. The cases being, then, in no way analogous, there is no need for the various emendations that have been suggested or the idea of interpolation, *perinde* rel., see Chlamtacz, Rechtl. Nat., 122 n. 2; Bonfante *ad* Windscheid, 5. 466.

---

4. IULIANUS *libro septimo decimo digestorum* Idemque est et si mortis causa traditurum mihi iusserim uxori tradere, nec referre, convaluerit donator an mortuus sit. neque existimandum est, si dixerimus valere donationem, non fieri me pauperiorem, quia sive convaluerit donator, condictione tenebor, sive mortuus fuerit, rem, quam habiturus eram, in bonis meis desinam propter donationem habere.

That there must have been transfer of ownership to H. follows from *condictione tenebor* (incorrect, Chlamtacz, *loc. cit.*), unless we impute to Julian a glaring *petitio principii*. This is what Beseler does, Z., 444, by adding *si mihi tradita esset*, without even mentioning the resulting conflict with 5. 13, *etc.*, and the insuperable analytical difficulties thus raised, or noticing the significant absence of those words in the parallel text, 56. The mention of the condiction seems to prove that the gift was upon a resolutive condition, otherwise the personal action would not lie until the vindication had been lost.

---

5. ULPIANUS *libro trigesimo secundo ad Sabinum* Si sponsus sponsae donaturus tradiderit Titio, ut is sponsae daret, deinde Titius tradiderit post nuptias secutas: si quidem eium interposuerit maritus, donationem non valere, quae post contractas nuptias perficiatur: si vero mulier eum interposuerit,

iamdudum perfectam donationem, hoc est ante nuptias, atque ideo quamvis contractis nuptiis Titius tradiderit, donationem valere.

As to interpolation see Beseler, Z., 469, who by recognizing the validity of the distinction impliedly admits his mistake, 4. 204 *ad* 11. 7, that it cannot be important who interposed. The theory of Last, J. J., 62. 36; Burckhard, 93 n. 94, that the decision depends on acquisition of possession by the fiancée is unsatisfactory for two reasons: first, because the possibility of such acquisition is violently disputed, cf. Beseler, 4. 54; Albertario, *cit.* Z., 1926, 472; second, because it fails to take account of the probability that the text dealt with mancipation. All difficulties are avoided if we assume in accordance with principle that Titius acquired ownership in either case, cf. Pininski, Besitzwille, 2. 217 n. 2. Thus, where W. is the mandator, H. has divested himself of every right and subsequent delivery does not impoverish him; otherwise, however, he is thereby deprived of his right of revocation.

---

1. Si maritus duos reos habeat Titium et mulieri accepto tulerit donationis causa, neuter liberatur, quia acceptilatio non valet: et haec Iulianus libro septimo decimo digestorum scribit. plane si mihi proponas Titio accepto latum, ipse quidem liberabitur, mulier vero manebit obligata.

It may be mentioned that this and the following four texts appear clearly contrary to De Medio's theory. The anomaly here is surprising, cf. 34. 3. 29, Gradenwitz, 236; Binding Korrealobl., 177 n. 29, 230 n. 56, but Beseler's claim of interpolation, Z., 444, is not convincing, because the second proposition follows from the first in view of the continually observed policy of allowing the transaction all possible validity, 5. 5; 5. 8; 7. 8; 17 pr. This is not to say that either decision is free from theoretical objections. If H. may free W. by suing the *correus*, why may he not do so by releasing the latter? Where W. is released, is it necessary that it be done *donationis causa* to her or to C.? *i. e.*, would it be void if H., who had never intended to sue W., released her solely as a gift to the absent C.? In short it seems unjust to C. that the law allows a gift to W. at his expense, which it refuses if he benefits. Practically the passage may be justified by the assumption that C. had agreed with W. for contribution; such a common event that H. would usually have the *animus donandi* in giving the release, but cf. 34. 3. 3. 3, 4. Query if he released W. merely as a gift to C. mistakenly believing that C. had no recourse against her?

---

2. Generaliter tenendum est, quod inter ipsos aut qui ad eos pertinent aut per interpositas personas donationis causa agatur, non valere: quod si aliarum extrinsecus rerum personarumve causa commixta sit, si separari non potest, nec donationem impediri, si separari possit, cetera valere, id quod donatum sit non valere.

The second sentence is so obscure that there is much to be said for Beseler's idea, Z., 444, that it is a gloss, cf. Cugia, Adjectus, 6. A satisfactory illustration of the principle has never been offered, cf. Gentilis, 1. ch. 13. Savigny, 82 ff., mentions cases of urgent need or those like 5. 15, 28. 2, *etc.*, where circumstances alter the *animus;* even more unconvincing is Accursius, who cites 21. 1. 34. 1 as to things, *id.* 40. pr. as to persons, by which interpretation the transaction would appear to be valid if a pair of horses worth 50 together and 10 separately were sold *an. don.* for 40. Perhaps the best case is offered by Pothier: that of a servitude granted by H. in favor of land held in common by W. and another. Even here the *animus* should be decisive, so that if there were a b. f. attempt only to benefit the other he should be allowed the value on partition, till which time W. only has the use. The passage has, however, been taken seriously by Haymann, 47 n. 2, as proving the often reiterated rule, cf. Regelsberger, Pand., 611, that a *negotium mixtum* is treated as two transactions, a gift *sub modo* as one. If Haymann's attempt, 48 ff., to distinguish these types in regard to 39. 5. 18 be read with the *n. m.* of 5. 5. in mind, it is believed that his confusion will become apparent, cf. *infra* 13. 2. For example, after citing our text to show that a *n. m.* is void *pro tanto*, and 59 to show the contrary rule for a *don. sub. m.*, he is at pains to prove that 49, where the gift is wholly void, is an example of the *n. m.* The truth appears to be that the distinction between the transactions rests upon whether the intent was that supposed by Julian in 39. 5. 2. 7, or that of B. G. B. § 527, which has caused the difficulties of Haymann and his follower Mitteis, 201, by purporting to deal with a gift *sub. m.* Thus, whatever else it may be, it is not a *n. m.* if as in 5. 5 a slave is sold on credit *don. an.* for half his value, and the price, which corresponds to the charge, is not paid, *provided that* the sale would not have been made without the gift. As regards our prohibition a gift *sub. m.* was usually valid because of the rule of 17, 18, which was not the case of the *n. m.* of 5. 5, otherwise of that in 39. 5. 18, cf. 7. 8 with 49. Forgetfulness of the principle that a gift of the use is permissible causes a fundamental error on Haymann's part, Z., 1917, 225 n. 5, 239 n. 4; cf. *infra* 5. 8; 9. 2.

---

3. Si debitor viri pecuniam iussu mariti uxori promiserit, nihil agitur. 4. Si uxor viri creditori donationis causa promiserit et fideiussorem dederit, neque virum liberari neque mulierem obligari vel fideiussorem eius Iulianus ait, perindeque haberi ac si nihil promisisset.

Although this is contrary to the usual rule in delegation, 46. 2. 13, Savigny, 591, gives a good reason for it, cf. also the *S. C. Velleianum*, Gradenwitz, 97 ff. His explanation of the rule in our field, 247, is not applicable to the situation after the *oratio*.

---

5. Circa venditionem quoque Iulianus quidem minoris factam venditionem nullius esse momenti ait: Neratius autem (cuius opinionem Pomponius non improbat) venditionem donationis causa inter virum et uxorem factam nullius esse momenti, si modo, cum animum maritus vendendi non haberet, idcirco venditionem commentus sit, ut donaret: enimvero si, cum animum vendendi haberet, ex pretio ei remisit, venditionem quidem valere, remissionem autem hactenus non valere, quatenus facta est locupletior: itaque si res quindecim venit quinque, nunc autem sit decem, quinque tantum praestanda sunt, quia in hoc locupletior videtur facta.

Cf. 31. 3; 32. 26; 16. 1. 17. pr.; 18. 1. 38; Regelsberger, Pand., 611 n. 3; Savigny, 101 ff.; convalescence is not involved, but cf. Lotmar, Causa, 59. Lammfromm, 144 ff., thinks the passage interpolated from *quatenus*, forgetting that, in our field at least, enrichment is as necessary for a gift as the *animus donandi*. In answer to his ingenious suggestion that Julian's view depended on lack of certainty of the price, it seems that this is true only of the sale that ought to have been made and not the actual transaction. The idea that Neratius' distinction itself is interpolated occurred simultaneously to Partsch, Z., 1921, 266, and Pringsheim, *id.* 325; *acc.* Beseler, *infra* 7. 5; 49. The weakness of Pringsheim's thesis that *animus donandi* is always interpolated may be seen from the fact that if property is given to one that it be returned in a year to the donor's daughter, it is only the intention which decides whether the transaction is *commodatum*, *precarium*, mandate, *do ut facias*, gift *sub modo*, or *negotium mixtum*, cf. Haymann, *pass.* It would aid in the understanding of his view if he explained whether *donationis causa* is always also interpolated, cf. 326 n. 1, and if not, how it differs from the expression objected to; for a revolt in favor of *animus* see Mél. Cornil, 1. 427 ff. Partsch's argument that the decision depends upon the idea that property had a just price fails because the only important point is what the donor thought was the just price, cf. *infra* 7. 4. The statement that *remittere* must mean a later release is refuted not only by a glance at H. S. but in terms by the fact that in 31. 4 it is stated to be the same whether the gift was later or not. The view that the text is interpolated is belied in the clearest fashion by the words of 39. 5. 18. pr. and involves a failure to comprehend the nature of Aristo's *negotium mixtum*, which could not help occurring to Neratius, cf. Karlowa, 1. 704 n. 4. The *autem* also becomes incomprehensible, for no satisfactory explanation of the real view of Neratius and Pomponius has been offered. It seems perverse to balk at the consideration of the *animus* in a case where that alone is admittedly decisive as to whether the transaction was a gift or a sale, nor is this the only case of the kind; in the next two passages without the *animus* the transaction would have been valid, in the former case for lack of impoverishment, in the latter as an accident.

---

6. Si donationis causa vir vel uxor servitute non utatur, puto amitti servitutem, verum post divortium condici posse.

Cf. 44; 47; Savigny, 575; Ascoli, 56 ff.; Burckhard, 111; v. Mayr, Condictio, 325; De Medio, 380 ff.; Pflüger, 30. This is the clearest of several texts which show that acceptance was not needed to constitute a gift, against which conclusion a desperate but hopeless struggle is maintained. The words *post divortium* are difficult; of the various explanations the most seductive is that of Pflüger, who suggests that the passage dealt with the *retentio*. His conclusion that the condiction did not lie involves the impossible affirmation that the Romans were unable to manipulate their procedure to make the prohibition work both ways; if anything is certain, it is that if W. has no remedy, neither has H. As Savigny shows, the servitude is lost because there is no transaction which can be called void; the donor did nothing but let the law take its course *don. an.* Even if it is assumed that a *negotium* was unanimously held to be necessary for the *condictio*, its absence here should not surprise us in view of the number of *singularia* created by our law, cf. also 58. 2. Nevertheless the *condictio* has greatly puzzled modern scholars. De Medio regards it as a remnant of the old law, Pflüger as an interpolation. This disagreement is natural, for if both were right there would have been no action to recover a gift before Justinian. Since condiction of a servitude is called *incerti* in 12. 6. 22. 1, our remedy is subject to all the suspicions which have lately centred on that institution. Those who discuss the subject, are prone to forget a fact of which they make great use as regards the *condictio certae rei*, cf. Pflüger, 38 n. 2; *i. e.*, the condemnation is equally indefinite in either case; cf. H. Krüger, Z., 1900, 423 ff.; as for the distinction between *dare* and *facere* there is little to choose between *condictio operarum* and that of a "real" servitude or even a *cautio*.

---

7. Si uxor vel maritus exceptione quadam donationis causa summoveri voluerint, facta a iudice absolutione valebit quidem sententia, sed condicetur ei, cui donatum est.

Cf. 17. 1. 29. 5. As there is here *datio* of a sum of money Pflüger's suspicions seem groundless.

---

8. Concessa donatio est sepulturae causa: nam sepulturae causa locum marito ab uxore vel contra posse donari constat, et si quidem intulerit, faciet locum religiosum. hoc autem ex eo venit, quod definiri solet eam

demum donationem impediri solere, quae et donantem pauperiorem et accipientem faciet locupletiorem: porro hic non videtur fieri locupletior in ea re quam religioni dicavit. nec movit quemquam, quod emeret, nisi a marito accepisset: nam etsi pauperior ea fieret, nisi maritus dedisset, non tamen idcirco fit locupletior, quod non expendit.

Cf. 5. 17; 7. 1. For a radical expurgation of this and the following passages see Beseler, 4. 204, who might have informed us of his view of the gift had the wife otherwise had to buy the land. The argument, intended as a makeshift, is obviously wrong, as Gothofredus remarks, citing 46. 3. 47. 1, cf. 12. 6. 65. 7; Windscheid, § 421 n. 13. No *a priori* explanation for this rule will be successful, cf. v. Mayr, Condictio, 327.

---

9. Haec res et illud suadet, si uxori maritus sepulturae causa donaverit, ita demum locum fieri intellegi mulieris, cum corpus humatur: ceterum antequam fiet religiosus, donantis manet. proinde si distraxerit mulier, manet locus donatoris.

These rules are derived from those developed for the case in 7. 8. The result, as yet doubted apparently by nobody (not even by Haymann, Z., 1917, 225 n. 5, cf. 240 n. 1, who fails to escape the problem, equally pressing whether the term is a year or a day), that the mancipation is subject to a condition has been noticed by few, of whom Buckland, 631 n. 1, tries to dismiss it with the remark that the condition *inest*, as upon release of a conditional debt, cf. Mitteis, 170 n. 13. Although the inadequacy of the analogy is obvious, it is true that in the usual fiduciary mancipation the condition is imposed by law contrary to the will of the parties. But to say with Buckland that this text does not prove that an express condition can be appended to a mancipation involves the absurdity that one cannot expressly intend a result which is imposed upon one when he intended something else, that is, that one can obtain the desired effect only by pretending that it was not desired. Such seem to be consequences of the theory entertained by Rabel, 516 n. 3, Biondi, 15 n. 2, and Senn, 72, that H. and W. could not make a mancipation *mortis causa*, cf. *infra* 9. 2, a view which is furthermore belied by 40. 1. 15, cf. 23. 3. 43. pr. Even if the maxim of 50. 17. 195, which was not applied to legacies, cf. 30. 3; 35. 1. 107; Bufnoir, Condition, 53 ff., was always preserved in full force, it only forbids use of the word *si;* and that the conditional effect may be reached by a *lex* is shown by the case of a slave sold for export, Mitteis, 181 ff. Because the gift is valid only if used in one way, there arise here none of the problems of relation attendant upon a gift *m. c.*, cf. 11. 9, but there are the same academic difficulties about the suspensive condition that are mentioned *infra* 8.

---

10. Secundum haec si uxori suae monumentum purum maritus magni pretii donaverit, valebit donatio, sic tamen, ut, cum fit religiosus, valeat.

Because of the inaccessibility of Haymann's Freilassungspflicht, it cannot be determined whether his grounds for the interpolation mentioned by Kr. are more serious than those of repetition. Beseler, 3, 159, eradicates the whole text as a "worthless example."

---

11. Sed et si ipsa fuerit illo illata, licet morte eius finitum est matrimonium, favorabiliter tamen dicetur locum religiosum fieri.

Beseler, *cit.* 5. 8, is equally merciless with this passage, without stating whether it is suspicious because it conflicts with 8, or because it is too obvious. The latter conclusion would be plausible if it were not for the rule of 8, for which it is hard to find a reason, as death offers no presumption of a change of heart.

---

12. Proinde et si maritus ad oblationem dei uxori donavit, vel locum, in quo opus publicum quod promiserat facere, velut aedem publicam, dedicaret, fiet locus sacer. sed et si quid ei det, ut donum deo detur vel consecretur, dubium non est, quin debeat valere: quare et si oleum pro ea in aede sacra posuerit, valet donatio.

Cf. 7. 1. The public interest is an unnecessary factor here, otherwise perhaps in 14.

13. Si maritus heres institutus repudiet hereditatem donationis causa, Iulianus scripsit libro septimo decimo digestorum donationem valere: neque enim pauperior fit, qui non adquirat, sed qui de patrimonio suo deposuit. repudiatio autem mariti mulieri prodest, si vel substituta sit mulier vel etiam ab intestato heres futura.

Cf. Savigny, 30 ff. Burckhard, Begriff der Sch., 12 ff., remarks that the goods would be *bona materna* if a wife did this in favor of her son, a conclusion which, appealing as it may be, seems to be refuted by 23. 3. 5. 5.

---

14. Simili modo et si legatum repudiet, placet nobis valere donationem, si mulier substituta sit in legato vel etiam si proponas eam heredem institutam.

The first person plural excites Pampaloni's suspicion, A. G., 55. 515, but his promised explanation, *op. cit.*, 505, has not been found. It is true that, very strictly speaking, the decision is perhaps contrary to the Sabinian view of a real legacy, which prevailed in the Digest, cf. 8. 6. 19. 1; 28. 1. 16. 1; see, however, Windscheid, § 643 n. 2. Since, however, Julian appears to have adopted a somewhat modified theory (cf. 30. 86. 2; 46. 3. 13; Wlassak, Z., 1910, 314) and since in another connection in the same book of his Digest, Lenel, 279, 285, he made no distinction against a legacy, it would seem that the result is certainly genuine.

---

15. Si quis rogatus sit praecepta certa quantitate uxori suae heredidatem resituere et is sine deductione restituerit, Celsus libro decimo digestorum scripsit magis pleniore officio fidei praestandae functum maritum quam donasse videri: et rectam rationem huic sententiae Celsus adiecit, quod plerique magis fidem exsolvunt in hunc casum quam donant nec de suo putant proficisci, quod de alieno plenius restituunt voluntatem defuncti secuti: nec immerito saepe credimus aliquid defunctum voluisse et tamen non rogasse. quae sententia habet rationem magis in eo, qui non erat deducta quarta rogatus restituere et

tamen integram fidem praestitit omisso senatus consulti commodo: hic enim vere fidem exsolvit voluntatem testatoris obsecutus. hoc ita, si non per errorem calculi fecit: ceterum indebiti fidei commissi esse repetitionem nulla dubitatio est.

This decision is held by Windscheid, § 289 n. 5, to depend on the existence of a natural obligation in spite of the fact that the minimum requirement of that institution, the *soluti retentio*, is shown by the last sentence to be lacking, cf. Meyerfeld, Schenkung, 356; more inadequate is the interpretation of Pernice, 3. 255 n. 6, who maintains the absence of the obligation and yet holds the last sentence interpolated, completely disregarding the other texts supporting his statement, 22. 6. 9. 5, 6; 36. 1. 70. 1; C. 6. 50. 9, with the strange remark that in these cases there is never any question of mistake. Finally Vassalli, St. Senesi, 30. 44 n., alleges the interpolation of all from *et rectam*, on the ground that *voluntatem defuncti secuti* is in contradiction to the case supposed, thereby overlooking the fact that the same is said by Celsus, *officio fidei . . . functum*, admitted by him to be genuine. The explanation of this difficulty is certainly not furnished by Ascoli, 132, who supposes that H. somehow knew that the *praelegatum* was given only to fulfil the law; *sine deductione*, however, refers to the Pegasian fourth, not to the *praeceptio*, which was accepted but was less than the fourth (on the method of computation see Vangerow, 2. 419). The testator's purpose is thus fulfilled, the *praelegatum* being naturally construed as an intended substitute for the fourth; hence the *aliquid voluisse* clause. If such an intent cannot be made out, as where the *praelegatum* itself is transferred, or H. directed to retain the fourth, the transaction would appear to be void on the ground of impoverishment, since ownership is necessarily acquired in the whole inheritance, cf. Savigny, 86 n. *g*, who, citing 36. 1. 69. 3, seems mistaken in saying that no rights are acquired by one forced to enter under the Pegasian. There, however, to repress an attempt to evade the caduciary laws it was necessary, contrary to logic, to hold that the testator was the real donor of the fourth, while here logic and policy are at one. More difficult from this point of view is the case where a legatee receives the property without the intent to acquire for himself but for W. Since he expressly repudiates and W. cannot acquire through a free person without a mandate, who has the title in the mean time? Textually improbable and analytically impossible seems Vassalli's theory of this subject that both the consideration of the testator's intent, and the distinction between mistakes of law and fact are interpolated, although every text in the sources uses one or the other of these criteria, cf. Paul, 4. 3. 4. An inquiry into the testator's purpose is quite indispensable: (*a*) in every case of overpayment with knowledge, to decide whether the transaction is invalidated by our prohibition or the *Lex Cincia;* (*b*) in the cases of overpayment by mistake, at least of a *fideicom.* (on C. 4. 5. 7, cf. G. 2. 213), to distinguish the situation from the ordinary *solutio indebiti;* thus the simple view that recovery is never allowed is impossible if the heir is requested to deduct the fourth. In the usual case where nothing is said, no more reasonable and just distinction can be imagined than that between mistakes of law and fact, cf. 22. 6. 9. 5, 6, which speaks for itself, even Vassalli, 39, admitting that the mention of ignorance of law is classical. It is more doubtful whether the distinction was employed where the intent was clear, *i. e.*, whether the heir could recover: (*a*) for a mistake of law when requested to retain the fourth, cf. 36. 1. 22; (*b*) for a mistake of fact when requested not to retain it. Except that the intent is not express but implied the latter case is decided in the last sentence of our text, in favor of the genuineness of which is the fact that the result is more consonant with the law of a period when there was no tendency to hold that the testator could deprive the heir of the fourth, cf. Nov. 1. 2. 2*i. f.* It was entirely natural to treat the point in this connection, for H., failing in his claim under our prohibition, would then attempt to succeed on the ground of mistake, whence it is probable that the discussion was abridged rather than inserted by the compilers. Although this case is one where there is no *soluti retentio*, yet payment with knowledge is not a gift, since the latter peculiarity rests solely upon the desire of the testator, express or implied; there is no justification either for Accarias' doubt, 2. 633 n. 2, whether ours is a case of a natural obligation, or for Meyerfeld's deductions, *loc. cit.*, from this to the case of payment of a real *n. o. donandi animo*, cf. *infra* 32. 9.

---

16. Cum igitur nihil de bonis erogatur, recte dicitur valere donationem. ubicumque igitur non deminuit de facultatibus suis qui donavit, valet, vel, etiamsi deminuat, locupletior tamen non fit qui accepit, donatio valet. 17. Marcellus libro

septimo digestorum quaerit, si mulier acceptam a marito pecuniam in sportulas pro cognato suo ordini erogaverit, an donatio valeat? et ait valere nec videri locupletiorem mulierem factam, quamvis mutuam pecuniam esset acceptura et pro adfine erogatura.

Cf. 7. 1. This decision by Marcellus, cf. 7. 3, should embarrass Girard, 633 n. 1, and Windscheid, n. 26, who follow Savigny's view that the *oratio* first introduced the defense of consumption. Although it is merely an application of a constitution of Pius, 42, the general principle may be very ancient, 29, pr.; 31. 9.

18. In donationibus autem iure civili impeditis hactenus revocatur donum ab eo ab eave cui donatum est, ut, si quidem exstet res, vindicetur, si consumpta sit, condicatur hactenus, quatenus locupletior quis eorum factus est.

Cf. De Medio, 395, Beseler, 3. 92; Pflüger, 36 ff., whose suspicions are excited by the repetition of *hactenus*. The latter's discussion serves as a reminder of our ignorance of the substantive and adjective law of the condiction. His thesis that the rule of 46. 3. 78 is to be applied to all fungibles is hardly an improvement upon the usual view that that principle is exceptional, for Niemayer, Z. für Handelsr., 42. 20, has shown that it is meaningless in every case. As regards procedure the difficulty is of course to reconcile the supposed strictness of the *intentio* with a liability which was limited to enrichment. Some, like v. Mayr and v. Tuhr, Aus Röm. und Burg. Recht, 301, suggest a *taxatio;* Pflüger conjectures that the plaintiff elected to treat the money as a *certa res,* which illustrates the logical impossibility of distinguishing among condictions. For our purposes it is enough that given the plethora of analogies it is quite possible that abridgments rather than additions were made by Justinian. It is difficult to suggest interpolation until a more coherent theory has emerged, for lack of which nobody has yet discovered anything Byzantine in the substance of this text, cf., however, Perozzi, Ist. 2.2 87 n. 2. Savigny seems mistaken in the assertion, 180, that the condiction lies if the donee parts with the *res;* for while a vindication exists there is no impoverishment, nor in the case of a sale, any enrichment.

6. GAIUS *libro undecimo ad edictum provinciale* quia quod ex non concessa donatione retinetur, id aut sine causa aut ex iniusta causa retineri intellegitur: ex quibus causis condictio nasci solet.

See Pflüger, Z., 1911, 178, who regards the passage like 12. 5. 6, as interpolated on the ground that the *cond. ex inj. causa* is a Byzantine name for extensions of the *cond. furt.* Indeed the term is strange for a defendant who was treated as well as, if not better than, a b. f. p. It may refer to the fact that our law was so strict that an action was given in cases where it would otherwise fail for lack of a *negotium*, cf. 5. 6; 31. 1, 2; 20. 1. 1. 4; 58. 2; see also De Medio, 379 n. 1. In view of *retinere*, which hints at a liability only for enrichment, it is strange that Girard, 633 n. 6, should cite Gaius to show that the *oratio* introduced the defense of enrichment, cf. Huvelin, Furtum, 345 n.

---

7. ULPIANUS *libro trigesimo primo ad Sabinum* Quod autem spectetur tempus, an locupletiores sint facti, utrum tempus litis contestatae an rei iudicatae? et verum est litis contestatae tempus spectari oportere idque imperator noster cum patre rescripsit.

The older writers, cf. Gentilis, 1. ch. 31, had much difficulty in reconciling this decision with 5. 3. 36. 4. Whatever the explanation of that text (cf. Francke, Comm. über H. P.), ours represents the rule, cf. 46. 3. 47. pr., and does not involve the problems discussed by Pernice, 2. 2. 155 n. 1; Marchi, St. Scialoja, 1. 167; Maria, Ét. Girard, 2. 237.

---

1. Si maritus pecuniam uxori in unguenta dederit eaque eam pecuniam creditori suo solverit, mox ea de sua pecunia unguenta emerit, non videri locupletiorem factam Marcellus libro septimo digestorum scribit. idemque et si lancem ob eandem causam ei dederit eaque lancem retinuerit, de sua autem pecunia unguenta emerit, vindicationem cessare, quia non est locupletior, quae tantundem in re mortua impendit.

On *res mortuae* cf. Cujas, Obs. 9. 30; Gentilis, 1. ch. 33. The latter properly cites 15. 3. 7. 3 to show that this text presents the same anomaly as 5. 8. The expression *res mortua*, cf. also 32.9, implies the incorrectness of Windscheid's statement, 365 n. 14, that the donee was released even by consumption of necessaries, upon which theory few of the difficulties in regard to *annui* could ever have arisen. cf. *infra* 21. 1. Though it is true that one might be enriched by consumption of unnecessaries, that possibility was disregarded, perhaps by interpretation of the constitution of Pius, 42. This decision raises a considerable number of problems, one of which is mentioned by Savigny, 75. In relating the money to the object the test would seem to be that of causation, cf. 50. 1, rather than the donor's intent, *i. e.*, consumption or loss does not preclude enrichment if either would have occurred without the gift, cf. F. Mommsen, Beiträge, 1. 321. The same ought to be true of loss even after mixture, as where the donee is robbed of a like amount by a thief who heard of the gift, cf. Savigny, 65. Is the gift *in unguenta* immediately valid or treated like that in 5. 8? If the latter is true, as it should be, what will happen if H. has begun or finished vindicating the coins or the plate from the creditor before the perfume is bought? If the vindication follows the purchase the creditor must be protected by the *exceptio doli*. What is the answer if the coins are given outright and the wife after paying the debt is later caused to buy perfumes? In view of the uncertainty of the law as to change of position both in our system and that of modern Europe the Romans cannot be blamed for not foreseeing cases which apparently do not arise.

---

2. Si vir et uxor quina invicem sibi donaverint et maritus servaverit, uxor consumpserit, recte placuit compensationem fieri donationum et hoc divus Hadrianus constituit.

In advocating the *exceptio doli* Beseler, Z., 444, overlooked 67, an even stronger case, properly cited by Gentilis, 2 ch. 21. Although it is quite clear from 32. 9; 32. 14 that there was as a rule no compensation as regards mutual gifts, this exception is justified by their identity. All claims are held to be cancelled when the claimant receives that to which he is entitled, no matter what the *animus*. It would be strange to hold that each has a claim paralyzable by an extraordinary exception, when the situation is exactly the same as if nothing had happened. Further, the *exceptio doli* is not fitted to a field where all defenses are interposed in Gradenwitz's words, not only *officio*, but *ex officio, judicis*, cf. 5. 7; 44. 4. 10 is a case where there may have been no intent whatever to make a gift, *infra* 31. 2. The decision would of course be different if the donee had repaid after consumption, 32. 9.

---

3. Aestimari oportere, in quantum locupletior facta sit mulier. proinde et si praedia hodie vilissimo sunt, consequenter dicemus litis contestatae tempore aestimationem eorum spectandam. plane si magni pretii praedia sunt, summa tantum numerata erit restituenda, non etiam usurae pretii.

The refusal of interest, cf. 15. 1, after the donee has alienated the gift should be pondered by those like Huvelin and Haymann, *infra* 63, who speak of theft and the actions *ad exh.* or *de tigno* between H. and W. In this and the following and other texts which deal with purchase by the donee it must be assumed that the coins have been mixed, *supra* 5. 18.

---

4. Eleganter tractabitur, si mulier quindecim praedia emerit et maritus non totum pretium numeraverit, sed duas partes pretii, hoc est decem, uxor de suo quinque, deinde haec praedia valeant nunc decem, maritus quantum consequatur. et magis est, ut consequi debeat duas partes decem, ut quod periit ex pretio, utrique perierit et marito et uxori.

This truly elegant and certainly genuine decision, probably by Pomponius (cf. 28. 2; 3. 31 ff.), is directly counter to Pringsheim's thesis in Kauf mit Fremden Geld, and affords another example of that affinity of the classical Roman law to our equity jurisprudence which causes scepticism about the interpolation in 44. 4. 4. 31. The case is obviously that of 50. 1 as distinguished from 50. pr., cf. *infra* 7. 7. It is not easy to state the reason why the rule of 5. 5. (cf. 31. 3) was not followed and H.'s recovery restricted to the amount of W.'s enrichment. It seems to rest upon the *animus:* the gift in 5. 5 is made possible only because the donor adverts to the value of the slave; here this is neither necessary nor probable. It is then analytically correct to regard the former transaction as if the gift consisted of the amount by which the value exceeded 5, and this case as if the gift was ⅔ of the slave, because the intentions actually differed in this respect. No more striking example of the importance of *animus* could be desired, nor should such a brilliant distinction be attributed to the compilers.

---

5. Si maritus aestimationem rerum quas in dotem accepit dicat se donationis causa auxisse, remedium monstravit imperator noster cum divo patre suo rescripto, cuius verba haec sunt: 'Cum donationis causa pretium auctum adfirmes, qui super ea re cogniturus erit, si pecuniae modum recusabis, ipsa praedia restitui debere sumptuum deductis rationibus arbitrabitur.' in arbitrio igitur mariti erit, quid praestitum malit. idem iuris est et si e contrario mulier de minore aestimatione queratur. nec aliud in commodato aestimato dato observari solet, ut Pomponius libro quarto variarum lectionum scribit.

Partsch, Z., 1921, 271, believes that the election shows an interpolation, failing to notice that, as the marriage has ended, H. may properly pay the valuation as a new gift. Beseler, Z., 469 *ad* 23. 3. 12. pr., apparently carries the former's theory of 5. 5 to a logical conclusion by supposing the transaction wholly void, although it is not clear what is meant by "Hinundherzahlung" when H. promised only later payment. Beseler's objections to 12 pr. *cit.* are more plausible if confined to the last sentence, for a gift before marriage to take effect after its end cannot be reproached upon any ground, cf. *infra* 32. 22. Even our decision can be explained only by an overemphasis on the analogy to a sale, for in substance the gift is merely *divortii causa*, cf. 10.

---

6. Si uxor a marito suo praedia, quae ob dotem pignori acceperat, emerit eaque emptio donationis causa facta dicatur, nullius esse momenti, pignoris tamen obligationem durare imperator noster cum patre suo rescripsit, cuius rescripti verba ideo rettuli, ut appareat venditionem inter virum et uxorem bona fide gestam non retractari. 'Si tibi maritus pignora propter dotem et pecuniam creditam data non donationis causa ven-

didit, quod bona fide gestum est, manebit ratum. at si titulus donationis quaesitus ostenditur atque ideo venditionem irritam esse constabit, iure publico causam pignorum integram obtinebis.'

For interpolation cf. Beseler, Z., 469. From the analogous examples of this use of *publicum ius* in Bonfante, Ist. 7 ed., 13, it would appear to be the equivalent of our "public policy," and as such contrary to Alibrandi's thesis that the origin of our prohibition is statutory, cf. also 32. 24.

---

7. Si uxor rem emit et maritus pretium pro ea numeravit, interdum dicendum est totum a muliere repetendum, quasi locupletior ex ea in solidum facta sit: ut puta si emit quidem rem mulier et debebat pecuniam, maritus autem a venditore eam liberavit: quid enim interest, creditori solvat an venditori?

Cf. *infra* 50. It is strange that Pringsheim should have cited, Kauf, 97 n. 3, this case which is an exception, without noticing the rule 29. pr.; 50. 1, or the modification in 7. 4. The distinction is clear, the general principle that the donor bears the risk and does not benefit by appreciation, 28. 3, does not apply where the donee had made the contract before the gift, so that the required causation, *supra* 7. 1, is absent. The great difficulty with the last principle exemplified here and in 50. pr. is the statement that the donee is freed, contradicted in 50. 1. Savigny, 593, attempts to explain the result on the assumption that the creditor has mixed the coins. While this interpretation is satisfactory where the *datio* was made by the donee, it would not prevent a condiction if, as it here assumed, the donor directly paid the creditor, cf. 46. 3. 38. 1. That Ulpian and Javolenus reach their decision without the effort, or any mention of the fiction found in 3. 12, is a puzzling anomaly which might conceivably be laid to Byzantine abridgment, assuming the rhetorical question here and repeated in 50. pr. to be interpolated; for it is foolish to assume that the creditor case is so clear. Unfortunately the texts do not seem to offer much ground for suspicion.

---

8. Uxori quis donavit servum ita, ut eum intra annum manumitteret: an, si mulier non obtemperet voluntati,

constitutio divi Marci imponat ei libertatem, si vir vel vivit vel etiam diem suum obierit? et ait Papinianus, cum Sabini sit sententia recepta, qui putat tunc fieri servum eius cui donatur, cum coeperit libertas imponi ideoque nec si velit mulier post exactum tempus possit manumittere, recte dici non esse constitutioni locum nec voluntatem mariti posse constitutioni locum facere, cum proprium servum possit manumittere: quae sententia mihi quoque probatur, quia venditor sive donator non sibi vult legem imponi nec potest, sed ei qui accepit: dominio igitur penes se remanente nequaquam effectum habebit constitutio.

For a discussion of this constitution, see Buckland, 628 ff. Whether or not these passages have been formally tampered with, Buckland, 630 n. 7, in view of 5. 8, it is obviously inadequate to say with Pernice, 3. 137 n. 1, that the interpolation is proved by the condition, cf. however, Haymann, Z., 1917, 240 n. 1, who attempts to avoid the issue as in 5. 8. Beseler's objection, Z., 469, that the constitution applies after death is not serious, because the text says nothing to the contrary. The passage seems to support Haymann's view reported by Buckland, 634, that such a mancipation was irrevocable. From his reproach of *nec si velit* Beseler seems to adopt the older theory that the *jus poenitentiae* is classical, but his treatment at least shows the incorrectness of Lotmar's thesis, Z., 1912, 370, that the terms of our text support that view. If the phrase implies anything, it is that W.'s will is sovereign before the period has elapsed. Papinian's authority is the more impressive in view of the strange decision of 28. 5. 77, cf. *infra* 11. 10. Not only is it difficult to understand why *fides* allows revocation of a transaction which was intended to be irrevocable and is being properly carried out by the donee, but the weakness of the grounds for assuming that *fiducia* was always revocable is not often remarked. In the first place it is by no means certain that the texts in question, 17. 1. 27. 1; *id.* 30, were not written of mandate, cf. Heck, Z., 1889, 115 ff., 120; secondly, assuming the contrary, it would seem from 39. 5. 18. 1, that this revocation was not allowed where the fiduciary had an interest (on which text cf. Jacquelin's difficulties, Fiducie, 372), a conclusion especially telling if applied to gifts *m. c.*, cf. *infra* 11. 10; Haymann, Z., 1917, 237.

9. Manumissionis causa donatio facta valet, licet non hoc agatur, ut statim ad libertatem, sed quandoque perducatur. proinde si, ut post certum tempus manumittat, uxori suae tradidit, tunc demum eius fiet, cum tempore impleto manumittere coeperit: quare antea manumittendo nihil agit. nam et illud sciendum est: si uxori quis suae donaverit, ut intra annum manumittat, deinde non manumiserit ea intra annum, postea manumittendo nihil agit.

Cf. 49; Savigny, 62 n. *d*. On the origin of this exception cf. Paul, 2. 23. 2; it dates from a time when relations between patron and freedman were not commercialized; the illogical nature of the rule that patronal rights were invaluable was later recognized, cf. 19. 1. 425. 2.

---

8. GAIUS *libro undecimo ad edictum provinciale* Si, antequam servus manumittatur, morte aut divortio solutum fuerit matrimonium, resolvitur donatio: inesse enim condicio donationi videtur, ut manente matrimonio manumittatur.

The fact that death revokes the gift is not easy to justify, *supra* 5. 11. This passage offers as much support for the irrevocability as 11. 10. The word *resolvitur* is interesting and ought to have been held interpolated by Vassalli, Bull., 27. 192 ff., and other writers on conditions if it had been noticed, but cf. 11. 10; 52. 1. It shows not only how uninterested were the Romans in such barren points of doctrine but also that if one is so interested, the legal results in this case, as in 5. 9, can be better explained by assuming a resolutive than a suspensive condition. If the latter alternative is taken, as it was by Sabinus, Papinian, and Ulpian, it is difficult to decide when the property passes, for it cannot do so until the manumission is effective, for which result a prior transfer of title is necessary. The word and the consideration that a resolutive condition, if anything but manumission is accomplished, is in substance exactly the same as a suspensive condition upon manumission, may give food for thought to those who suppose that ownership could not revert in classical law.

---

9. ULPIANUS *libro trigesimo secundo ad Sabinum* Si eum uxori donet maritus, qui eius erat condicionis, ne umquam ad libertatem perduci possit, dicendum est omnino nihil agi hac donatione.

Cf. 31. 31; 35. 1. 27; Buckland, 630 n. 4.

---

1. Si pecunia accepta mulier manumiserit vel operas ei imposuerit, ait Iulianus operas quidem eam licito iure imposituram et tenere obligationem nec videri mulierem ex re viri locupletiorem fieri, cum eas libertus promittat: quod si pretium ob manumissionem acceperit mulier et sic manumiserit, si quidem ex peculio suo dedit, nummos mariti manere, si vero alius pro eo dedit, fient nummi mulieris: quae sententia recte se habet.

The rule as to *operae* depends rather upon 28. 2 than upon the refusal to value patronal rights, cf. 12. 6. 65. 5. The phrase *nummos . . . manere* contradicts De Medio's thesis, *supra* 3. 10.

---

2. Inter virum et uxorem mortis causa donationes receptae sunt.

This and the following texts till 13. 1 are held "seriously altered" by Haymann, Z., 1917, 239 n. 4. His view is not clear; how, by assimilating a gift *m. c.* to a legacy, did the compilers make that institution any less revocable than in classical law? His remarks on this subject as on gifts *sub modo*, *supra* 5. 2, 8, seem to show a double mistake: first, the intent that the donee shall enjoy the use of the property does not necessarily render the transaction void, usually the contrary; second, even if the donor attempts to bind himself not to reclaim the object in the meantime, the fact that he remains free to do so in no sense requires that the gift upon death shall be equally revocable. In other words, the fact that the transaction is necessarily subject to a condition precedent as regards the intermediate enjoyment is without influence on the revocability of the condition itself or upon the method of treating it after fulfilment.

---

10. GAIUS *libro undecimo ad edictum provinciale* quia in hoc tempus excurrit donationis eventus, quo vir et uxor esse desinunt.

11. Ulpianus *libro trigesimo secundo ad Sabinum* Sed interim res non statim fiunt eus cui donatae sunt, sed tunc demum, cum mors insecuta est. medio igitur tempore dominium remanet apud eum qui donavit.

It is observed both by Enneccerus, 459, and Lenel, Ulp. 2768, that the first sentence is repeated from 39. 6. 2. It may be remarked that Ulpian sticks to his idea of a suspensive condition even though he has to admit in the next passage that the distinction is not academic as in 5. 9 and 7. 8.

---

1. Sed quod dicitur mortis causa donationem inter virum et uxorem valere, ita verum est, ut non solum ea donatio valeat secundum Iulianum, quae hoc animo fit, ut tunc res fiat uxoris vel mariti, cum mors insequetur, sed omnis mortis causa donatio.

Faber, De Err., D. 44 E. 8 believes *sed omnis rel.* to be interpolated because an attempt to transfer immediate ownership must be void, *acc.* Senn 77; a view which seems refuted by the considerations mentioned *supra* 5.9.

---

2. Quando itaque non retro agatur donatio, emergunt vitia, ut Marcellus animadvertit in specie huiusmodi. maritus uxori mortis causa donatum voluit: interposuit mulier filium familias, qui a marito acciperet eique traderet: deinde, cum moritur maritus, pater familias invenitur: an valeat traditio? et ait consequens esse dici traditionem valere, quia sui iuris effectus est eo tempore, ad quod traditio redigitur, id est cum maritus moriebatur.

Cf. Lenel, 2. 1142 n. 2. Glasson, Don. M. C., 109 n. 1, is probably right in assuming the son to be an *extraneus* (*invenitur*). The suggestion that there may be retroactivity is considered interpolated by Vassalli, Bull., 27. 244; Senn, 153; Suman, Saggi Min., 24 n. 1; Beseler, Z., 220, who have to say the same of 11. 9, and (except for Senn) of 39. 6. 40; cf. with which suggestion the more reasonable view of Cugia, 88, that the passage is suspicious because retroactivity is not applied to the case discussed, which can be explained either by supposing that an express suspensive condition was affixed to the mancipation, *supra* 5. 9, or that there was tradition of a *res mancipi*, or that the *res* was *non mancipi*. The first answer to this theory is that it takes no account of the clearly contrary decision in 20. Another objection is that it is based on a conviction that the classical law did not allow persons to impose a resolutive condition with a real, not personal effect, a doctrine which has no application to a case where ownership is meant to pass with a mere obligation to restore but where the law imposes a condition contrary to the intent, cf. also *supra* 5. 9. Further, even by the freest attribution of interpolations the resulting views remain incoherent. Thus in an attempt to show that a transaction subject to a suspensive condition was never granted any effects till fulfilment, Vassalli, 215 n. 1, objects to the result in 45. 3. 26 and yet holds that the similar rule favoring the father, 45. 1. 78. pr., is due to the influence of *potestas*, which indeed seems more a description than an explanation. He is then left with a hopeless anomaly in these texts, especially 11. 4, which, however, he approves, 203, for all traditions as in accord with his thesis, cf. Suman, *op. cit.*, 20 ff. Senn, who was not bold enough to impugn the apparently genuine 39. 6. 40, arbitrarily (cf. Gradenwitz, 213) assumes, 140, that it refers only to stipulations, so that for no satisfactory reason a stipulation *m. c.* between H. and W. follows the rule of 45. 1. 78. pr., because it is an exception to the exception of 39. 6. 22. Aside from the improbability of this hypothesis it involves a confusion of thought, because 78. pr. *cit.* is not analogous, cf. *infra* 20, for the father is held immediately to acquire the chance without reference to whether the transaction is retroactive. More superficial is the view of Bonfante, 223 n. 1, who seems to disregard 9. 2; 10, in comparing this case to those under the *oratio*, C. 5. 16. 25; *infra* 32. 1. The existence of retroactivity is not only clearly evidenced but analytically right and necessary, for a transaction allowed between H. and W., which would have had immediate and lasting effect between strangers, ought, when the point is material, to be treated as if it had been valid from the first, cf. the excellent remarks of Bufnoir, Condition, 413 ff. It is material here and not in 5. 9; 7. 9, because there the donee could do only one thing with the object (cf. the analogy of *summissio*, Petravycki, Einkommen, 1. 102 ff.), but here he can without violating the condition alienate it or dispose of it in any way, cf., however, *infra* 11. 9. The rule of this and the following texts is clear, but in view of 39. 6. 22 its applicability to all traditions is denied by Beseler, and Rabel, 516, though affirmed by Enneccerus, Vassalli, and Bufnoir, *op. cit.*, 418 ff. Although the contrary rule for stipulations appeared worthy of note (*in stipulationibus*) and was even infringed on occasion, cf. 45. 3. 40; Mandry, Familiengüterrecht, 1. 270; Beseler, 1. 112, it would appear from the principle of 50. 17. 18, that the former view is correct, cf. 39. 6. 44.

---

3. Idem ait: placuisse scio Sabinianis, si filiae familias uxori maritus tradet, donationem eius cum omni suo emolumento fieri, si vivo adhuc marito sui iuris fuerit effecta. quod et Iulianus libro septimo decimo digestorum probat.

The word *Sabinianis* is important for the history of the schools, and it has to be declared interpolated by Baviera, S. G., 116 ff.; cf. Z., 1900, 397.

---

4. Proinde et si uxor marito filio familias mortis causa tradat et is sui iuris effectus sit, sine dubio dicemus ipsius fieri.

Beseler, Z., 220, regards this as too obvious to be classical. The same might, however, be said of 3, 5, and 6.

---

5. Per contrarium quoque si uxor donaverit mortis causa patri familias marito et mortis eius tempore filius familias inveniatur, patri erit nunc emolumentum quaesitum. 6. Consequenter Scaevola apud Marcellum notat, si servum interposuit mulier, ut ei tradatur mortis causa, isque adhuc servus dederit mulieri, deinde mortis tempore liber inveniatur, tantundem esse dicendum. 7. Idem Marcellus tractat, si is qui interpositus est, posteaquam dederit mulieri, decesserit vivo adhuc donatore, donationem evanescere, quia debeat aliquo momento interposito fieri et sic ad mulierem transire: quod ita procedit, si ea cui donabatur eum interposuit, non is qui donabat. porro si a marito interpositus est, et res ipsius statim facta est et, si ante mortem mariti tradiderit et deces-

serit, traditio eius egit aliquid, ut tamen haec traditio pendeat, donec mors sequatur.

As Vassalli shows, Bull., 27. 206 n. 2, the interpretation of Senn, 144, is vitiated by forgetfulness of the fact that the *int.* is first thought of as *alieni juris*. If he is *sui juris*, the identity of his *mandator* cannot be decisive as to his acquisition of ownership; it will not do to say with Enneccerus, 466, that conditional transfer by the *mandator* is impossible because the mandate will be extinguished by his death: first, because redelivery will take place usually, if not necessarily, *infra* 11. 8, before that event; second, because the transfers in all the preceding cases were conditioned by the fact that the *int.* was *alieni juris*. Hence we must agree with Beseler, 4. 204, that *quod ita . . . marito* is interpolated; in this case it cannot matter who interposed. On the other hand, in alleging that *et res* rell. is interpolated, *acc.* Beseler, Z., 220, Vassalli seems to overlook the fact that an *int. sui juris* is meant, who alone can acquire *statim*. The point of the contrast is thus that where the redelivery is void because the *int.* is in *potestas*, his subsequent death precludes rehabilitating the transfer, probably even where retroactivity is allowed; but where the *int.* is *sui juris*, by delivery he has done all he could, *traditio egit aliquid*, cf. 46. 2. 14. 1; subsequent death is no more significant than if he had been a mere *nuntius*.

---

8. Si uxor rem Titio dederit, ut is marito mortis causa traderet eaque defuncta invitis heredibus eius Titius marito dederit, interest, utrum a muliere sit interpositus Titius an vero a marito cui donabatur: si a muliere interpositus est, obligabit se condictione, si marito tradiderit, si autem a marito sit interpositus, mortua muliere confestim fundus efficietur eius quem maritus interposuit et actionem ipse maritus cum eo habebit.

Beseler, *loc. cit.*, suspects this entire passage, without being able to point out any mistake of substance. The assumption of Burckhard, 62 ff., that the donee learned of the gift only after the death is unsupported by any evidence, cf. 5. 6; 47, and the interpretation of v. Scheurl, Beiträge, 2. 2. 46, that the gift is not "perfect," 5. pr., neglects the *statim* clause in the preceding passage. Although the case of refusal to transfer after the death would create difficulties, Vat. Fr., 286; Rabel, 504 n. 4, it is hard to see why performance of the charge subjects Titius to liability to the heirs. Though no reasonable ground can be seen for supposing the tacit condition that the delivery must take place before death, yet in view of 8 this may be the explanation of the text, so Beseler, Gentilis, 4. ch. 24. The common explanation is that the mandate expires with death, 46. 3. 108, cf. C. 4. 11. To this, one objection is that this rule apparently did not apply to *fiducia*, 17. 1. 27. 1. Furthermore, even for a mandate the rule was far from absolute, cf. the same Marcellus in 17. 1. 12. 17; *id.* 13, which can with difficulty be supposed interpolated because of G. 3. 117, see Buckland, 515; Karlowa, 2. 664. The charge in 12. 7 *cit.* seems no more "highly personal" than ours.

---

9. Si uxor rem, quam a marito suo mortis causa acceperat, vivo eo alii tradiderit, nihil agitur ea traditione, quia non ante ultimum vitae tempus mulieris fuit. plane in quibus casibus placeat retro agi donationem, etiam sequens traditio a muliere facta in pendenti habebitur.

The second sentence is thought interpolated by all those who object to 11. 2, and who overlook the decision of Javolenus, 20. It may be remarked that, even where there is no relation, a transferee for value is protected in equity, 6. 1. 72; 21. 3. 2; 44. 4. 4. 32; cf. Appleton, Prop. prétorienne, 1. 153 n. 9, 2. 208 n. 65.

---

10. Si maritus uxori donaverit mortis causa eaque diverterit, an dissolvatur donatio? Iulianus scripsit infirmari donationem nec impendere.

Cf. Senn, 148. How can the transaction "dissolve" if, as Ulpian says in the pr., nothing happens till death? It seems difficult to reconcile this decision with the doctrine that gifts *m. c.* were revocable at will. In that event, except in the rare case of forgetfulness rather than lack of time, Levy, 79 n. 3, failure to reclaim upon divorce should amount to an affirmance to bar the heirs of the donor. In other words, though the transaction is valid until revoked upon the principle that the donor's intent is sovereign, this rule would usually defeat his intent; the very fact that this situation is treated differently from that of the *oratio* by the compilers, 32. 10 ff., in whose time they were identical, shows that that was not the case in classical law where there was in our situation no question of intent; that is, just as in 8, where the evidence is in favor of irrevocability, this decision does not appear sensible unless Biondi's thesis is adopted that gifts *m. c.* were irrevocable in the absence of reservation of a power to revoke, cf. 39. 6. 13.1; *id.* 35. 4. Biondi does not attempt to extend his hypothesis to gifts between H. and W. Yet because of the principle expressed in 28. 2 it might be argued that here if anywhere would revocation be refused, a conclusion which may be supported by the absence of the insertion of that right in 7. 8 ff., so in part Haymann, Z., 1917, 241, who is lead astray by the view mentioned *supra* 5. 8; 9. 2. There is, however, a statement which seems explicitly contrary in 28. 5. 77; cf. 22, that decision seems to imply both that the gift could not be revoked if it were not a case of H. and W. and that even then there was doubt, *et quoque*. Whether it is to be explained because Papinian held a stricter view of our prohibition, cf. 7. 8 with 8. 23, or by the expedient always used in any difficulty of assuming tradition instead of mancipation, it does not seem that the passage is enough to remove all doubt on the subject, cf. 39. 5. 18. 1; *supra* 7. 8, and the fact that the point was worthy of treatment in the Questions is enough to show that it is not as simple as the common opinion would have it.

---

11. Idem ait, si divortii causa facta sit donatio, valere:

12. PAULUS *libro septimo ad Sabinum* quae tamen sub ipso divortii tempore, non quae ex cogitatione quandoque futuri divortii fiant:

It is not clear why Rabel, 513, supposes this to show that Paul disagreed with the preceding text, for the same point is decided really in the same way in 39. 6. 43. The *bona fides* there required has, however, to be objectively supported where the happening of the condition is in the power of the donor.

---

13. ULPIANUS *libro trigesimo secundo ad Sabinum* sed si mors sit insecuta, non videri factas res mulieris, quia donatio in alium casum facta est.

Faber, De Err., D. 46, E. 3, 12, to the contrary notwithstanding, it may well be argued that a gift intended on divorce is *a fortiori* intended on death.

---

1. Proinde et si mortis causa uxori donaverit et deportationem passus est, an donatio valeat, videamus. et alias placet in casum deportationis donationem factam valere, quemadmodum in causam divortii. cum igitur deportatione matrimonium minime dissolvatur et nihil vitium mulieris incurrit, humanum est donationem, quae mortis causa ab initio facta est, tali exilio subsecuto confirmari, tamquam si mortuo marito rata habebatur, ita tamen, ut non adimatur licentia marito eam revocare, quia et mors eius exspectanda est, ut tunc plenissimam habeat firmitatem, quando ab hac luce fuerit subtractus, sive reversus sive adhuc in poena constitutus.

Since Cujas, Obs., 3. 10, this text has been supposed interpolated by comparison with C. 5. 16. 24, cf. Faber, Conj., 12. 17, De Err., D. 46, E. 3. Although the fact seems certain, there is to this day so little knowledge of the law in question that Glasson, Don. M. C., 118 n. 1; cf. De Retes, 8. 14, is to be excused in holding it genuine. In an article cited by Coli, Saggi Crit., 1. 31, Lusignani drew attention to the fact that there is a large discrepancy between the Code provision and the original C. Th. 9. 42. 1, where, among other matter, the clause *cum . . . dissolvatur* is missing. For our purposes such passages as 48. 20. 5. 1; C. 5. 17 . . . are inconclusive, and the authorities are unable to decide what, if any, changes in the classical law are contained in Tribonian's language. Desserteaux, 2. 469, holds that the preservation of the right of revocation is interpolated because the donor was formerly considered dead in this case, cf. *infra* 32. 6; Bonfante, 243 n. 3, taking the opposite view, thinks that the gift failed. Both theories seem unlikely; a marriage between a Roman and a peregrine is certainly a marriage, cf. 48. 5. 14. 1; Karlowa, 2. 182; and Coli, *loc. cit.*, n. 3, cites many instances of W. following H. into exile. The existence of a real marriage, though not "just," would certainly preclude the application of a fiction so hesitatingly used. The result may have been that if the *de facto* marriage continued, the gift was unaffected;

if not, the fisc claimed by the rule of the pr. Constantine's statute probably did no more than state what had become the customary rule, cf. Desserteaux, 434 ff., that the fisc would not intervene against children and spouses; furthermore it applied only to W.'s chance under the *oratio*. The interpolation as to the right of revocation is an argument in favor of the view expressed *supra* 11. 10, for the words are unnecessary if that right already existed. The real difficulty in the passage is the mention of a gift *deportationis causa*, Cohn, Beiträge, 217, the creation of which strange phenomenon was perhaps the occasion for the interpolation, cf. *infra* 43.

---

2. Cum quis acceperit, ut in suo aedificet, condici ei id non potest, quia magis donari ei videtur: quae sententia Neratii quoque fuit: ait enim datum ad villam extruendam vel agrum serendum, quod alioquin facturus non erat is qui accepit, in speciem donationis cadere. ergo inter virum et uxorem hae erunt interdictae.

Beseler's harsh comments, 3. 43, upon this passage are thoroughly deserved. In its present condition it makes two remarks which have no connection with each other or with gifts between H. and W. The first point is as to the possibility of condiction upon refusal to perform a charge. The proper rule for such a case, which cannot be improved, limited, or explained away, is given by Julian in 39. 5. 2. 7, to the effect that recovery of all is allowed if nothing would have been given had the failure been foreseen. The decision of Neratius is not opposed to this, for it is rare that such will be the intent accompanying a *modus simplex*, where the charge will amount merely to advice, because its purpose is in general the same as that of the gift. Thus if one gives money to a beggar to buy whiskey, a condiction might not be allowed if he bought bread, though it would in the converse case. Influenced by B. G. B., 527, which applies the rules of a *negotium mixtum* to a *don. sub m.*, Haymann, 30, 124 ff., asserts that such a condiction is proper only if the *modus* is in favor of the donee, cf. Mitteis, 200 ff., who holds the condiction proper only if the donee is *not* at fault! It seems impossible to comprehend the grounds for such a distinction which could never have prevailed among the Romans, who show no sign of having ever conceived the idea of distinguishing varieties of *modi*. The fact that there are few and suspicious illustrations of the condiction in the sources, but cf. Vat. Fr., 268, Schultz, Fests. f. Zitelmann, is due to the later popularity of the action to require fulfilment, as to allowing the condiction in concurrence with which a discussion would be irrelevant. The next consideration mentioned is *quod alioquin, etc.*, which is adduced to prove the *animus donandi* and is considered very significant by Pernice, 3. 198 n. 1, who even reproaches Windscheid for adopting Byzantine ideas in disregarding it, *id.* 200 n. 6. In truth, however, this clause is the one which can be explained by no effort of ingenuity, cf. Haymann, 32 n. 2. In deciding whether the donor wished to live in the house nothing could be more unimportant than the question whether the donee would otherwise have built it. In fact, in the only connection in which this inquiry is relevant, *i. e.*, as to enrichment after consumption, loss, or deterioration, the distinction ought to be the opposite of the one made here. Finally, as to gifts between H. and W. there is not the slightest doubt that a *modus simplex* does not save the transaction; the rules as to a *modus qualificatus* may be found in 5. 8, 9; 7. 9; 49. If a conjecture as to the origin of the text may be hazarded it is that Neratius was drawing the line between a gift and an innominate or other obligation in cases like that of 17. 1. 16, and that Ulpian was applying his conclusion in our field. The *alioquin* clause was an interpolation on the analogy of 50. 1 by the same confused spirit who attacked 11. 7 and 32. 27. Haymann's interpretation of the passage seems unconvincing. He assumes that Ulpian and Neratius denied the condiction between H. and W., for which the reason adduced is that "it seems rather to be a gift," and upon which hypothesis the last sentence containing the only reference to the subject, must be disregarded, and a mere *quis* interpreted, without parallel in the title, as *vir* or *uxor*. He then attempts ingeniously to connect the passage with 63, supposing that Neratius here allowed the *actio de tigno*, although no *tignum* is mentioned.

---

14. PAULUS *libro septuagesimo primo ad edictum* Quod si vir uxori, cuius aedes incendio consumptae sunt, ad refectionem earum pecuniam donaverit, valet donatio in tantum, in quantum aedificii extructio postulat.

This decision, a real infringement of principle because the expense is for necessaries, is justified both on the ground of public utility, cf. C. 8. 53. 36. 2; Machelard, 261 n. 1, and because the event is of a nature to supply a motive for the gift other than those reprobated by the law, cf. 36. 1; De Retes, 5. 19. The words *in tantum rel.* are not superfluous as maintained by Beseler, Z., 444, but refer to the case where a surplus from a reasonable gift remains to W., caused, for example, by a fall in building prices. The transaction being valid, W. might be allowed to keep this, as where she later is found to have had the best of the bargain in a sale, but as the rule itself involves an exception it is exceptionally confined.

---

15. ULPIANUS *libro trigesimo secundo ad Sabinum* Ex annuo vel menstruo, quod uxori maritus praestat, tunc quod superest revocabitur, si satis immodicum est, id est supra vires dotis.

This is the first of the texts presenting the problem "than which there is none more complicated in the title," De Retes, 5. 5 *i. f.* In alleging the interpolation of the *immodicum* clause, Beseler, Z., 444, does not appear to realize that it is certain that H. may contribute a reasonable amount towards the household expenses, *infra* 18; 21. 1. Without it the text would hold that W.'s savings from her dress allowance can be recovered, which would indeed violate the principle of 28. 2, cf. Gentilis, 2. ch. 14, and is refuted by 31. 8, 10. More suspicious is the last clause in view of Justinian's tendency to equiparate the *onera* and the income of the *dos*, cf. Czyhlarz, 104 ff.; Bonfante, 512. H. should not be able to recover money given for the household expenses on the ground that the value of the *dos* had depreciated, cf. Bonfante, 218 n. 8.

---

1. Si maritus uxori pecuniam donaverit eaque usuras ex donata pecunia perceperit, lucrabitur. haec ita Iulianus in marito libro octavo decimo digestorum scribit.

For the distinction which probably was felt between interest and fruits, see Savigny, 40 ff.; Petražycki, Einkommen, 2. 204 *et pass.*; Regelsberger, Pand., 396 n. 12; *contra* Riccobono, 386 n. 4; but cf. 7. 3 with 22. 1. 45.

16. TRYFONINUS *libro decimo disputationum* Quid ergo si ex centum, quae vir uxori donavit, quinquaginta apud debitorem ex his perierint et alia quinquaginta duplicata usuris uxor habet? non plus quinquaginta eius donationis nomine maritus ab ea consequetur.

---

17. ULPIANUS *libro trigesimo secundo ad Sabinum* De fructibus quoque videamus, si ex fructibus praediorum quae donata sunt locupletata sit, an in causam donationis cadant. et Iulianus significat fructus quoque ut usuras licitam habere donationem.

The apparent conflict in the texts as regards fruits is excellently resolved by Windscheid, § 365 n. 6; as in the *negotium mixtum* of 5. 5 so in that of 49, the *animus* is decisive. Riccobono's contrary view, 386 n. 4, that gifts of the fruits were allowed by exception, and his invocation of interpolations cannot be supported; if 19. pr. is spurious, why not 17. 1? As between H. and W. a gift of fruits can be supported on either of two grounds. The first follows from the principle that our prohibition required the attempt to grant a legally enforceable claim, cf. 46, a mere revocable license was not considered a gift, cf. 43. 26. 1. 2, 3; thus any advantage which could have been enjoyed by a *precario tenens* is licit in principle, 18., 28. 2, *etc.*, even though the donor might have derived commercial advantage from the use of the object. The other point is that whatever the donee acquires through the object by his own labor, skill, or luck, he is entitled to keep, because the donor is not thought of as impoverished any more than in the first case, even if he can prove that he would have made an equally good bargain, cf. the similar rule for legacies, 31. 70. 1. It is not considered a loss not to have made a gain, cf. 5. 13. On the other hand, the Romans forbade the attempt to create whatever resembled a usufruct, cf. 39. 5. 9. 1; *id.* 11, as distinguished from *precarium*, *commodatum*, or *usus*, cf. 49. The distinction is none the less clear for being one of fact, cf. 7. 9 with 39. 5. 18. 1; Savigny, 62, n. *d.* It is of such a forbidden gift that the author of 39. 5. 9. 1 is thinking in 22. 1. 45, cf., however, Petražycki, Fruchtvertheilung, 204 ff.; Pernice, 2. 1. 358 n. 2; Perozzi, *cit.* Albertario, Bull., 26. 250, who overlook 9. 1 *cit.* Even though the gift is void the donee may keep the results of his skill or labor, 7. 3.

1. Sed si quid servus donatus adquisiit, ad eum qui donavit pertinebit.

This is because the donor owns the slave, cf. 19. pr.; 28. 5.

18. POMPONIUS *libro quarto ex variis lectionibus* Si vir uxoris aut uxor viri servis aut vestimentis usus vel usa fuerit vel in aedibus eius gratis habitaverit, valet donatio.

Such advantages amount to no more than *de facto* revocable use. Since support of the wife in so far as she is a member of the household is allowed, 35. 2. 81. 2; Rabel, 417 ff., and since proper clothes were an element thereof, 34. 1. 6; 50. 16. 43, this text must be understood either of clothes belonging to the donor, cf. the learned note of Glück, 26. 33 n. 79; 34. 2. 23. 2, or, as in 29. 1 ff., of extras, cf. 31. 8; De Retes 5. 4.

19. ULPIANUS *libro trigesimo secundo ad Sabinum* Si uxor filio donaverit servum, qui in patris mariti sit potestate, deinde is servus ancillam acceperit, dominium mulieri quaeretur: nec interesse Iulianus ait, ex cuius pecunia haec ancilla empta sit, quia nec ex re sua quicquam adquiri potest per eum qui donatur ei cui donatur: hoc enim bonae fidei possessoribus concessum est, virum autem scientem alienum possidere.

This passage and 41. 1. 57 are held interpolated by Pernice, 2. 1. 409 n. 6, eagerly followed by De Medio, 395 n. 1; Riccobono, 386 n. 4; *contra* Salkowski, 148. Nothing objectionable is discovered by anybody either in the form or the content of the texts, which agree in attributing the rule to Julian, except that it is supposed to be surprising that the donee is thought an unjust or m. f. possessor. This is obviously incorrect; what is meant is only that he is not for this purpose a b. f. p.; although for most other purposes he is treated better than the b. f. p. The purpose referred to is the establishment of a *peculium*, which would be natural in this case, though just as void as if attempted by a commodatary. It is merely this special provision of slave law which prevents an acquisition which ought to enure to the donee, and there is not only no conflict with 29.1, 22. 1. 45 as Pernice thinks, but none with the better analogy of 7. 3. Thus the donee would not acquire by *iussum*, 46. 3. 33; Buckland, 349, or *nominatio*, Buckland, 380, but could where the slave was a mere *nuntius* or *minis-*

terium, cf. Salkowski, 166; Buckland, N. R. H., 1925, 355 ff. The rule for slaves may be crudely phrased by saying that acquisitions may be made by or with but not through them.

---

1. Idem quaerit, si ex re mariti ea ancilla comparata fuerit, an adversus agentem mulierem de dote maritus pretium possit per exceptionem retinere. et dicendum est posse maritum et exceptionem habere, si dos ab eo petetur, secundum Marcelli sententiam et, si solverit, secundum Iulianum condicere posse.

In objecting to the whole passage on the score of *exceptionem habere*, Beseler, Z., 444, seems to forget that the original read *retentionem*. The decision shows that the donee is not an "unjust" possessor, cf. Buckland, 355. The condiction is allowed to prevent undue enrichment, cf. 36. pr., and the decision recalls the possibility that the rule of 19. pr. may on occasion have to yield to our prohibition, where the donee takes advantage of the law of slavery to make a gift, simulating a transaction *ex re*.

---

20. IAVOLENUS *libro undecimo epistularum* Si is servus, qui uxori mortis causa donatus est, prius quam vir decederet stipulatus est, in pendenti puto esse causam obligationis, donec vir aut moriatur aut suspicione mortis, propter quam donavit, liberetur: quidquid autem eorum inciderit, quod donationem aut peremat aut confirmet, id quoque causam stipulationis aut confirmabit aut resolvet.

This evidently genuine passage containing a real example of retroactivity has been inexplicably disregarded by those authors who attack 11. 2, 9. It also illustrates the confusion in which Senn, *supra* 11. 2, was involved when he cited 45. 3. 78. pr. as a case of retroactivity, when it merely decides that whatever the nature of the condition the *stipulator alieni juris* cannot acquire. Citing 39. 6. 39, Haymann, Z., 1917, 239 n. 4 *i. f.*, asserts a difference between this and the usual gift *m. c.*, but the analogy is not easy to grasp.

---

21. ULPIANUS *libro trigesimo secundo ad Sabinum* Si quis pro uxore sua vectigal, quod in itinere praestari solet, solvis-

set, an quasi locupletiore ea facta exactio fiat, an vero nulla sit donatio? et magis puto non interdictum hoc, maxime si ipsius causa profecta est. nam et Papinianus libro quarto responsorum scripsit vecturas uxoris et ministeriorum eius virum itineris sui causa datas repetere non posse: iter autem fuisse videtur viri causa et cum uxor ad virum pervenit. nec interesse, an aliquid de vecturis in contrahendo matrimonio convenerit: non enim donat, qui necessariis oneribus succurrit. ergo et si consensu mariti profecta est mulier propter suas necessarias causas et aliquid maritus expensarum nomine ei praestiterit, hoc revocandum non est.

Cf. 23. 4. 26. 3. Lenel, Ulp. 2772, is led by *exactio* to suppose that the passage dealt with the *retentio*, cf. Zanzucchi, R.I. S. G., 42. 43, a view which is supported by the meaningless *an vero* clause, which seems to have been added by "completomania" to refer to the vindication. Beseler's suspicions, Z., 444, seem to miss the point. The beginning of any discussion of the obscure subject of *annua* or the like must be with the surely classical distinction of 31. 10; 58. 1. It was not W.'s necessary expenses which were important, but those in connection with life in common. It is thus hardly credible that Ulpian, after quoting Papinian's statement of this well-known rule, should proceed to overturn it without a sign of the consciousness of so doing. Hence from *ergo*, and perhaps from *non enim*, there is excellent cause for alleging the interpolation. The statement that a gift is valid if for W.'s necessary expenses in connection with the rule of 7. 1, would reduce our prohibition almost to a nullity.

---

1. Si uxor viro dotem promiserit et dotis usuras, sine dubio dicendum est peti usuras posse, quia non est ista donatio, cum pro oneribus matrimonii petantur. quid tamen, si maritus uxori petitionem earum remiserit? eadem erit quaestio, an donatio sit illicita: et Iulianus hoc diceret: quod verum est. plane si convenerat, uti se mulier pasceret suosque homines, idcirco passus est eam dote sua frui, ut se suosque aleret, expeditum erit: puto enim non posse ab ea peti quasi donatum, quod compensatum est.

Cf. *infra* 54. This passage with its mention of compensation has proved more troublesome than almost any other in the title. Paradoxically the difficulties begin with *plane.* Bechmann, 2. 77, cites 23. 3. 69. 3; 24. 3. 42. 2, which are not analogous because the support there referred to is of the kind which H. might bear regardless of the source from which he paid. Another view represented by Czyhlarz, 105 n. 3, would remove all difficulties on the subject, for as the donee is merely spared an expense it can never be invalid for one spouse to contribute to the other's support, cf. *supra* 7. 1. The usual interpretation, cf. Gothofredus; Hellman, Z., 1892, 357 n. 1; Beseler, Z., 444, that the release is void unless the wife makes the promise, shows most clearly the confusion implicit in the assertion that the transaction is void if the money is given for a certain purpose, but valid if the wife promises to apply it to that purpose. The case seems to be as follows: H. collects the *dos* and interest, for *passus* cannot mean a release, cf. Gradenwitz, Mél. Gerardin, 289. In return for W.'s promise to support herself and her *familia* H. then contributes to that end from the fruits of the *dos.* It must be apparent that the promise is legally immaterial, for the validity of the gift is judged by the method in which it is applied; a promise to do something which the promisor must do anyway is not an equivalent depriving the transaction of its gratuitous character. The validity of the gift may perhaps be explained in the following manner. A promise of *annua* was always void, 28. 7; 33. pr.; 23. 4. 22, because it was fixed without regard to the fact that the reasonable needs might vary from year to year. An actual gift of *annua* from H.'s pocket was valid only if it was for the support of W. as a member of the household, 31. 10; 58. 1, and would presumably not be allowed if W. was spending the summer with her family. But since in such a case H. enjoyed the *dos* while relieved of the *onera* it may well have been recognized as permissible for the fruits of the *dos* to be used for reasonable maintenance of W. wherever she was. The *suosque* here must not be understood to refer to W.'s *venalicium* nor perhaps even to her "domestic family," 31. 10; although the amount of *onera* must have been a question of fact. As for the compensation it may, as in analogous cases, 28. 7; 32. 9; 24. 3. 42. 1, have referred to the *retentio* and have been retained by the compilers from an idea that it might refer to the promise, which for the above reasons it does not seem plausible to impute to Ulpian. If the theory of *annua* submitted is correct, it may of course mean that W. is entitled to support if she is away because the saving on her maintenance compensates for her absence.

---

22. Idem *libro tertio ad Sabinum* Uxori suae quis mortis causa servum donavit eumque cum libertate heredem scripsit: an valeat institutio, quaeritur. et puto, si hoc animo eum scripsit heredem, quod donationis se dixit paenituisse, valere institutionem et necessarium heredem domino servum fieri: ceterum si, posteaquam heredem instituit, donavit, donatio praevalebit, vel si ante donavit, non tamen adimendi animo libertatem adscripsit.

It is fairly clear that this text is interpolated, see Cugia, 88 ff.; Biondi, 49; Bonfante, S. G., 1. 427 n. 2. If the fact that the parallel text, 28. 5. 77 (neglected by Suman, Favor Testamenti, 207), is untouched is taken into account together with *puto* it seems likely that Ulpian decided against the right of revocation, cf. Accursius, *ad h. l.*; Haymann, Z., 1917, 239 n. 4, 241 n. 1. The case of forgetfulness of the gift becomes, however, no less troublesome with the elimination of *vel si, etc.*, as Byzantine, although its practical importance is too slight to justify the extensive treatment of the case by Julian, Papinian, and Ulpian.

---

23. Idem *libro sexto ad Sabinum* Papinianus recte putabat orationem divi Severi ad rerum donationem pertinere: denique si stipulanti spopondisset uxori suae, non putabat conveniri posse heredem mariti, licet durante voluntate maritus decesserit.

For various views upon the dispute which this passage has occasioned see Vangerow, 1. 419 ff.; Windscheid, n. 35; Accarias, 1. 813 n. 3, who in asserting an interpolation seems to have overlooked Nov. 162. The most elaborate attempt to show that the other rule is a creation of Justinian is that of Bremer, Arch. 51. 175 ff., to whom two objections may be made. First, he makes the assertion, 187, that a stipulation *m. c.* was at once valid, when the rule was that for all practical purposes it did not take effect till death, 39. 6. 22, cf. Senn, *supra* 11. 2. Second, he holds in common with Beseler, Z.,

444, that Papinian's theory is justified by the principle that an obligation cannot begin with the heir, an argument which is impaired both by the possibility of construction used by G. 2. 232, 3. 100 and by the assimilation of benefits from the *oratio* to those by testament 32. 1, cf. also G. 3. 117. The attempt of Cuq, 531 n. 1 to justify Papinian is shown to be artificial by the fact that it has occurred to nobody who believes in the revocability of gifts *m. c.* to apply his argument to such stipulations, and it amounts at most to a presumption of fact which might be easily rebutted (*licet, etc.*), cf. also Costa, Papiniano, 4. 192. As the passage seems to depend upon a formalistic conception of convalescence like that which leads De Medio to his theory, cf. the excellent remarks of Lenel, Exceptio, 119 ff., Savigny's view that Ulpian's disagreement suffered by abridgment is appealing; as it is, he does not express approbation, for *pertinere* need not be translated with Vangerow as "restrict." The insoluble problem remains, as to the reason for such procedure on the part of compilers who approved the contrary view. The substance of the passage is the least of the puzzles which it raises: The title is constructed in an attempt to portray the law historically; there is, except here, not a mention of the effect (cf. 3. pr.) of the *oratio* until it appears in 32. pr. with an almost dramatic introduction. Furthermore, there is nothing in the present context which could even remotely justify the unsymmetrical insertion of our text. In addition to all this the rubric is false, for the 6th book dealt with the acquisition of inheritances. Lenel, who had formerly, Pap. 183, assigned the text to the 36th book, later, 2. 1034 n. 1, suggests the 46th on novations, for otherwise the passage would not have been separated from 33, the only other excerpt from the 36th in our title. Such reasoning appears to involve a *petitio principii* if it is remembered that the position of this passage is already an anomaly which needs explanation. The resulting probability that the text formed the introduction to the decision in 33, at least allows the conjecture that the latter is not interpolated, for the same hand would not have there made an alteration to express a view contrary to that resulting from the manipulation of this passage. No hypothesis has been imagined to account for these peculiarities, which seem to deprive the text of some of its persuasiveness.

---

24. Paulus *libro septimo ad Sabinum* Si inter extraneos facta sit donatio et antequam per tempus legitimum domi-

nium fuerit adquisitum, coierint, vel contra si inter virum et uxorem facta sit donatio et ante impletum tempus supradictum solutum sit matrimonium, nihilo minus procedere temporis suffragium constat, quia altero modo sine vitio tradita est possessio, altero quod fuerit vitium, amotum sit.

Lenel, 1. 1271 n. 2, suspects that this passage originally dealt with the interdict *utrubi*, because the decision is in conflict with 41. 6. 1. 2, an affirmation which seems correct in spite of the labored attempt of Savigny, 115 n. *e*; cf. Machelard, 258, at a reconciliation; cf., however, Pothier, Pand., De Usurp. et Usuc. no. 66, who supposes that the solution depends on the *oratio*. In view of 41. 6. 3, *id.* 1. 2 must be understood to refer to tradition by the owner of a *res mancipi*. If, however, it is assumed that our text dealt with a *res aliena*, it conflicts with the next passage in substance even if the results are not different, and the reconciliation of the older writers is no more successful than that of Savigny on the other hypothesis, cf. Gentilis, 2. ch. 28 (259). The further possibility that the difference between this and the next decision is due to the fact that here the donor is usucapting while there he cannot, as where he has bought from a lunatic, is disposed of by the arguments to be mentioned as to the donor's use of the interdict. If Lenel's suggestion is adopted the question may be either as to the use of the interdict between H. and W. or between W. and a third person. The former possibility seems unlikely for the following reasons. First, although the transferor for consideration was probably prevented by *accessio temporis* from immediately recovering by the interdict, Ubbelohde-Glück, 43. 596 ff.; 44. 3. 14. 3, it is not so clear that this was true of a donor, cf. Vat. Fr., 311. Hence it is doubtful whether our text is correct even in the fiancé situation. It is far more difficult to justify the decision in the case of divorce, where it must be assumed that the donor was prevented by *accessio* from attacking the now valid (but cf. 41. 6. 1. 2) possession of W., which as regards him had always been thoroughly void. It is an unparalleled nullification of our prohibition that the law should strain to uphold a transaction against the will of the donor which it usually had difficulty in maintaining even in accord with that will. That the passage concerned the question of the interdict between W. and a stranger is thus proved by the process of elimination, and also by the fact that the donor's intent and the manner of divorce are not mentioned. It may be remarked that only by a perverse reading can the *vitium* be referred to *accessio*, that is, that the donee has always been able to use the interdict, but only after the divorce can she add the donor's possession. Such a rule would be thoroughly arbitrary, for if the prohibition does not forbid the interdict, it ought not to forbid *accessio*, since the whole transaction is by the consent of the donor. All becomes clear if the view advocated *infra* 46, is adopted, that the donee could not use the interdict. Her possession *prò possessore* was exactly of the kind to count indirectly once the *vitium* had been removed, cf. G. 4. 151.

---

25. TERENTIUS CLEMENS *libro quinto ad legem Iuliam et Papiam* Sed et si constante matrimonio res aliena uxori a marito donata fuerit, dicendum est confestim ad usucapionem eius uxorem admitti, quia et si non mortis causa donaverat ei, non impediretur usucapio. nam ius constitutum ad eas donationes pertinet, ex quibus et locupletior mulier et pauperior maritus in suis rebus fit: itaque licet mortis causa donatio interveniat, quasi inter extraneas personas fieri intellegenda est in ea re, quae quia aliena est usucapi potest.

On Cujas' manipulation of the negative, Obs., 18. 15, see Lenel, *ad h. l.*; cf. Fitting, Arch., 52. 16 n. 111. Most writers on *usucapio* find the decision correct, Bonfante, S. G., 2. 539 n. 2; Windscheid, § 176 n. 6, cf. § 178 n. 7; as for 41. 3. 32. 1 see Pernice, 2. 1. 470 ff.; Cuq, 528 n. 9, forgets the rule *plus est in re;* Accarias, 1. 810 n. 3. Adler's objections, J. J. 33. 189 n. 1, seem unconvincing, for there is a gift if one parts with all that he has even if it is not enough for our prohibition, cf. 18. Upon the question of impoverishment, Savigny, 117, supposes that the donor could not usucapt on account of bad faith, *acc.* Appleton, Prop. prétorienne, 1. 17 n. 34. If the dominant view is correct that alienation in bad faith was theft, Windscheid, § 452 n. 8, this theory would limit the text to very exceptional cases like those mentioned by Bonfante, *op. cit.*, 566 n. 3. Even on this hypothesis the passage contradicts 46, however that is interpreted. It appears to be this problem which leads Beseler, Z., 227, to eradicate *quia, etc.*, but he does not explain the matter of impoverishment, 41. 6. 1. 2. The distinction seems to rest upon the nature of possession, which is both a valuable incident of ownership and an almost reluctant recognition by the law of a fact. Thus if H. gives W. property that he has stolen, there is no impoverishment, and W. clearly acquires possession, which is not thought of as a *res*, Buckland, T., 205, whereas if he gives his own property, the law will not grant W. an interest therein enforcible against everybody, thus partially maintaining a transaction which it reprobates *in toto*. It is not surprising that more is permitted when H. is trying to enrich W. at another's expense. Besides the difficulty of applying it to movables, which must have been the commonest subjects of such gifts, the general language of the texts is counter to Savigny's view, cf. Fitting, *loc. cit.*, n. 110. There are many difficulties in the way of the theory that the chance of *usucapio* was held a *res* of value, cf. Fitting, Arch., 51. 261; *supra ad* 9. 2. 11. 8. Whatever its scope, our passage presents a case where the gift is valid; in the other situation where there is clearly impoverishment, as where the donor is "bonitary" owner, many difficulties are created by the rule of 41. 6. 1. 2, which would seem to allow the paid seller to vindicate from the donee, *acc.* Savigny, *loc. cit.* It is of course possible to translate *cessat* "withhold itself," *i. e.*, from the donee, cf. H. S., *cessare* (5), especially since the question is only whether and when he may acquire. Adler's attempt, followed by Rabel, 440, to prove that the quiritary owner is barred fails in the following respects. He gives no explanation of 1. 2 *cit.*, which he wrongly identifies with 24, and cites in his favor our passage and 41. 6. 3, which, as they deal with a valid gift, do not even present the problem. In discussing the case of a usucapting donor, where he follows Savigny's view that the gift was void, he finds what to him, but not perhaps to everybody, seems an absurdity which is lacking in the much clearer case of the bonitary donor. Nor can his view be justified by the analogy of the pledgor, 41. 3. 16, or the *tradens* under a condition, Bufnoir, Condition, 426, who continued to usucapt, because in this case the donor wished to deprive himself of all his interest, cf. 41. 2. 1. 4. It thus appears probable that Adler and Rabel are wrong and that 1. 2 *cit.* is to be naturally construed; the fact that the donor did not want the object is more important than his preference of the donee to the seller, cf. 12. 6. 65. 2.

---

26. PAULUS *libro septimo ad Sabinum* Si eum, qui mihi vendiderit, iusserim eam rem uxori meae donationis causa dare et is possessionem iussu meo tradiderit, liberatus erit, quia, licet illa iure civili possidere non intellegatur, certe tamen venditor nihil habet quod tradat.

Pernice, 2. 1. 419 n. 4, makes the obscure and extraordinary statement that *jure civili poss.* here is certainly (*sic*) not the same as *civilis poss.* in 43. 16. 1. 8. On the contrary this passage seems to support the view advocated *infra* 46, that the donee did not enjoy interdictal protection. If possession had been transferred which was valid as against all the world but H., Paul would certainly not have had to rest his decision solely on the fact that the seller lost something. The result, like that of 7. 7, is in strange contrast to that of 3. 12, and to justify it on the ground of natural possession is more of a description than an explanation. As the question of mancipation does not seem significant, cf. Bechmann, Kauf, 3. 90 n. 2, the land will be assumed to be provincial, and the problem is what became of the legal possession. If this was acquired by H., the seller has fulfilled his obligation and there is no claim for cession of the vindication, which troubles Salkowski, 44 n. 80. It is, however, impossible to comprehend how H. can be held to acquire possession without the use of the fiction in 3. 12. Paul seems to have been misled by the rule that the seller need not transfer ownership, which was important only if he did not have it. Otherwise the rule that he must transfer possession is equivalent to saying that he must transfer ownership so that the situation is indistinguishable from 3. 12. The case seems analogous to that of transfer to a lunatic, 41. 2. 1. 3, where it would seem that possession remains with the *tradens*, but cf. *id.* 1. 4; 1. 20; 18. 1; 34. pr.; Kohler, Arch., 67. 197; Beseler, 4. 163, 220. Whatever the proper analogy or analysis, it may be repeated in conclusion that the decision is incomprehensible unless H. acquired at least the right to bring an interdict, and that this result cannot be explained by Paul's reason but only by that of Celsus in 3. 12.

---

1. Ex quibus causis inter virum et uxorem concessae sunt donationes, ex isdem et inter socerum et generum nurumve concessas Neratius ait. ergo socer genero mortis vel divortii causa donabit, sed et gener socero mortis suae vel divortii causa.

27. Modestinus *libro septimo regularum* Inter eos qui matrimonio coituri sunt, ante nuptias donatio facta iure consistit, etiamsi eodem die nuptiae fuerint consecutae.

---

28. Paulus *libro septimo ad Sabinum* Si id quod donatum sit perierit vel consumptum sit, eius qui dedit est detrimentum, merito, quia manet res eius qui dedit suamque rem perdit.

This passage is contrary to De Medio's theory.

---

1. Si quid in pueros ex ancillis dotalibus natos maritus inpenderit aut in doctrinam aut alimenta, non servatur marito, quia ipse ministeriis eorum utitur: sed illud servatur quod nutrici datum est ad educendum, quia pro capite quid dedisset, quemadmodum si a praedonibus redemisset servos dotales.

As Pothier saw, and for the reasons mentioned *infra* 45, this passage cannot originally have been here included, but belongs with 25. 1. 2; it was displaced on account of the Byzantine confusion of recovery of expenses with that of gifts. Since the case has not the remotest connection with our subject it may be dismissed with references to 21. 1. 30. 1; 25. 1. 15; H. S. *s. v. caput;* Riccobono, 345 n. 2.

---

2. Si quas servi operas viri uxori praestiterint vel contra, magis placuit, nullam habendam earum rationem: et sane non amare nec tamquam inter infestos ius prohibitae donationis tractandum est, sed ut inter coniunctos maximo affectu et solam inopiam timentes.

The last sentence is invariably cited to explain any hard text in the title. Beseler's grounds, 2. 21, for holding it interpolated are not of the strongest. *Amare* is said by dictionaries to occur in Plautus and Seneca; the last four words do not seem incomprehensible as applied to a revocable license, nor can the "analytical" justifications supposedly supplied by Paul be easily imagined.

3. Si ex decem donatis sibi mulier servum emerit et is quinque sit quinque petenda esse apud Plautium placuit, quemadmodum, si mortuus est, nihil peteretur: si vero quindecim dignus sit, non plus quam decem potest peti, quoniam eatenus donator pauperior factus esset. 4. Quod si ex decem duos servos emerit et eorum alter mortuus sit, alter decem dignus sit, solet quaeri. et plerique et Pomponius interesse putant, utrum uno pretio venierint an diversis: si uno, tota decem petenda, quemadmodum si una res empta deterior facta est, vel grex vel carrucha et aliqua pars inde perisset: si diversis, hoc solum petendum quanti sit emptus qui superest.

Cf. 31. 3. Though this elegant decision does not contain the word *animus* it seems to offer an example of the classical preference for subjective tests. Instead of stating facts from which the intent might be inferred or remarking that one or the other result will be presumed in the absence of contrary evidence, Pomponius assumed that the *animus* is a definite and decisive factor in a case where it would be particularly difficult to prove.

---

5. Iulianum putasse Pomponius refert, si quid per eum servum, quem ex nummis a marito donatis mulier adquisisset (forte legatum, hereditatem) aut partus editus esset, eo quoque nomine petitionem faciendam esse.

Cf. Lenel, *ad h. l.*, Pernice, 2. 1. 409 n. 5, mildly terms this an "extension" of the rule of 19. pr. Indeed, since the slave belongs to the donee, the decision involves a direct contradiction of what has been said in the preceding passages, as well as 7. 3. It is in the highest degree forced to suppose, with Accursius, that the slave has died (*quoque*) or with Mancaleoni, St. Sassaresi, 1. 14 n. 3, that he is worth less than his price (an assumption not only not made in our field, cf. 67, but also universally neglected where it should have been treated *ex professo*, cf. Windscheid, § 394 n. 1), and hence to interpret *eo nomine petitionem* as merely referring to the calculation of the enrichment. Indeed it is more than probably incorrect to include in the category of enrichment such acquisitions as legacies, even made with respect to the slave, cf. 16 *supra;* 17. pr.

The only explanation that can be suggested is that Pomponius was referring to a curious mistake of Julian, whose view was approved by the compilers following their predilection for the subrogation theory. On any interpretation of the text the appearance of such a view as early as Julian is another indication of the incorrectness of the theses of Pringsheim and Mancaleoni.

---

6. Illud constat, si, antequam a viro annuum acciperet, mulier ipsa de suo aut etiam mutuata impenderit, videri tantum iam ex annuo consumptum.

The term *annuum* refers to an allowance given to W. for her personal use, not limited in amount to maintaining the household or her position therein. The case is the converse of 7. 1 in that the expense precedes the gift, but governed by the same principle, cf. Accursius, *ad* 5. 3. 25. 12, 13, a text which is not analogous, for the question cannot be asked how one consumed a fund which was never acquired, cf. Francke, Comm. über H. P., 295.

---

7. Illud recte dictum Celsus ait: si dotis usuras annuas uxor stipulata sit, licet ei non debeantur, quia tamen quasi de annuo convenerit, peti quidem dotis iudicio non possunt, compensari autem possunt. idem ergo dicemus in qualibet pactione annui nomine facta.

The rule is stated that the stipulation for an allowance is void, of course because it does not vary with the amount actually needed by W. for her support, 33. pr.; 23. 4. 22; C. 5. 16. 11; incorrect, Hellman, Z., 1892, 358, 360. But according to 21. 1 what has actually been paid and used for maintenance cannot be recovered by H. Instead of interpreting the word compensation to refer to this fact, with Pothier and Keysser, *cit.* Hellman, it seems better to relate it to the case of divorce, where, as H. is making his claim in the form of a set-off, disallowance of the claim for these gifts may be called compensation for W. in so far as it cannot be used for that purpose by H.; *i. e.*, in so far as it is subtracted from his total claim. As to Hellman's objection that no *datio* is here mentioned, the answer is that without its assumption the decision does not seem sensible. The stipulation either falls under our prohibition or it does not. If the former, it can obviously not be used indirectly; if the latter, it is impossible to comprehend its invalidity. Hellman attempts to explain this by saying that the "congruence between question and answer produced nothing but the invalid interest liability." By such reasoning every "abstract" stipulation between H. and W. must have been void; furthermore, the redeeming cause might easily, and usually would, be expressed. His thesis that a natural obligation is created by a nude pact is thus not supported by this passage, but it is by 24. 3. 22, assuming the agreement there to have been informal, though in our text the word *convenire* is used of a stipulation. Girard's interpretation of that text, 654 n. 1, appears quite inadequate; the supposed pact was *ad augendam obligationem.*

---

29. Pomponius *libro quarto decimo ad Sabinum* Si mulier ex pecunia donata emptum servum vendidisset et alium emisset, posteriorem periculo mulieris esse Fulcinius scripsit: quod non est verum, licet non ex re mariti emptus sit.

Not only the decision of Pomponius, but the suggested restriction of the risk by the older Fulcinius to acquisitions *ex re mariti* is quite irreconcilable with Pringsheim's thesis in Kauf, cf. 7. 4. The text shows that the principle applied in 55 ought to be, and hence presumably was, nearly as old as Augustus. Pomponius' rule is hard to explain if consumption were not an excuse in his time, cf. supra 5. 17; 4. 2. 18.

---

1. Si vir uxori lanam donavit et ex ea lana vestimenta sibi confecit, uxoris esse vestimenta Labeo ait:

Here, as elsewhere, 6. 1. 5. 1; 41. 1. 27. 1; Ferrini, Bull., 2. 232, Pomponius follows the Proculian theory. The decision in 13. 1. 13 throws little light on Fulcinius' view, a reference to whom has probably been eradicated, cf. 31. 49. 2; Ferrini, *loc. cit.* It is difficult to follow the connection with 19. pr. discovered by Pernice, 2. 1. 410 n. 1.

---

30. Gaius *libro undecimo ad edictum provinciale* utilem tamen viro competere.

Cf. Pampaloni, A. G., 31. 417 ff.; Erman, Z., 1892, 216 n. 2; v. Mayr, *id.* 1905, 90, Condictio, 274; Lenel, Ed., 181 n. 10 (Mancaleoni's work was inaccessible). The widely held view that this text is interpolated may be correct for the so-often-forgotten reason that the principles of impoverishment forbid any claim by the donor to the completed object, cf. *infra* 55. In view, however, of the *utilis* action of G. 2. 78, conclusively proved by Bortolucci, Bull., 33. 151 ff., to be real, and of the excellent observation of Erman that that case is logically indistinguishable from this, those who insist upon the interpolation would do well first to explain that remedy, so puzzling to civilians, but so obvious to those acquainted with the constructive trust of English equity. Fortunately the words *praestat pretium* in 31. 1 make it unnecessary to inquire what is meant by *quibusdam* in G. 2. 79; Pernice, 2. 1. 323; Buckland, T., 218 nn. 6, 7, or to decide why the *condictio furtiva* applies to the completed *res*, or whether 13. 1. 14. 2 is a case of specification, on all which points the difficulties seem to be evaded by Pernice; Levy, Konkurrenz, 2. 112; cf. Girard, 326 n. 1; Bonfante, Ist., 8 ed., 258 n. 3; and above all why, given a *datio*, the condiction would not lie in all cases of specification. For 31. 1 proves that that lay in our case, and that there is no need of presenting such strange creations as v. Mayr's *utilis* condiction; any other result would be inexplicable, as there is a *datio* with subsequent consumption, destruction, or disappearance enriching the donee. There is then no reason for the usual view that Labeo refused any remedy.

---

31. Pomponius *libro quarto decimo ad Sabinum* Sed si vir lana sua vestimentum mulieri confecerit, quamvis id uxori confectum fuerit et uxoris cura, tamen viri esse neque impedire, quod in ea re uxor tamquam lanipendia fuerit et viri negotium procurarit.

This and the next passage show that the person who orders the work done is the one who acquires, which seems to prove that *occupatio* is not the basis of the institution, cf. Buckland, T., 218; 41. 1. 25; *id.* 27. 1, 2. If H. asks W. to make him a coat intending to give it to her, the later gift is void; otherwise, if she is told to make the coat for herself. What if in the former case she made it for herself? If she was ignorant of his intent, the problem of 13. 1. 13 is presented in the *a. rerum amotarum;* query, if she knew. Her services in the sewing room are of course not a gift, cf. 38. 1. 48. pr.

---

1. Si uxor lana sua, operis ancillarum viri, vestimenta sui nomine confecit muliebria, et vestimenta mulieris esse et pro operis ancillarum viro praestare nihil debere: sed viri nomine vestimenta confecta virilia viri esse, ut is lanae uxori praestet pretium: sed si non virilia vestimenta suo nomine mulier confecit, sed ea viro donavit, non valere donationem, cum illa valeat, cum viri nomine confecit: nec umquam operas viri ancillarum aestimari convenit.

Lenel, *ad h. p.*, regards *virilia* and *non virilia* as glosses, a suggestion more plausible as to the latter. The irrelevance of the idea of *occupatio* is shown even more clearly than in the preceding text. Since the donee can acquire neither *ex operis* nor *ex re*, the decision needs explanation, which is well supplied by Salkowski, 51 ff., 119, who cites 7. 8. 12. 6; *id.* 14. pr. to show that specification is not *ex operis.* If a thief of a slave employs him to cut down a tree on the thief's land, the tree does not become the property of the slave's owner, any more than he would acquire upon the thief's contract for the slave's labor, 12. 6. 55. As this would be true if the slave made a coat for the thief out of the latter's wool, so it would be the same if the wool were the property of anyone else, and so in our case. Although the rule is logical, it leads to the artificial result that the donee may use the slave for specification where work is involved but not for occupation where possession is involved, thus acquiring, according to Ferrini, Bull., 2. 199, in hunting, not the dead animal but its parts on separation. The case of making *viri nomine* is explained by the ownership of the slaves; they acquired for their master since in view of the wife's intent they could not acquire for her.

---

2. Si vir uxori aream donaverit et uxor in ea insulam aedificaverit, ea insula sine dubio mariti est, sed eam impensam mulierem servaturam placet: nam si maritus vindicet insulam, retentionem impensae mulierem facturam.

This passage is held interpolated by De Medio, 392, as to the vindication, with the suggestion that the *retentio* was meant; by Riccobono, 382, because the *exceptio doli* is not mentioned. The former's view is unlikely because a *retentio* would not be the natural word for W.'s claim, because the vindication is allowed in the parallel text, 44. 4. 10, and because it does not explain *mariti est.* The latter seems to have confused this case with that of the b. f. p.; cf. 426. Thus he discovers, 266 n. 3, Bull., 20. 244, a new case of a natural obligation in 20. 1. 1. 4, supposing that the claim might be made only by a *retentio.* Both on the principle of the preceding texts and upon authority including Sabinus, 25. 1. 11. 1, cf. Ulp. 7. 3; Bechmann, 2. 329, it seems certain that an invalid gift might be made by improving the property of one's spouse, not the *dos,* infra 45. The condiction would lie as in 31. 1 (cf. 5. 6; 47, as regards the *datio:* 12. 6. 40. 1; Pflüger, 52; 30. 60; Riccobono, 180 n. 1, as regards expenses), so that there is no natural obligation in 20. 1. 1. 4; the question of our text and 44. 4. 10 is whether the *retentio* would also be granted, which would infringe the rule of 32. 9 that there was no compensation of mutual gifts. It was finally allowed here, although its original function was to aid one who had no other remedy. The spouse is in the reverse situation from an ordinary possessor, the former's claim was made certain by knowledge of the lack of ownership which would entirely defeat that of the latter, a contrast which may have suggested the distinction in C. 3. 32. 2. 1, cf. Z., 1921, 320. If W. believes in the validity of the transfer of land, her expenditures do not form a gift, at least of the kind infringing our prohibition, so that she needs the *exceptio doli* like any b. f. p. In conclusion, the absence throughout this subject of the *ius tollendi* may be remarked, *infra* 45.

---

3. Si duo mancipia fuerint singula quinis digna, sed utrumque unis quinque donationis causa a viro mulieri vel contra venierint, melius dicetur communia ea esse pro portione pretii nec tandem spectandum esse, quanti mancipia sint, sed quantum ex pretio donationis causa sit remissum: sine dubio licet a viro vel uxore minoris emere, si non sit animus donandi.

Partsch and Pringsheim are led by their view of 5. 5 to hold this passage interpolated. The former finds in the common ownership an example of the Greek principles discerned by the latter in Kauf, thereby overlooking the surely genuine analogous decision more than probably of the same Pomponius (cf. 28. 4) in 7. 4. He also asserts that in classical law this transaction was void, citing 32. 26 but disregarding the contrary preceding text, which forces Pringsheim to maintain that 26 is entirely spurious. In addition it is not clear how the supposed nullity of the simulated sale accords with Partsch's main thesis. In an Inaug. Diss., Erlanger, Kaufvertrag unter Ehegatten, 30 ff., apparently for the first time attempts to resolve the antinomy between this decision and that of Pomponius in 5. 5. He holds that common ownership follows where the price is fixed too low; otherwise, where a proper price is accompanied by a release; and asks how, if a thing worth 10 is sold for 5, can 5 more which was never promised be claimed. The answer is that the claim is not upon a promise but by virtue of our prohibition. The solution is unconvincing not only because of the lack of any such hint in the texts but because it seems arbitrary and improbable, for it would be rare that the price of 10 would be demanded accompanied by a simultaneous release of 5. The importance of the mention of the release may be seen by reference to Pomponius' distinction in 28. 4. Supposing two slaves worth 5 each are sold for 5, and A dies, B appreciating to 7; if they are sold for one price the rule of 5. 5 applies. But if they are sold for "diverse" prices, the gift in effect consists of a release of the price of one. This is the case with which Pomponius is dealing, and his solution is the only possible one, not because it is impossible to prove which one was the intended subject of the gift, but because there was actually no definite intent. The text, like 7. 4, shows the refinements of which the Romans were capable in judging the *animus*. In the case supposed, if H. says: "Here is a valuable team of horses which I will sell for 5," he recovers 2; if he says: "Here are two horses worth 5 each which I will sell for 5," he recovers $3\frac{1}{2}$; if he says: "Here is B which I will sell for 5 throwing in A in case B turns out to have cancer," he recovers nothing. In answer to Lammfromm, 146, it is very doubtful whether the common ownership is more than an expedient analogous to our constructive trust, cf. 7. 4; *i. e.*, whether the wife cannot transfer to a third person a clear title in either slave; in these cases Pomponius was dealing exclusively with the matter of enrichment. As for the question of the donee's ignorance of the intended gift, see *infra* 47.

4. Si vir uxori vel contra quid vendiderit vero pretio et donationis causa paciscantur, ne quid venditor ob eam rem praestet, videndum est, quid de ea venditione agatur, utrum res venierit et totum negotium valeat, an vero ut ea sola pactio irrita sit, quemadmodum irrita esset, si post contractam emptionem novo consilio inito id pacti fuisset actum. et verius est pactum dumtaxat irritum esse. 5. Idem dicemus, si donationis causa pacti sint, ne fugitivum aut erronem praestent, id est integras esse actiones aedilicias et ex empto.

These decisions show clearly that there is nothing to the distinction proposed by Partsch (whether the release follows the sale), and are indistinguishable from the case in 5. 5, supposed to be interpolated.

---

6. Quod vir uxori in diem debet, sine metu donationis praesens solvere potest, quamvis commodum temporis retenta pecunia sentire potuerit.

This is merely a gift of the use of the money, 17 pr., 18. De Retes, 4. 12, remarks the contrary rule for fraudulent conveyances, 42. 8. 10. 22, but there is no need to invoke 28. 2, because the rights of creditors were naturally in other ways more extensive than those of donors, 42. 8. 18; Windscheid, § 463 n. 15. If H. had promised to pay interest, acceptance would be a gift by W.

---

7. Quod legaturus mihi aut hereditatis nomine relicturus es, potes rogatus a me uxori meae relinquere et non videtur ea esse donatio, quia nihil ex bonis meis deminuitur: in quo maxime maiores donanti succurrisse Proculus ait, ne amore alterius alter despoliaretur, non quasi malivolos, ne alter locupletior fieret.

For interpolation, see Beseler, 3. 14, who omitted to notice Kübler's remarks, Z., 1890, 47. This passage is too often neglected in discussions of 3. 13. De Medio, 374, well shows the improbability of Alibrandi's hypothesis in connection with Proculus' reasoning.

8. Si vir uxori munus immodicum calendis Martiis aut natali die dedisset, donatio est: sed si impensas, quas faceret mulier, quo honestius se tueretur, contra est.

Cf. 15 pr., the *immodicum* appears to have escaped Beseler's suspicions. These *impensas* should be distinguished from *annua*, which are not limited to maintenance of the position in the household.

---

9. Non videtur locupletior facta esse mulier, si aut in opsonio aut in unguentis aut in cibariis familiae donatam sibi pecuniam impenderit.

This passage seems another blow to the hypothesis that the *oratio* introduced the defense of consumption, *supra* 5. 17.

---

10. Quae vir cibaria uxoris familiae iumentisve praestiterit, quae in usu communi erant, non condicentur: quod si familiam domesticam uxoris aut venaliciam pavit, contra puto observari debere.

The "domestic family" is that not in common use, 55. 1. Instead of using this text to support his view that consumption was no defense before the *oratio*, Savigny rightly holds, 74 n., that one is enriched by consumption of necessaries, cf. the omission of this case in 5. 3. 25. 11. In attempting to explain away the text, Windscheid, § 365 n. 14, is forced into the unlikely hypothesis for a slave-dealing wife that her stock would otherwise have starved.

---

32. ULPIANUS *libro trigesimo tertio ad Sabinum* Cum hic status esset donationum inter virum et uxorem, quem antea rettulimus, imperator noster Antoninus Augustus ante excessum divi Severi patris sui oratione in senatu habita auctor fuit senatui censendi Fulvio Aemiliano et Nummio Albino consulibus, ut aliquid laxaret ex iuris rigore.

For a recent attempt at reconstruction, see Z., 1903, 450.

---

1. Oratio autem imperatoris nostri de confirmandis donationibus non solum ad ea pertinet, quae nomine uxoris a viro comparata sunt, sed

ad omnes donationes inter virum et uxorem factas, ut et ipso iure res fiant eius cui donatae sunt et obligatio sit civilis et de Falcidia ubi possit locum habere tractandum sit: cui locum ita fore opinor, quasi testamento sit confirmatum quod donatum est.

The theoretical nature of convalescence is well discussed by Gradenwitz, 191 ff., the situation produced by C. 5. 16. 25, by Labbé, Machelard, 319 ff. These gifts are treated for Falcidian purposes like those *m. c.*, C. 6. 50. 5; Savigny, 279 n. *h.*; cf. 35. 2. 81. 2. The question what, if any, differences existed between the two types has been often and lengthily discussed, without very satisfactory results, see Brinz, 3. 798 n. 24; Bremer, Arch., 51. 192 ff.; De Retes, ch. 9; Gentilis, 3. chs. 24–26; cf. also Machelard, 311 n. 2. Although the only evidence for retroactivity before Justinian is 32. 23, and there may be some force in Bremer's argument a *contrario* from C. 5. 16. 25 and 31. 77. 17 is better understood with De Retes to mean confirmation by will, practical considerations lead to a belief therein; *e. g.*, suppose an Aquilian action accrued just before the death. Besides the question of retroactivity the other chief difference concerns the right of revocation; even if this existed for gifts *m. c.*, it appears that more was required to revoke such a transaction, cf. *infra* 32. 5. For another situation, cf. 53. pr.

---

2. Ait oratio 'fas esse eum quidem qui donavit paenitere: heredem vero eripere forsitan adversus voluntatem supremam eius qui donaverit durum et avarum esse.'

Beseler, 3. 87, apparently regards this passage as ridiculous, specifying his objection only to *forsitan*, a word which seems reasonable in view of 32. 4; the heir might often fail to prove an intent to revoke which really existed. As for *fas*, cf. 3. 1 and Vassalli there cited.

---

3. Paenitentiam accipere debemus supremam. proinde si uxori donavit, deinde eum paenituit, mox desiit paenitere, dicendum est donationem valere, ut supremum eius spectemus iudicium, quemadmodum circa fideicommissa solemus, vel in legatis

cum de doli exceptione opposita tractamus, ut sit ambulatoria voluntas eius usque ad vitae supremum exitum.

Cf. 34. 4. 3. 11; *id.* 4; Beseler, 3. 50, 4. 161, with whom cf. Appleton, Testament, 47; Cugia, 92 ff.

---

4. Sed ubi semel donatorem paenituit, etiam heredi revocandi potestatem tribuimus, si appareat defunctum evidenter revocasse voluntatem: quod si in obscuro sit, proclivior esse debet iudex ad comprobandam donationem.

The objections of Beseler, 1. 90, seem based upon a too simplified view, cf. 32. 15.

---

5. Si maritus ea quae donaverit pignori dederit, utique eum paenituisse dicemus, licet dominium retinuit. quid tamen, si hoc animo fuit, ut vellet adhuc donatum? finge in possessionem precariam mulierem remansisse paratamque esse satisfacere creditori. dicendum est donationem valere: nam si ab initio ei rem obligatam hoc animo donasset, dicerem vim habere donationem, ut parata satisfacere mulier haberet doli exceptionem: quin immo et si satisfecisset, potuisse eam per doli exceptionem consequi, ut sibi mandentur actiones.

The rule, cf. C. 5. 16. 12, was changed by Justinian, Nov. 162. 1, and was not observed for legacies, according to Paul, 3. 6. 16, and hence presumably not for gifts *m. c.*, the absence of any discussion of ademption in connection with which is another argument for their irrevocability. From *ut parata* this text is impossible to comprehend and as hopelessly confused as 30. 57, on which see Ferrini, Legati, 286 ff., which it originally preceded, cf. Lenel, *ad h. l.* The first clause must refer to a suit by the heir, cf. 20. 6. 12. 1. It is difficult then to comprehend the reason why W. must exonerate without a hint at the usual question whether H. knew of the pledge. Even more inexplicable is the mention of the *exceptio doli.* Faber, De Err., D. 46. E. 7, holds that the ownership remains with the heir from lack of a proper *traditio*, thus apparently referring to the *precarium.* Since, however, possession could never be transferred, 46, and if it could, it apparently would have been here, 43. 26. 6. 4, the impossible result is that the benefit of the *oratio* always had to be claimed by that plea, cf. Perozzi, *cit.* Siber, Leipz. Rechtw. St., 11. 9 n. 1, on *obligatio civilis* in 32. 1. From *quin* the passage becomes, if possible, even more obscure. If, with Faber, the more natural assumption is made that the creditor is suing, cf. 20. 4. 19; 30. 57, the rule directly contradicts the previous statement that W. must exonerate. If, on the contrary, Gentilis is right, 3 ch. 12, that the heir is suing, it is difficult to imagine what claims W. in possession can have against the satisfied creditor. If there is some such action as the Aquilian, either W. may bring it anyway by retroactivity, or she may not and it belongs to the heir, in which case it is strange that she can use the heir's suit as an excuse to obtain something that the law did not otherwise grant her. For these reasons Beseler's view, 3. 186; cf. Z., 1919, 314 n. 2, is plausible that from *ut* the passage is interpolated, cf. Ferrini, *cit. ad* 30. 57. It suggests, however, many interesting and unanswerable questions as to the procedural effect of the *oratio*.

---

6. Si donator servus fuerit effectus privati, dicendum est non impletam, sed peremptam donationem, quamvis morti servitus comparetur: proinde et si ipsa in servitutem redigatur cui donatum est, extincta erit donatio.

The decision is in accord with the general principles of gifts *m. c.*, 39. 6. 7, though contrary to Constantine's principle as to a spouse who becomes *servus poenae*, C. 5. 16. 24; *supra* 13. 1. It is, therefore, often supposed that *privati* is interpolated, cf. Cohn, Beiträge, 369; Ratti, Bull., 35. 161 n. 1, which depends upon the gratuitous assumption that Constantine's statute represents an innovation. The distinction is quite reasonable, for the sovereign might generously resign his own rights in favor of the criminal's family, but not those of another. Desserteaux, 2. 395 n. 1, regards *quamvis ... comparetur* as Byzantine, following a theory that the classical jurists made the comparison only for the *servus poenae*. The reasons for this are obscure; it is arrived at merely by rejecting our text and believing others like 35. 1. 59. 2; 36. 1. 18. 6; 48. 20. 5. pr., the last of which is widely suspected. A still more peculiar fact is that he yet holds, 428, that Constantine's enactment is an innovation. Most important of all, without the comparison to death, he cannot explain, 395 n. 3, our decision as to the donee, cf. the maintenance of the conditional legacy in 36. 2. 14. 3.

---

7. Si maritus uxori donaverit et mortem sibi ob sceleris conscientiam consciverit vel etiam post mortem memoria eius damnata sit, revocabitur donatio: quamvis ea quae aliis donaverit valeant, ˊsi non mortis causa donavit. 8. Si miles uxori donaverit de castrensibus bonis et fuerit damnatus, quia permissum est ei de his testari (si modo impetravit, ut testetur, cum damnaretur), donatio valebit: nam et mortis causa donare poterit, cui testari permissum est.

These decisions merely follow the law as to gifts *m. c.* and legacies, see 39. 6. 15; 48. 21. 3. pr.; C. 6. 21. 13; Mommsen, Strafrecht, 438 n. 8, 987 n. 1; for which reason a suspicion as to their genuineness is voiced by Cugia, 52 n. 1.

---

9. Quod ait oratio 'consumpsisse,' sic accipere debemus, ne is qui donationem accepit locupletior factus sit: ceterum si factus est, orationis beneficium locum habebit. sed et si non sit factus locupletior, dederit tamen tantam quantitatem eaque exstet, dicendum est, si is decessit, qui factus est locupletior, posse repetere id quod dedit nec compensare id quod consumpsit, quamvis divortio secuto haec compensatio locum habeat.

Cf. Beseler, Z., 444 *sub* 7. 2; Pflüger, 31; Nolde *ad* Nikolsky, Z., 1903, 449 n. 1, who follows Dernburg, Comp., 2 ed., 185 n. 2, who had formerly, *id.* 1 ed., 185 n. 1, spoken of convalescence of a consumed gift. The passage clearly implies that there may be consumption with enrichment, cf. *supra* 7. 1. The point of the decision lies in the tense of *factus*. If H. gives W. 10, which are consumed without enrichment, H'.s claim is lost; if thereupon W. gives H. 10 and he dies enriched, W. may recover from his heirs, and there is no compensation because there is nothing to compensate. Thus, *quamvis, etc.*, is senseless; it must have referred to the *retentio* and been inserted by a misunderstanding. Its original function may be arrived at by a process of elimination; the only case to which it could apply is that of mutual incommensurable (7. 2) gifts, or probably in the case of 5. 5 if a horse had been exchanged *don. an.* for a cow. Here there was evidently no compensation to the vindication or condiction of either party, but there would be in the *retentio*, cf. *supra* 28. 7. The text shows as well as 32. 14 that "remunerative" gifts are void, with the probable exception of the case in Paul, 5. 11. 16; 39. 5. 34. 1 (on *id.* 27 reff. in Beseler, 3. 137); justified by the principle of 14; 36. 1; cf. Meyerfeld, Schenkung, § 19; Windscheid, § 368 n. 11. It is otherwise in the case of a natural obligation, 39. 5. 19. 4, 5; *i. e.*, where there is the *soluti retentio*, which may occur between H. and W. in cases like 2. 2. 3. 7; 12. 6. 19. pr., cf. Siber, Leipz., Rechtswiss. St., 11. 60. This distinction does not depend upon the *animus*, as Siber suggests, 78; correct, Meyerfeld, *op. cit.*, 357; payment of the natural obligation would presumably be valid though made, not from a sense of duty, but *donationis causa* in a burst of affection or gratitude for a service rendered. The point is that the amount of the claim is definite, so that payment of the exact sum may be supported on the principle of 7. 2; 67, here as in the latter text the donor is merely cancelling a former enrichment at the donee's expense. Of course if more than the proper amount is paid the transaction may be avoided, and, as Gradenwitz acutely suggests, 219 ff., the rules of the *condictio indebiti* were perhaps affected by our prohibition to permit the vindication even in case of mistake. This conclusion is not, however, supported by 39, where the *ignorans* is an *extraneus;* the consequences depend upon the intent, not of the mandatary, but of the prohibited donor, who was there *sciens*. As in 67 a difficulty arises if the donor, unjustly released from an obligation to transfer a slave *generaliter*, gives *don. an.* an immensely valuable painter, a case which illustrates the doubtful correctness of the exception in favor of natural obligations. Because the Romans were not interested in purely theoretical controversy, it is not easy to guess at their conception of *animus donandi* as between H. and W.; *i. e.*, how they would have treated a gift of a fierce dog in the hope that he might injure the donee, or how they distinguished a sale for too low a price under pressure of poverty from a case where the pressure was exercised by the family or public opinion, cf. 34. 4. 18. The treatment of "remunerative" transactions seems to show that the important point was that the donor should not be acting as a business man, with the hope of receiving the best possible commercial advantage. It is also probable that they would never have thought of speaking of a gift without some pecuniary advantage to the donee, but cf. Haymann, 66, *et pass.*

---

10. Si divortium post donationem intercessit aut prior decesserit qui donum accepit, veteri iuri statur, hoc est, si maritus uxori donatum vult, valeat donatio, quod si non vult, exstinguitur: plerique enim cum bona gratia discedunt, plerique cum ira sui animi et offensa.

Kübler, Z., 1890, 48, objecting to the double *plerique*, believes that this and the next four passages are largely interpolated. It should be obvious, but cf. Levy, 146, that the *hoc est* clause is anything but a statement of the old law, by which there was no convalescence. Pothier's ingenious but strained interpretation of *vult* as a testamentary gift is impossible in view of *prior decesserit*. While formerly an express or implied reiteration of his will by a divorced donor was undoubtedly valid as a *traditio brevi manu*, cf. 41. 6. 1. 2, there is plainly no such declaration involved here; *bona gratia*, cf. 60. 1 and Bonfante, 263, is an expression clearly adapted to the *novum jus*. De Medio, 394, regards the evidence of interpolation as so strong that he refuses to accept the only text which supports his theory. Indeed it is probable that the passage is wrong even for later law, Solazzi, Bull., 34. 305. The opposite rule is stated in 62. 1, and a reconciliation can be effected with Gotofredus, Machelard, 312, only upon the arbitrary hypothesis, in disaccord with the context, that in the latter passage the divorce is not *bona gratia*. From the discussion in the next text and 32. 13, and especially from the express words of 32. 14, *quia vivis, etc.*, it can be assumed with some assurance that the *oratio*, either in terms or by unanimous interpretation, applied only to death during marriage, a result which should not be explained, with Solazzi, on a theory that divorce necessarily showed a change of intent to the classical lawyers. He is right in his contention that the purpose of the interpolation was to equiparate a gift with a legacy, 34. 2. 3.

---

11. Quid ergo, si divortium factum est, deinde matrimonium restauratur, et in divortio vel mutata est vol-

untas vel eadem duravit, restaurato tamen matrimonio et voluntate donatoris reconciliata an donatio duret, si constante matrimonio donator decesserit? et potest defendi valere.

The words *constante mat.*, which frequently recur, cf. 32. 20, support the view just advocated. Solazzi's contention that Ulpian said *non valere* is improbable for two reasons. First, it would make it unnecessary to consider the intervening changes of intent. Second, it seems illogical that a transaction wholly void at the beginning can be impaired by the divorce, which can have no more effect than any other intermediate change of mind. The requirements of the *oratio* are fulfilled by death during marriage with the proper intent; see further, Levy, 13 n. 4.

---

12. Quod si divortium non intercesserit, sed frivusculum, profecto valebit donatio, si frivusculum quievit.

The dispute whether the *b* of *fribusculum* should be read as a *g*, or a *v*, still continues, cf. Lewis-Short; H. S.; Glück, 26. 142 n. 41. Kübler's claim of interpolation has some force, cf. Levy, 15 n. 1.

---

13. Si mulier et maritus diu seorsum quidem habitaverint, sed honorem invicem matrimonii habebant (quod scimus interdum et inter consulares personas subsecutum), puto donationes non valere, quasi duraverint nuptiae: non enim coitus matrimonium facit, sed maritalis affectio: si tamen donator prior decesserit, tunc donatio valebit.

Cf. 35. It seems impossible to explain this passage unless death *constante matrimonio* was required. The interpolation of *affectio* assumed by Levy, 11 n. 3, following Kübler, does not seem likely in view of Vat. Fr., 253b; cited by Bonfante, 191 n. 1.

---

14. Si ambo ab hostibus capti sint et qui donavit et cui donatum est, quid dicimus? et prius illud volo tractare. oratio, si ante mors contigerit ei cui donatum est, nullius momenti donationem esse voluit: ergo si ambo deces-

serint, quid dicemus, naufragio forte vel ruina vel incendio? et si quidem possit apparere, quis ante spiritum posuit, expedita est quaestio: sin vero non appareat, difficilis quaestio est. et magis puto donationem valuisse et his ex verbis orationis defendimus: ait enim oratio 'si prior vita decesserit qui donatum accepit': non videtur autem prior vita decessisse qui donatum accepit, cum simul decesserint. proinde rectissime dicetur utrasque donationes valere, si forte invicem donationibus factis simul decesserint, quia neuter alteri supervixerit, licet de commorientibus oratio non senserit: sed cum neuter alteri supervixerit, donationes mutuae valebunt: nam et circa mortis causa donationes mutuas id erat consequens dicere neutri datam condictionem: locupletes igitur heredes donationibus relinquent. secundum haec si ambo ab hostibus simul capti sint amboque ibi decesserint non simul, utrum captivitatis spectamus tempus, ut dicamus donationes valere, quasi simul decesserint? an neutram, quia vivis eis finitum est matrimonium? an spectamus, uter prius decesserit, ut in eius persona non valeat donatio? an uter rediit, ut eius valeat? mea tamen fert opinio, ubi non reverterunt, ut tempus spectandum sit captivitatis, quasi tunc defecerint: quod si alter redierit, eum videri supervixisse, quia redit.

Cf. 34. 5. 8; *id.* 10. 1; 28. 6. 34. pr.; for the relation of captivity to *cap. dem.* see Desserteaux, 1. 135 ff. The result is supposed to be Byzantine by Solazzi, *op. cit.*, 302; De Medio, Bull., 13. 245 n., who appear to disregard the fiction usually applied, cf. Buckland, 298 ff. The former makes no reference to Beseler, who, following the recent tendency to eradicate completely retroactivity, has declared both fictions to be interpolated, Z., 192 ff. In so doing he overlooks this passage and 24. 3. 10. pr., which are irreconcilable with his view (the more unconvincing because the question was mooted in the time of Gaius, 1. 129, or even then already decided in favor of the fiction, cf. Ratti, Bull., 35. 112 n. 2). On *postliminium* between spouses, see C. 5. 16. 27; Ratti, *op. cit.*, 161, who shows that De Medio's suspicions of our passage are as groundless as those of Beseler of the others. The first case there given follows our decision; as for the second, retroactivity need not be assumed if in Justinian's time the death did not have to occur during marriage, 32. 10, cf. Glück, 26. 157, who sidesteps the question. In classical law a "benignant" interpretation would have been necessary, 49. 15. 8, cf. Lenel, Paul, 941; Buckland, 297; Ratti, 161 n. 2.

---

15. Qui quasdam res ex his quas donaverat legasset, quasdam non, non videbitur ceteras noluisse ad uxorem pertinere: plerumque enim antea legat, postea donat: vel alia causa fuit legandi.

Cf. Glück, 26. 172 ff.; W. is legatee. This apparently genuine decision, so extreme if the legacy follows all the gifts, may vindicate 32. 4.

---

16. Oratio non solum virum et uxorem complectitur, sed etiam ceteros, qui propter matrimonium donare prohibentur: ut puta donat socer nurui vel contra, vel socer genero vel contra, vel consocer consocero qui copulatos matrimonio in potestate habent: nam ex mente orationis his quoque omnibus permissum est in eundem casum donare. et ita et Papinianus libro quarto responsorum sensit: sic enim scribit: socer nurui vel genero donavit: postea filius eius vel filia constante matrimonio vita decessit: quamquam vitium donationis perseveret, tamen, si socer nullam quaestionem donationibus intulit, post mortem eius contra heredes orationis sententia videtur intervenire: nam quae ratio donationem prohibuit, eadem beneficium datum implorabit. ut igitur valeat donatio ista, Papinianus exigit, ut et filius eius qui donavit ante decesserit, et socer postea durante voluntate.

Because of Pothier's interpretation, followed by Glück, 26. 130 n. 14, it must be emphasized that Ulpian does not expressly approve Papinian's view, cf. *infra* 32. 19, from whose case no rule can be made out as it is the easiest imaginable, *viz.*, death of the child during marriage and *potestas* and death of the father before that of the donee. From 53. pr. it may be assumed that he did not allow convalescence if the son survived the father and was married. Supposing that the marriage had ended otherwise than by divorce, 32. 19, two problems arise according to whether the son predeceases the father or not. In the first case Papinian probably would have upheld the gift, for the ground upon which validity was refused in the case of divorce was a presumed intent to revoke, which was absent in all except possibly the last of the other situations in which the marriage ended, *e. g.*, captivity, slavery, perhaps exile, and adoption, 23. 2. 67. 3 (of the donor's child by the donee's father, unless the gift were between the fathers). Thus the phrase *constante mat.* is meant only to exclude the case of divorce, not that of death of the donor's child in captivity and is properly omitted by Ulpian in his résumé. Where the son survives his father, regardless of any question of Cornelian retroactivity or comparison of slavery to death it must be clear that the gift may convalesce; the survival of the son on Papinian's theory and perhaps that of Ulpian, 32. 20, is important only if he is married. Thus reasonably restricted, Papinian's view may be summarized by saying that at the father's death the marriage must have ended in a manner which in the absence of other evidence justified no presumption of the intent to revoke.

---

17. Si filius familias, qui castrense peculium habet vel quasi castrense, uxori donet, filii personam et mortem spectabimus.

Krüger credits the suggestion of interpolation of *quasi castrense* to Albertario, but see Pothier; Schilfordeger, reported by Albertario, Studi Pavia, 2. 114. For an explanation by one who believes it genuine, see Fitting, Peculium Q. Cast., 388 ff.; cf. also Cuq, 148 n. 7.

---

18. Si nurus socero donaverit, mortem nurus et perseverantem in supremam diem voluntatem spectare nos oportet. quod si socer ante decesserit, dicemus exstinctam donationem an, quia maritus vivit, si uxori suae supervixit, admittimus vim habere donationem? et si quidem maritus solus socero heres exstitit, quasi nova donatio potest servari in maritum collata, ut illa finita sit, alia coeperit: sin vero filius heres patri non est, finita erit donatio ratione nova.

For the various attempts at emendation of *ratione nova*, see Krüger, *ad h. l.;* Glück, 26. 133 n. 26, who shows that the words are open to a sensible interpretation as they stand. This text lays down a rule which in our field, cf. 43. 26. 4. 4, is revolutionary, and renders unnecessary all the preceding and following discussion. If a new gift may here be presumed from mere inactivity after the old one has failed, why should not the same be true in the last sentence, or if the gift was to the husband in *potestas* after the latter's death, or in favor of the heirs as to all gifts between H. and W. when the donee dies first? It is of course possible to limit the decision to the case where the spouse benefits, so that mere inactivity + *affectio maritalis* = an express declaration, but cf. 53. pr. where there should be a new gift if the son inherits. Moreover, as the decision raises so many difficult questions where the donor is ignorant or forgetful of the gift, and since, as Accursius remarks, it leads to co-ownership if the donee inherits *pro parte*, with all the attendant possibilities as to ignorance or mistake of the donor about the amount of his share, it may well be suspected of interpolation. The classical lawyers would have required something more than passivity.

---

19. Si socer nurui nuntium miserit, donatio erit irrita, quamvis matrimonium concordantibus viro et uxore secundum rescriptum imperatoris nostri cum patre comprobatum est: sed quod ad ipsos, inter quos donatio facta est, finitum est matrimonium. 20. Proinde et si duo consoceri invicem donaverint, idem erit dicendum, si invitis filiis nuntium remiserint, inter ipsos irritam esse donationem. in hac autem donatione inter soceros facta mors desideranda est eius qui donavit constante matrimonio et iure potestatis durante: idemque et in his qui sunt in eorum potestate.

Solazzi, *op. cit.*, 15, finds much to object to in these texts but, perhaps on account of the intricacy of the situation, avoids reconstruction. Following Vat. Fr., 116, he objects to the clause *quamvis . . . comprobatum*. It is unnecessary to comment on the audacity of impugning many explicit texts in favor of one so mutilated, cf. Buckland, 117; Bonfante, 250 n. 2. His grounds for objection here are as follows. First he declares that the existence of the marriage has no effect on the validity of the gift, a contention which is refuted by 53. pr. He cites in his favor *vitium . . . perseveret* in 32. 16, remarking that the gift continues to be void, but failing to mention that it convalesces and is thus as valid as it is possible for it to be. Further, the case in 16 is quite different: there the question is whether the gift is valid, given the favorable intent; here, it is whether the intent can be called favorable. There it is held that the gift is not confirmed if the marriage subsists at death (53. pr.); here the attempt to end the marriage, though abortive, and whether by donor or donee, raises a presumption of the intent to revoke, even though, if the donor survived his child, the other requisites for validity would be present. On the other hand it is hard to comprehend Levy's remark, 146, that the divorce allows revocation *vetere jure*, according to which the transaction was at once void. As for *inter vivos*, Solazzi inquires for whom the gift is valid if void as between donor and donee, perversely refusing to understand the point that the gift fails only if the repudiation proceeds from these parties, cf. the gift *divortii causa* in 53. pr.; *i. e.*, it would be otherwise as between father and daughter-in-law if the divorce were attributable to the latter's father or the former's son. (The doubts as to a son's power to divorce himself, Solazzi, 27; Ferrini, Pand., 881, do not seem justified, the tendency to restrict his father's right conclusively implying a right in the son, cf. also Brini, Mat. e Div., 3. 151.) All is clear until *in hac, etc.*, where the phrase *constante mat.* implies dissent from 32. 16; 53. pr. On account of the word *potestas* Pothier's attempt to relate *c. m.* to *donavit* fails, cf. Glück, 136 ff., who does not notice the resulting antinomy. The phrase is here part of the rule and cannot be explained as an immaterial fact as in 32. 16. The difficulty was caused by the impossibility of the application of the *oratio*, which required death of the donor, during, and hence ending, the marriage, 32. 10, conditions which could be fulfilled here only if the father and son died simultaneously. Papinian for some reason regarded the ending of the marriage as the most important factor. His view is analytically incorrect as it is the patrimonial identity of father and son which is significant, and even if this exists, the son inheriting, the rule of 32. 18 would permit confirmation as a new gift. The sentence is thus in accord with that doubtful decision. It is also incorrect in that, although on one hand it rectifies Papinian's view in a minor degree, it seems to exclude the clearest cases of validity like that in 32. 16. It is hard to avoid the conclusion that the presence of the phrase *c. m.* is as objectionable here as its absence in 32. 10. The proper view would seem to be to refuse either to consider whether the marriage subsisted or to allow a *nova donatio*, but merely to inquire whether on the death of the donor his *married* child would be impoverished by convalescence. The last sentence appears also very suspicious and may have been added by completomania, for one in *potestas* could not make a gift. If H. gave to W. in *potestas*, the gift would presumably not convalesce if she died first, though H. died next, cf. 32. 18; 39. 6. 23; Cugia, 82.

---

21. Si consocer consocero donaverit et alter eorum vel uterque copulatos emancipaverit, debet dici donationem ad orationem non pertinere et ideo infirmari donationem.

Pertinere is not clear; it seems that emancipation was treated like divorce, the intent to revoke being assumed. It may be significant that *consoceri* are mentioned as showing that the emancipation must proceed from a party to the gift.

---

22. Si sponsus sponsae donaverit in tempus matrimonii collata donatione, quamvis inter virum et uxorem donatio non videatur facta et verba orationis minus sufficiant, tamen donationem dicendum est ad sententiam orationis pertinere, ut, si duraverit voluntas usque ad mortem, valeat donatio.

It is usually held, Machelard, 249 n. 2; Savigny, 122 n. *b*, 175 n. *l*; Gentilis, 4. ch. 6, that this passage and 5. pr. represent the rule that fulfilment of an antenuptial stipulation is void. No justification for such a strange doctrine can be seen either in reason or policy; such a transaction is of course *solutionis*, not *donationis causa*. Against it speaks 45. 1. 97. 2, since the invalidity there is based upon the *turpis causa*, cf. Levy-Bruhl, Denegatio Actionis, 63; the implication is that the stipulation would otherwise be valid, and no doubt seems to exist in Celsus' mind as to the possibility of suit after marriage. These considerations point to the conclusion that ours is a case like C. 5. 3. 4., where no legal liability arose before the marriage, and that 23. 3. 12. pr. is not to be trusted, cf. 7. 5. Only in Justinian's day when a "nude" pact was binding is the decision illogical.

23. Sive autem res fuit quae donata est sive obligatio remissa, potest dici donationem effectum habituram: ut puta uxori acceptum tulit donationis causa quod debeat: potest dici pendere acceptilationem non ipsam, sed effectum eius. et generaliter universae donationes, quas impediri diximus, ex oratione valebunt.

Gradenwitz's attempt, 254, to reconcile this passage with 23 by citing 4. 2. 9. 3, fails to account for the last sentence, which, however, might be now suspected by some, see Bull., 33. 104, *s. v. generaliter*. The passage is discarded as interpolated by Bremer, Arch., 51. 230. It clearly expresses the rule of retroactivity, which, as applied to a formal transaction of this kind, should surprise nobody, cf. *supra* 32. 1. Gradenwitz makes some interesting remarks on the difficulty of applying the *oratio* to releases by a third person, cf. 39, which seem equally to apply to tradition. Celsus' fiction must be employed unless the donee's chance under the *oratio* is to be dependent upon the caprice of the *extraneus*.

---

24. Si inter virum et uxorem societas donationis causa contracta sit, iure vulgato nulla est, nec post decretum senatus emolumentum ea liberalitas, ut actio pro socio constituatur, habere poterit: quae tamen in commune tenuerunt fine praestituto, revocanda non sunt. idcirco igitur pro socio actio non erit, quia nulla societas est, quae donationis causa interponitur, nec inter ceteros et propter hoc nec inter virum et uxorem.

On *fine* cf. Vat. Fr., 294. Since such a contract was void by partnership law, 17. 2. 5. 2, this passage is perhaps the strongest evidence that Ulpian did not agree with 23; it is not clear how Bremer, *op. cit.*, 213, avoids it. The distinction here is clearly that between executed and executory transactions; an acceptilation in the course of partnership business would presumably convalesce; Ulpian is referring only to claims that would have to be made in the partnership action.

---

25. Idem erit dicendum et si emptio contracta sit donationis causa: nam nulla erit.

The passage is very difficult to comprehend; its result not only violates the logical rule expressed by Windscheid, § 75 n. 3, Brinz, § 524 n. 7, the policy continually observed in our field of allowing the transaction its maximum effect and the preceding decision as to common ownership, but also the principle expressed by the next passage. The *nam* clause does not explain *idem*, it contradicts it. If any text on the subject of simulated sales is interpolated it is this one, approved by Pringsheim, Z., 1921, 325. It really amounts to nothing less than a punishment for the simulation.

---

26. Plane si minoris res venierit donationis causa vel postea pretium sit remissum, admittemus donationem valere ad senatus consultum.

The confusion of Partsch and Pringsheim is well brought out by their treatment of this passage, for in the attempt to maintain the same thesis one appeals to this text as a genuine reproduction of the old law, while the other repudiates it as Byzantine.

---

27. Si quis sponsam habuerit, deinde eandem uxorem duxerit, cum non liceret, an donationes quasi in sponsalibus factae valeant, videamus. et Iulianus tractat hanc quaestionem in minore duodecim annis, si in domum quasi mariti inmatura sit deducta: ait enim hanc sponsam esse, etsi uxor non sit. sed est verius, quod Labeoni videtur et a nobis et a Papiniano libro decimo quaestionum probatum est, ut, si quidem praecesserint sponsalia, durent, quamvis iam uxorem esse putet qui duxit, si vero non praecesserint, neque sponsalia esse, quoniam non fuerunt, neque nuptias, quod nuptiae esse non potuerunt. ideoque si sponsalia antecesserint, valet donatio: si minus, nulla est, quia non quasi ad extraneam, sed quasi ad uxorem fecit et ideo nec oratio locum habebit.

Cf. Savigny, 172 (mistranslated); Windscheid, n. 19; for Beseler's view, *supra* 3. 1. In showing the hopeless muddle created by interpolation in this and the next passage it is hardly possible to do more than retail the brilliant researches of Faber, De Err., D. 79, E. 6, ignored not only by Beseler but by Pampaloni, A. G., 55. 516, 505. The first objection to this decision is that to avoid a conflict with 65 it is necessary arbitrarily to suppose either with Accursius that *sponsalia* had there taken place, or with Savigny that the invalidity was known. Second, if the reason for the invalidity is the ignorance, the existence of *sponsalia* is irrelevant. Third, the ignorance itself is as unimportant as possible. It would be a strange rule that a gift valid by law and accompanied by an eminently just cause should be revocable because the giver mistakenly believed in facts which would have invalidated the gift contrary to his intent. Fourth, having arrived at this senseless conclusion that the gift is void, the text then makes the amazing assertion that it cannot convalesce, and all this in a case where neither party is at all at fault as in 3. 1 or the next passage. The decision is the unusually inept attempt of an amateur who was reading Ulpian's discussion in 23. 1. 9 to apply our prohibition to that case.

---

28. Sed si senator libertinam desponderit vel tutor pupillam vel quis alius ex his, qui matrimonium copulare prohibentur, et duxerit, an donatio quasi in sponsalibus facta valeat? et putem etiam sponsalia inprobanda et quasi ab indignis ea quae donata sunt ablata fisco vindicari.

As Faber's arguments, *loc. cit.*, E. 4, from 23. 1. 16 are not powerful, the genuineness of that text need not be discussed, although it may be that Riccobono's objections, St. Fadda, 1. 305 ff., valid for *id.* 15, do not apply to the type of marriage in 16. The first difficulty with this passage is that it is thoroughly arbitrary to employ a harsher rule between putative fiancés than between putative spouses, C. 5. 16. 7, cf. *supra* 3. 1. Accursius tries to reconcile the decision with that in the Code by supposing that here the invalidity of the gift was known, a factor which would be present in most gifts between legal spouses, cf. Pothier, *ad h. l.* It is uncertain whether this is the view of Savigny and Windscheid, who justify the decision on the grounds of fault in the donor. If they mean that he is the law-breaking party the result is in glaring contradiction with the principles applied to the point, cf. 23. 2. 63; 30. 128; 34. 9. 2. 2. Faber's conjecture should be adopted that the decision represents a false analogy of Tribonian's from 34. 9. 2. 1, where the rule is quite correct; see Windscheid, § 548 n. 9; incorrect, Di Marzo, Lezioni sul Mat., 24, who accepts the text without question. It seems strange that the validity of gifts between *sponsi* should have been even doubted, for the objection in 3. 1 has no application.

---

33. IDEM *libro trigesimo sexto ad Sabinum* Si stipulata fuerit mulier annuum, id ex stipulatu petere constante matrimonio non potest. sed si manente matrimonio decessisse maritus proponatur, puto, quia in annuo quoque donatio vertitur, posse dici stipulationem confirmari ex senatus consulto. 1. Si uxor marito annuum versa vice praestiterit, restituetur ei hoc et poterit vindicare id quod exstat: credo poterit et condicere, in quantum locupletior factus est, quia non tam sollemne est annuum, quod maritus uxori pendit et quod uxor marito praestat, immo incongruens est et contra sexus naturam. 2. Et si forte maritus ab uxore stipulatus sit id annuum decesseritque mulier constante matrimonio, dicendum erit ex oratione donationem convalescere.

Cf. *supra* 23. This text is placed by Lenel under the rubric *De Retentionibus*, but it is hard to discover any relation between those and confirmation of a promise by death, cf. De Medio, 387 ff. It is more likely that it occurred in a discussion of dotal pacts, cf. 2. 14. 49; 23. 4. 32. De Medio is forced to hold *vindicare* interpolated, one of the few words accepted by Beseler, Z., 445, who suggests that Ulpian said that H. might give money for W.'s support. If properly limited, 21. 1; 31. 10, this hypothesis is plausible, as it explains 1. There is no reason for eradicating 2, for it is probable that the original dealt with all four cases: promise and payment by either party. Gradenwitz, 253 ff., tries to show that some instalments had been paid, overlooking the general terms of 2, while in view of 45. 1. 16. 1 the importance of that factor may be doubted.

---

34. IDEM *libro quadragesimo tertio ad Sabinum* Sive uxor marito res donasset isque eas in dotem pro communi filia dedisset, sive post donationem, quam in maritum contulit,

uxor passa est eum pro filia in dotem dare, benigne dici potest, etsi prima donatio nullius momenti est, attamen ex sequenti consensu valere dotis dationem.

It seems strange that Lenel should place this text before 23. 3. 34; Vat. Fr., 269, for it represents a special and "benign" consequence of that rule. The fact that W. was allowed to constitute a *dos* for her daughter in spite of H.'s expectancy therein is not easy to reconcile with the ostensible decision of 59, which would require that the *dos* be *recapticia*. What if W. gratuitously mancipates a slave to X, knowing that he has conditionally and gratuitously promised the property to H.? In the main case it is probable that the intent is decisive, *i. e.*, the transaction must be *dotandi*, not *donandi animo* as where W. constituted the *dos* to relieve H. of an enforcible obligation to do so whether by contract or law, cf. Rabel, 514 n. 4. Hence if W. may directly establish a *dos*, she may do it indirectly by giving the property to H. for that purpose, 23. 3. 5. 9. But if, as here, the property is given outright, it will not do with Bonfante, S. G. 3. 201, to hold that H.'s later establishment is valid, for he has no title to the property, cf. 41. 7. 5. pr. Three cases are possible, all of which are mentioned: where W. expressly consents to the transaction, where she knows and is silent, where she is ignorant. The text first decides the last case thus rendering mention of the others superfluous. It then speaks of benignity in connection with what seems an express ratification, the easiest hypothesis imaginable, involving as it does a *traditio brevi manu*. Such an absence of logical coherence arouses suspicions which are voiced by Beseler, 3. 37. Although there is room for nothing but vague conjectures as to the original, it seems reasonable to suppose that the "benignity" consisted in holding that the silence constituted a fresh manifestation of intent.

---

35. IDEM *libro trigesimo quarto ad edictum* Si non secundum legitimam observationem divortium factum sit, donationes post tale divortium factae nullius momenti sunt, cum non videatur solutum matrimonium.

The law referred to is that of Augustus, prescribing the manner of repudiation, 24. 2. 9; 32. 11. 1. 1. The decision seems to conflict with the rule implied by 32. 13; 64. A reconciliation is often made by assuming it to be interpolated, cf.

Solazzi, Bull., 34. 315. Another view is that of Glück, 26. 73 n. 67, cf. Bonfante, 248, who maintains that Augustus' legislation did not cover divorce by mutual consent. A far more satisfactory hypothesis has been offered by Levy, 34, *i. e.*, that the form had to be fulfilled by H. only in case of adultery in order to escape the charge of *lenocinium*, cf. 48. 5. 30 ff., *contra*, however, Bull., 35. 211. Not so appealing seems his theory that the form applied only to a *manus* marriage to permit emancipation of an absent wife. Two objections may be made: first, it is hard to understand the relevance of emancipation under the adultery statute; second, the same problem must often have occurred as to an absent child, in which case, if emancipation is impossible, disinheritance would seem to be an adequate remedy, cf. Buckland, T., 133. Furthermore, if this text is interpreted as such a case, with Levy, 45, the decision would be banal, and the problem, that of *manus*, thoroughly out of date in Ulpian's day.

---

36. Paulus *libro trigesimo sexto ad edictum* Si donatae res exstant, etiam vindicari poterunt: sed quia causam possidendi donatio praestitit, nisi reddatur res, aestimatio facienda est iusto pretio caverique possidenti debebit de evictione simpli, quanti ea res sit: idque etiam Pedio videtur.

Although De Medio attempts, 386, to refer this passage to *retentio*, it seems almost a conclusive proof against his theory. It is to a vindication only that the words *nisi reddatur* can refer, as well as the difficulty of the estimation caused by the *juramentum* peculiar to that action, which is refused because the donor might recover more than his impoverishment. Levy, Z., 1921, 493 n. 6 believes that the *cautio* is imposed because the defendant has the object *volente domino*, cf. 6. 1. 35. 2, which is not true after suit has been brought, cf. 37; F. Mommsen, Beiträge, 2. 103. The reason seems the same as usual, *viz.*, to prevent W.'s impoverishment by having to pay twice the value — a principle which would lead to rejection of Mommsen's view that the *interesse* is meant by the words *justo pretio;* for the method of computing the *cautio* cf. Machelard, 291 n. 1. It has recently been maintained by Albertario, Bull., 31. 9, that *sed quia . . . res sit* is interpolated, which, as Levy shows, Z., 1922, 534, is quite impossible, for in Byzantine law the question of *justum pretium* could not here arise. It is odd that Albertario, who believes that W. had the interdicts, should object to *causam possidendi*, which of course is to be interpreted in connection with 6. 1. 9, cf. *infra* 46.

---

1. Sponsus alienum anulum sponsae muneri misit et post nuptias pro eo suum dedit: quidam et Nerva putant fieri eum mulieris, quia tunc factam donationem confirmare videtur, non novam inchoare: quam sententiam veram esse accepi.

The words *fieri eum mulieris* speak against De Medio's view. The facts of this case make it extremely unlikely that the transaction was performed with the intent merely to make an exchange. The decision seems contrary to the principle of 32. 22, even if H. intended before marriage to give a ring of his own and from poverty or convenience gave another's ring as a sort of *arrha*. Since, as Gentilis shows, 1. ch. 1, the Romans observed the custom of the engagement ring, cf. Beseler, 4. 105, this exception may be explained like that in 14 as a case where there existed a strong independent motive for the transaction.

---

37. Iulianus *libro septimo decimo digestorum* Si mulier dolo fecerit, ne res exstaret sibi a marito donata, vel ad exhibendum vel damni iniuriae cum ea agi poterit, maxime si post divortium id commiserit.

On the strength of 10. 4. 14, Pernice, 2. 1. 409 n. 4, holds *maxime, etc.*, interpolated. These passages are those which suggested Savigny's theory, *supra* 5. 17, that the *oratio* introduced the defense of consumption. The conclusion depends upon a confusion in the conception of *dolus*, cf. *supra ad* 9. 2. 38. It is hard to understand what *dolus* there can be in one who obeys the request of the owner; it did not occur to the author of 10. 4. 14 to suggest the action *ad exh.* in 31. pr., cf. Rabel, 442 n. 2; see also 29. pr. It cannot be important whether there is consent to the specific act committed or whether it is general, as in any gift between H. and W. The *dolus* can consist only in the knowledge or suppressed suspicion (*culpa proxima dolo*, cf. 16. 3. 11) that the donor has changed his mind and wishes to reclaim the object, after which it is natural to hold the donee for *levissima culpa*, cf. C. 8. 55. 7. 2, and the remarks of Petražycki, Fruchtvert., 190. As to the action for damage, cf. *supra* 3. 10.

---

38. ALFENUS *libro tertio digestorum a Paulo epitomatorum* Servus communis viri et fratris eius puerum donavit uxori fratris: pro qua parte is servus qui donasset viri esset, pro ea parte munus non esse factum mulieris respondit.

The translation of this passage in Pothier shows how telling is Beseler's criticism, Z., 445. Not to mention the objectionable repetition of *frater*, it seems incredible that the validity of the gift should depend upon the ownership in the donor slave without the slightest reference to that in the one donated, yet cf. Buckland, 391. Hence Beseler supposes that the former had bought the latter, thus acquiring for each master, 10. 3. 24. pr.; 41. 1. 45. Since express authorization was needed for gifts of *peculium* it would not seem a very difficult case where such has been given by the brother. Even in the most complicated cases ownership in the donor slave would seem to be immaterial; *e. g.*, where on account of a usufruct the property was in suspense, 41. 1. 43. 2; Salkowski, 199 ff., or where in our case after an order by both brother and H. to give W. 10, the slave, obeying the former only, used by mistake the latter's *peculium.*

---

1. Idem iuris erit, si ex tribus fratribus unus uxorem haberet et rem communem uxori donasset: nam ex tertia parte mulieris res facta non est, ex duabus autem partibus reliquis, si id scissent fratres aut posteaquam donata esset ratum habuissent, non debere mulierem reddere.

Beseler, *loc. cit.*, regards this passage as a worthless illustration. He does not object to the ratification, cf. 34, a possibility which must always be remembered even where the donor survives the donee.

---

39. IULIANUS *libro quinto ex Minicio* Vir uxori pecuniam cum donare vellet, permisit ei, ut a debitore suo stipuletur: illa cum id fecisset, priusquam pecuniam auferret, divortium fecit: quaero, utrum vir eam summam petere debeat an ea

promissione propter donationis causam actio nulla esset. respondi inanem fuisse eam stipulationem. sed si promissor mulieri ignorans solvisset, si quidem pecunia exstat, vindicare eam debitor potest: sed si actiones suas marito praestare paratus est, doli mali exceptione se tuebitur ideoque maritus hanc pecuniam debitoris nomine vindicando consequetur. sed si pecunia non exstat et mulier locupletior facta est, maritus eam petet: intellegitur enim ex re mariti locupletior facta esse mulier, quoniam debitor doli mali exceptione se tueri potest.

The fiction of 39. 5. 21. 1 is inapplicable here because the promise had no effect whatever, differing in this respect from a tradition, 3. 12, which in fact changes the situation; the usefulness of the rule of nullity may be seen from the results of the attempt to employ the fiction made by Gradenwitz, 246 ff. As for the payment, Savigny's reconciliation, 592 n. *a*, of this text with 3. 12 on the ground that the transferor had here no intent to benefit H., though not conclusive on the theory there adopted that in neither case has H. the intent to receive the benefit, at least brings out the fact that this is a harder case for the fiction, so that it does not necessarily show a divergence between Julian and Celsus. It is more often said, Riccobono, Bull., 8. 201, 222; De Ruggiero, A. G., 63. 436, that this passage is in perfect accord with 46. 3. 38. 1, attributed to Julian, a remark which is so far from true that the difference may be said to be irreconcilable, cf. Beseler, 3. 187, whose suggestion of interpolation would have to be accepted if every citation from Africanus' Questions must refer to Julian. Such a result is open to doubt because this particular dispute is preserved in another connection, cf. 20. 5. 12. 1 with 21. 2. 38; v. Tuhr, Grünhut's Z., 25. 559 ff.; Dernburg, Pfandrecht, 2. 194 ff.; those who suspect these latter fragments, cf. Beseler, 3. 70; Riccobono, 610 ff., fail to consider not only the fortifying presence of our texts, but above all C. 4. 2. 2, inexplicably neglected by all, even Windscheid, on which cf. the Gloss; Schilling, Inst., § 226 n. *q*. As Julian or Minicius clearly states, the condiction of H. and that of the debtor, though like our action of assumpsit enjoying the same name, are substantially different actions, that of the latter being the usual claim by the giver for *tantundem*, that of the former being only for enrichment, *supra* 5. 18, and depending not upon a *datio* as in 12. 1. 11. 2, wrongly cited by

Gradenwitz, but upon the *negotium* of permission, assuming that Julian required a *negotium* in our field, 12. 1. 33, but cf. 5. 6, 7; 25. 1. 11. 1. As the decision is thus contrary to Pflüger's requirement of a *datio*, he holds, 34, that it dealt with the *retentio*, failing to observe that if the debtor has the condiction H. has given nothing. Aside from its verbosity our decision is merely an application of the principle of 20. 5. 12. 1; the plural *actiones*, attacked by Beseler, may refer to the remedies of 37. Africanus, on the other hand, followed the practice employed by Ulpian in 21. 2. 38, allowing cession of an action which was not the same in the hands of the assignee as in those of the assignor. Beseler somewhat captiously objects to his omission to mention the vindication, which must have been rare in the case of money, cf. *supra* 5. 18; 7. 3 In conclusion it may be repeated that while this text is not in conflict with 3. 12, it cannot be reconciled with 38. 1. *cit.*, for Julian's direct concession of the condiction to H. would apply *a fortiori* if the debtor had paid for him and not in pursuance of his own promise.

---

40. Ulpianus *libro secundo responsorum* Quod apiscendae dignitatis gratia ab uxore in maritum collatum est, eatenus ratum est, quatenus dignitati supplendae opus est:

41. Licinius Rufinus *libro sexto regularum* nam et imperator Antoninus constituit, ut ad processus viri uxor ei donare possit.

42. Gaius *libro undecimo ad edictum provinciale* Nuper ex indulgentia principis Antonini recepta est alia causa donationis, quam dicimus honoris causa: ut ecce si uxor viro lati clavi petenti gratia donet vel ut equestris ordinis fiat vel ludorum gratia.

Cf. Ulp., 7. 1; *supra* 5. 17. The name of Gaius proves that D. Pius is meant; for learning on the point, see Glück, 26. 14 ff.

---

43. Paulus *libro singulari regularum* Inter virum et uxorem exilii causa donatio fieri potest.

Under Arcadius and Honerius, C. 9. 49. 9. 2, the rule laid down by Constantine, C. Th. 9. 42. 1, is repeated that gifts of this kind are void as a fraud upon the fisc, cf. 48. 20. 11. 1; our text is the more surprising as it seems to permit entire preemption of the sovereign, cf. the interpolated 13. 1. It is an additional peculiarity that a decision of such a delicate and doubtful point should occur in a beginner's manual, see Karlowa, 1. 747, for which reason it may be conjectured that *exilii* was interpolated for *divortii* by the same hand which dealt with 13. 1. The only other possible hypothesis, cf. Gentilis, 2. ch. 32, is that of Cohn, Beiträge, 217 (cf. Glück, 26. 77 ff.; Machelard, 271), that the text refers to support of an exiled spouse, 23. 3. 73. 1.

---

44. NERATIUS *libro quinto membranarum* Si extraneus rem viri ignorans eius esse ignoranti uxori, ac ne viro quidem sciente eam suam esse, donaverit, mulier recte eam usucapiet. idemque iuris erit, si is, qui in potestate viri erat, credens se patrem familias esse uxori patris donaverit. sed si vir rescierit suam rem esse, priusquam usucapiatur, vindicareque eam poterit nec volet 'et hoc et mulier noverit,' interrumpetur possessio, quia transiit in causam ab eo factae donationis. ipsius mulieris scientia propius est, ut nullum adquisitioni dominii eius adferat impedimentum: non enim omnimodo uxores ex bonis virorum, sed ex causa donationis ab ipsis factae adquirere prohibitae sunt.

The first gift is valid because, unlike the second, it was not made by a prohibited person. The only difficulty is as to the requirement of ignorance in the *extraneus* (Di Marzo's suggestion of interpolation has been unanimously rejected, A. G. 72. 255 n. 2), a factor which is immaterial from the point of view of our prohibition. The phrase supports the theory of Landsberg in the dispute mentioned by Windscheid, § 452 n. 8; cf. Bonfante, S. G., 2. 567 n. 2, who notices the possibility of collusion. Far more serious is this requirement in the case of the son, where, as Bonfante remarks, it is unimportant from the standpoint of *usucapio*, so that the rule ought to apply in all other cases, as where H. *sui juris* gives, mistakenly thinking that a divorce has occurred. It seems incredible that the policy of our prohibition could be thus nullified by a mistake; the situation is the converse of that in 32. 27, and open to much the same criticism; thus the words *credens se patrem familias* seem more objectionable than anything following. For various views on the substance and form of the remainder, see Machelard, 287 ff.; Glück, It. trans., 24. 16 n. *b*; Zanzucchi, A. G., 72. 264; Riccobono, St. Moriani, 1. 394 ff.; Bonfante, S. G., 2. 567 ff. As punctuated by Savigny the text implies that the transaction can be invalidated only by an understanding between H. and W. equivalent to a *traditio brevi manu* or attornment. Although Savigny's grounds for the belief that knowledge of H. alone is immaterial have been refuted by Machelard, the decision does not seem unreasonable enough to justify the extensive resort to interpolation made by Bonfante and Zanzucchi. As is remarked by Keysser, *cit.* Ancona-Glück, this case differs from 5. 6 in that here the gift is that of the *extraneus; i. e.*, there H. took advantage of the situation to make the gift, here he merely does not prevent the completion of a gift the origin of which is quite unconnected with him. It is then not only reasonable but perhaps correct to hold that it was not H. but another who made a gift even where H. knew of the transaction when it took place. As for W.'s knowledge the statement of its insignificance is correct as regards our prohibition, a fact which should give pause to those like Zanzucchi who hold that supervening bad faith prevented *usucapio pro donato*, cf. Cuq, 287 n. 1. Riccobono's view that the case is not one of supervening bad faith but of removal of the just cause involves a distinction difficult to grasp, for W., in learning of H.'s ownership, will not often suppose that he too intended a gift.

---

45. Ulpianus *libro septimo decimo ad edictum* Marcellus libro septimo digestorum scribit etiam eum detrahere sine mulieris damno et citra metum senatus consulti, quod detrahentibus negotiationis causa occurrit.

For a full discussion of this and the twin fragment, 30. 43. 1, see Riccobono, 453 ff. His view, shared by Lenel, Marcellus 89; Cujas, Obs., 5. 26, that the texts dealt with a gift seems untenable (see Schulz, Z., 1913, 64; Monier, Tignum Junctum, 93 n. 1) not only on the practical ground that the situation is exactly the same if the house had been built not as a gift but for H.'s temporary pleasure, but because it is theoretically impossible to make a gift by building on one's own land with one's own materials, cf. Bechmann, 2. 255 n. 1. It was an idea of Tribonian's to insert this passage in our title; it belongs in a discussion of the retentions for expenses, Lenel, Marcellus, 94. For these reasons it is impossible to follow or to agree to Riccobono's treatment of the passage. He supposes that this privilege, involving, not the *jus tollendi* of a non-owner, but the right of a promisor to alter his property, is classical as regards a gift, but interpolated as regards expenses, 489 ff. *ad* 25. 1. 9. The action *de tigno* has no connection with either case, but it is a further error to use it as an analogy to one only. For a discussion of the *S. Cta. Hosidianum* and *Volusianum* see Schulz.

---

46. IDEM *libro septuagesimo secundo ad edictum* Inter virum et uxorem nec possessionis ulla donatio est.

On this subject, see Fitting, St. Brugi, 233 ff. As was apparently first perceived by Cuperus, De Natura Poss., 104, this text dealt with the interdict *utrubi* and is to be placed after 41. 2. 13. 11 or 12; incorrect, Buckland, T., 205 n. 10. The almost unanimous modern view is that the donee acquired interdictal possession, Ferrini, Pand., 309 n. 1; Vangerow, 1. 352; the few who notice this passage, *e. g.*, Lenel, Ed., 469 n. 8, are therefore forced to interpret it as merely excluding the *accessio temporis*, and this in spite of the fact that *ulla donatio* seems as clear as any phrase could be, and that 41. 2. 13. 12 becomes thus irrelevant and almost incomprehensible. Before the modern scientific method of studying the texts was discovered, this view rested solely upon 43. 16. 1. 10, see Savigny, Besitz, 7 ed., Beil. 21. Yet in the course of a dispute on the meaning of "natural" possession, of two recent authors who agree that the latter text is hopelessly interpolated, each bases his interpretation on the fact, apparently so clear that it is not discussed, that in classical law the donee spouse enjoyed the protection of the interdicts, see Riccobono, Z., 1910, 348; Albertario, Bull., 27. 283 ff. Except for that passage everything in the Digest on the point seems clear. Possession was not only a privilege of value (thus inability to use the interdict was cause for recovery from the seller, 19. 1. 11. 13; 41. 2. 22; 45. 1. 38. 3) but also, Buckland, T., 205, to the contrary notwithstanding, apparently a *res* in view of the possibility of *furtum possessionis*, for which reasons a gift thereof would seem obviously to involve the necessary impoverishment and enrichment; further, it would constitute a true stultification of the law to help the donee to recover possession of a thing the transfer of which had been absolutely void, cf. 41. 2. 30. 1; Jhering, Besitzwille, trad. Meulenaare, 54. On the other hand there was no objection to giving effect to the transaction as far as it did not involve benefiting the donee; in fact, if the donor's vindication is ancient, the donee must always have possessed in this sense, 6. 1. 9; hence Julian did not make a very bold step if, as is possible, he introduced the rule that the donee might be sued in the *hereditatis petitio*, 5. 4. 13. 1; cf. 41. 2. 1. 4; 41. 6. 1. 2, the peculiar requirements of which exactly covered our case. As for 1. 10 *cit.*, whether it is an example of the Byzantine tendency to restrict self-help or whether it represents a classical extension, the term "natural" possession seems enough to mark it as an exception; for it does not seem plausible to hold that this was ever a generic term for interdictal possession. If it were so clear that the donee could bring the interdicts, in view of the certainty that he could not usucapt, such texts as this and 26 would be inexplicable. It is then probable that the donor was treated like a lunatic incapable of alienation, so that the donee was not allowed the interdict as a *precario tenens*, cf. 41. 2. 10. 1 with 32. 5.

---

47. Celsus *libro primo digestorum* Utrum negotium uxoris gerens an officio mariti ductus in rem eius impenderit vir, facti, non iuris est quaestio: coniectura eius rei ex modo et ex genere impensae non difficilis est.

As Lenel shows, this was taken from a treatise on *negotiorum gestio*, so that its bearing here is doubtful. The word *officio* may indicate a permitted gift where H. feeds W.'s slaves who are working for him, cf. Pothier, *ad h. l.* If this is not so, the decision is merely on the point of pleading; the Gloss is guilty of an anachronism in mentioning the *oratio*. The question of *neg. gestio* may excuse a digression against the widely maintained theory that acceptance was needed for a gift. Two of its supporters, Burckhard, 140; Ascoli, 61 ff., remark that the *an. don.* in *neg. gestio* is important only to prevent recovery of the expenses, which would not be true in our field, cf. *supra* 31. 2; 32. 9. Two cases should be distinguished: first, where the enrichment is not accepted, 5. 6, 31. 2; second, where it is accepted, but the fact of enrichment, 5. 7, 31. 3, or the identity of the giver, as in cases of interposition, is unknown. If anything in our title is sure it would seem to be that acceptance is immaterial, yet Accarias, 1. 785 n. 3, misled by 44, holds that here alone is it needed, cf. Ferrini, Pand., 846, who well exposes the lack of evidence for the theory in any connection.

---

48. Idem *libro nono digestorum* Quae iam nuptae maritus donavit, viri manent et potest ea vindicare: nec quicquam refert, quod ampla legata ab uxore ei relicta sunt.

De Medio, 588, must hold this passage interpolated, even to *viri manent.*

---

49. Marcellus *libro septimo digestorum* Sulpicius Marcello. Mulier, quae ad communem filium volebat, qui in potestate patris erat, post mortem patris fundum pervenire, eum patri 'tradidit,' uti post mortem restituatur filio. quaero, an donatio tibi videatur, ut nihil agatur, 'an valeat quidem, sed mulieri potestas datur, si noluerit, eum repetere,' respondit: si color vel titulus, ut sic dixerim, donationi quaesitus est, nihil valebit 'traditio,' idem si hoc exigit uxor, ut aliquid ex ea re interim commodi sentiret maritus: alioquin si solo eius ministerio usa est et id egit, ut vel revocare sibi liceret vel ut res cum omni emolumento per patrem postea ad filium transiret, cur non idem perinde sit ratum ac si cum extraneo tale negotium contraxisset, hoc est extraneo in hanc causam 'tradidisset'?

Cf. Beseler, 3. 101; Biondi, 46 ff.; Senn, 46 n. 4; Haymann, Z., 1917, 238 n. 2. There seems to be general agreement that the case was that of a fiduciary mancipation and that the mention of the right to revoke is interpolated, even though Senn later states, 72, that such a transaction is impossible between H. and W., and all believe revocation was always a matter of course, so that no motive for the change can be perceived. Beseler explains the decision by the remark that the mancipation is valid, so that ownership is apparently transferred, but is vitiated by the later transfer of "possession," cf. 46, thus arriving at a case of reversion of ownership by a resolutive condition implied in law, cf. 8; 9. 2. This theory is probably not even correct if the *animus donandi* had been conceived between mancipation and delivery. He goes on to say that *omni emolumento* is "absolutely inconceivable," as if the father could not keep a separate account of the farm profits. The idea that the delivery necessarily constitutes a *neg. mixtum* is refuted by 5. 8; 7. 8; equally false is the theory that the whole transaction is void if such is the case, which is belied in the clearest terms by 39. 5. 18. pr. and renders the term meaningless. The original decision is shown by *color*, but the point has been lost in the interpolation. The whole transaction is void only if the *modus* was a cloak to hide the sole intent to benefit H.; if there is an intent also to benefit the son, the rule of 7. 9 should apply, H. benefiting no more than in 17. pr., 18; cf. Savigny, 62 ff. For Haymann's attempt to show that this is not a gift *sub modo* cf. *supra* 5. 2.

---

50. IAVOLENUS *libro tertio decimo epistularum* Si, cum mulier viginti servum emisset, in eam emptionem vir quinque venditori dedit, divortio facto omnimodo vir eam summam exiget neque ad rem pertinet, an is servus deterior factus sit: nam et si mortuus esset, quinque exactio ei competeret. quaeritur enim, an mulier ex viri patrimonio locupletior sit eo tempore, quo 'de dote' agebatur: facta autem intellegitur, quae aere alieno suo interventu viri liberata est, quod potuisset adhuc debere, si vir pecuniam non solvisset: neque enim interest, ex qua causa mulier pecuniam debuit, utrum creditam an eam quam ex emptione praestare debeat.

---

1. Quod si mulier non emerat servum, sed ut emeret, a viro pecuniam accepit, tum vel mortuo vel deteriore facto servo damnum ad virum pertinebit: quia quod aliter emptura non fuit, nisi pecuniam a viro accepisset, hoc consumptum ei perit qui donavit, si modo in rerum natura esse desiit: nec videtur mulier locupletior esse, quae neque a creditore suo liberata est neque id possidet quod ex pecunia viri emerat.

It is hard to follow the connection between this passage and 39. 5. 2. 7 discovered by Cuq, 532 n. 5. The statement that W. is freed in one case and not in the other seems to show hopeless confusion, for if there is room for the distinction mentioned *supra* 7. 7 the exactly reverse result would be expected. Pernice suggests, 3. 199 n. 2, that the end of 1 is interpolated, but the pr. does not so easily lend itself to such measures. Why W. should there be freed in view of 3. 12; 5. 4; 39, is an anomaly for which no explanation can be suggested. It is none the less true that the decisions themselves are correct and the distinction of the greatest importance, *supra* 7. 1, which may tend to excuse Javolenus, if indeed it was he, who could justify the results no better.

---

51. POMPONIUS *libro quinto ad Quintum Mucium* Quintus Mucius ait, cum in controversiam venit, unde ad mulierem quid pervenerit, et verius et honestius est quod non demonstratur unde habeat existimari a viro aut qui in potestate eius esset ad eam pervenisse. evitandi autem turpis quaestus gratia circa uxorem hoc videtur Quintus Mucius probasse.

Some of the problems created by this presumption are discussed by Tenge, Arch., 45. 305 ff. (cf. Bonfante, 224 n. 2; Segrè, St. Brugi, 416 ff.) who identifies it with the *unus casus*, J. 4. 6. 2. Alibrandi's remark, St. e Doc., 13. 69, that its existence implies that such gifts are not "bad or unbecoming" is of slight force, for the policy of our law is not founded on the view that gifts are bad but requires only that they shall be freely revocable. Indeed when he held that this rule antedates our prohibition it is to be regretted that Alibrandi did not mention its original function, a point of some obscurity. Even as applied in our field its value is not clear, as it does not appear how the *turpis quaestus* (or *quaestio*, Mo. *ad h. l.*) is avoided. W. must be allowed to show that she got the property by sale, deposit, *etc.*, or as a birthday present from her uncle; and if she is shameless enough to prove that it was a gift from an adulterer or even an admirer, it is hard to see how H.'s claim thereto can be recognized, *contra* Segrè. The presumption will work against repentant wives and in favor of brazen defiance. Beseler thus declares, 3. 50, that the last sentence is interpolated, forgetting *honestius* and that a poor reason is better than none, but cf. Dernburg, Pand., 8 ed., § 412 n. 2. The rule must certainly be restricted to gifts during marriage; Tenge, 314 ff., seems to overlook the possibility that W. could prove possession of the property on her wedding day without being able to state its origin.

52. PAPINIANUS *libro decimo questionum* Si vir uxori donationis causa rem vilius locaverit, locatio nulla est: cum autem depositum inter eas personas minoris donationis causa aestimatur, depositum est. haec ideo tam varie, quia locatio quidem sine mercede certa contrahi non potest, depositum autem et citra aestimationem quoque dari potest.

In attaching such importance to *nulla* as contradicting 5. 5, Lammfromm, 141 ff., forgets the rule of 18. Unlike ownership, enjoyment may be given without any consideration, so that if the rent is not simulated, H. may collect it. All that is meant by *nulla* is that the donor may not resign his right of revocation at will. On the deposit, see Beseler, 2. 30, 3. 9, 4. 69, whose suspicions have increased, though he appears to agree with the result. The last sentence is indeed weak, for the fact that a *dos* can be given without estimation does not prevent a gift in 7. 5. A better reason might be that the deposit involves no benefit to the depositary; the question should rather be whether acceptance is a gift by her, which is not so because it amounts only to personal services as in 31. pr. The hypothesis seems odd because the pact would seem *pro tanto* to violate the rule of 16. 3. 1. 7, cf., however, 2. 14. 7. 15; *id.* 27. 3; Albertario, Bull., 25. 33 ff., should have considered this passage; furthermore, it smacks of a simulated transaction to say: "I deposit this property with you as to which you are not liable except for *dolus*, but if you should happen to be malicious, you need return only half the value." If a pact, to be liable for *culpa levis*, 16. 3. 1. 6, were given *donandi an.* the obligation might be valid as including no more than the duty of a good wife. The case is analogous to H.'s duty to support, neither fulfilment nor release of which is a gift, the latter because the duty is not legally enforcible, the former not from any idea of a natural obligation but because it falls outside the policy of our prohibition.

---

1. Uxor viro fructum fundi ab herede suo dari, quod si datus non fuisset, certam pecuniam mortis causa promitti curavit: defuncto viro viva muliere stipulatio solvitur, ut traditio, quae mandante uxore mortis causa facta est: nam quo casu inter exteros condictio nascitur, inter maritos nihil agitur.

It is not easy to follow De Medio's attack, 390, upon this passage. He agrees with Faber that 11. 1 is interpolated because it allows ownership to pass at once, a consequence which, on his theory, was permissible for all gifts between H. and W. before Justinian. In objecting to *traditio solvitur* Haymann, Z., 1917, 239 n. 4, forgets 8; 20.

---

53. IDEM *libro quarto responsorum* Mortis suae causa genero vel nurui socerum frustra donare convenit, quia mortuo socero nuptiae non solvuntur: nec interest, an pater filium vel filiam exheredaverit. divortii species eadem ratione diversa est.

Cf. 32. 19, 20; 39. 6. 11. No reason can be given for this decision except that it was due to a mistaken assimilation of gifts *m. c.* to those under the *oratio*. It seems indefensible where by disinheritance the patrimonial identity is severed at the time the gift takes effect; and it would even be possible to hold the transaction always valid on the analogy to a legacy.

---

1. Res in dotem aestimatas consentiente viro mulier in usu habuit: usu deteriores si fiant, damni compensatio non admittitur. easdem res non potest mulier sibi quasi donatas defendere ex illis verbis, quibus donationes ei a viro legatae sunt, cum eiusmodi species neque donari neque auferri videntur.

Cf. 18. Lenel suggests a connection with 23. 3. 69. 8.

---

54. IDEM *libro octavo responsorum* Vir usuras promissae dotis in stipulatum deduxerat easque non petierat: cum per omne tempus matrimonii sumptibus suis uxorem et eius familiam vir exhiberet, dote praelegata, sed et donationibus verbis fideicommissi confirmatis legato quidem dotis usuras non contineri videbatur, sed titulo donationis remissas.

Cf. 21. 1; Gothofredus *ad h. l.* The inactivity would constitute a gift even if W. supported herself, provided it was for reasons unconnected therewith, cf. *supra* 7. 1; 28. 6.

---

55. PAULUS *libro sexto quaestionum* Uxor marito suo pecuniam donavit: maritus ex pecunia sibi donata aut mobilem

aut soli rem comparavit: solvendo non est et res extant: quaero, si mulier revocet donationem, an utiliter condicticia experiatur? videtur enim maritus, quamvis solvendo non sit, ex donatione locupletior effectus, cum pecunia mulieris res comparata exstet. respondi: locupletiorem esse ex donatione negari non potest: non enim quaerimus, quid deducto aere alieno liberum habeat, sed quid ex re mulieris possideat. solo enim separatur hic ab eo, cui res donata est, quod ibi res mulieris permanet et vindicari directo potest: et erit deterior causa viri, si ei pecunia quatenus res valet, non ultra id tamen quod donatum est, condicatur, quam si dotis iudicio conveniatur. sed nihil prohibet etiam in rem utilem mulieri in ipsas res accommodare.

Upon the hypothesis that it offers an example of the suspicious *utilis* vindication the last sentence of this passage is generally held interpolated, cf. v. Mayr, Z., 1905, 113 ff. Such a conclusion is justified by the premise, for W.'s claim is not upon the *res* but only for the amount of the gift: v. Mayr's suggestion of the *exceptio doli* on the analogy of 12. 6. 26. 4; 50. 17. 84. pr. is obviously inadequate, for no praetor would frame a decretal action to which such a plea was needed, but cf. the authorities cited by Mancaleoni, St. Sassaresi, 1. 16 n. 1. The proper remedy is not an *actio in factum* as Lenel suggests, Ed., 182, but the *actio utilis hypothecaria*, which is properly described by the words *utilis in rem*, cf. 8. 1. 16; 20. 1. 16. 3. It seems impossible to doubt the genuineness of this remedy; not only are there many traces of the principle of "subrogation" in our field, 7. 4; 31. 3; 36. 1; 67, but any other result would be intolerable, as the donor bears the risk, 29. pr., a fact which makes a far stronger case than that of the pupil, where even Pringsheim, Kauf, 126, admits that the hypothec is classical. The word *condicticia* besides being formally suspicious, Beseler, 2. 63, presents the surprising phenomenon of a *utilis* personal remedy employed to achieve the result of a real action, and must replace the word *hypothecaria*. That and the last sentence are interpolated in order that W. may have a real and personal action. Such an idea was suggested by the *et*...*deterior* sentence. This can have nothing to do with the *beneficium competentiae*, which probably existed equally in the condiction, 42. 1. 20, but obviously referred to the *privi-*

legium exigendi, Czyhlarz, 406 ff.; with which it was quite natural to compare the proposed *utilis* action; incorrect, De Retes, 75. It is certain that the sense is more satisfactory if Faber's substitution of *nec* for *et* is adopted, Conj. 5. 9, a point which will be decided according to one's view of the nature of the *privilegium*, cf. Czyhlarz, 408. Finding the action compared to the obsolete *privilegium*, the compilers wished to preserve the analogy by granting W. the modern dotal remedies.

---

56. SCAEVOLA *libro tertio quaestionum* Si quod mihi mortis causa donare vellet, ego pure uxori donare vellem, non valet quod uxori iubeo dari, quia illo convalescente condictione teneor, mortuo autem nihilo minus pauperior sum: non enim habeo quod habiturus essem.

Cf. 4.

---

57. PAULUS *libro septimo responsorum* Ea, quae a marito suo pecuniam ex causa donationis acceperat, litteras ad eum misit huiusmodi: 'cum petenti mihi a te, domine carissime, adnuerit indulgentia tua viginti ad expediendas quasdam res meas, quae summa mihi numerata est sub ea condicione, ut, si per me meosque mores quid steterit, quo minus in diem vitae nostrae matrimonium permaneat, sive invito te discessero de domo tua vel repudium tibi sine ulla querella misero divortiumque factum per me probabitur, tunc viginti, quae mihi hac die donationis causa dare voluisti, daturam restituturam me sine ulla dilatione: spondeo.' quaero an, si eadem Titio marito suo repudium miserit, pecuniam restituere debeat. Paulus respondit pecuniam, quam vir uxori donavit, ex stipulatione proposita, si condicio eius exstitit, peti posse, quoniam ex donatione in pecuniam creditam conversa est: quod si stipulatio commissa non probetur, tunc tantum peti posse, quanto locupletior ex ea donatione factà probetur.

The passage is attacked by Beseler, 2. 445, on the ground that presence was invariably necessary for the validity of a stipulation, *acc.* Riccobono, Z., 1914, 282 n. 4. It is, however, not clear why the transaction is not valid as a loan, for which no promise was needed. Even without the consent of the lender an obligation would seem to arise upon Beseler's own theory, 3. 57, with regard to 12. 1. 18. 1; cf. *id.* 9. 8.

---

58. SCAEVOLA *libro secundo responsorum* Si praedia et mancipia Seiae data effecta sint eius tempore concubinatus ac postea tempore matrimonii aliis acceptis reddita sunt, quid iuris est? respondit secundum ea quae proponerentur negotium potius gestum videri, quam donationem intervenisse.

Cf. Z., 1921, 282; 36. 1.

---

1. Item cum quaereretur de cibariis mancipiorum, respondit: tempore quidem concubinatus data cibaria repeti non possunt, sed nec tempore matrimonii, si ea mancipia uxoris in communi usu fuerint.

Cf. 31. 10.

---

2. Filius rebus matris intervenire solitus pecunia matris consentiente ipsa mancipia et res mercatus emptionum instrumenta suo nomine confecit: decessit in patris potestate. quaestium est, an mater cum marito suo experiri et qua actione uti possit. respondit, si mater obligatum filium in ea pecunia voluit esse, intra annum, quam filius decessit, de peculio cum patre, in cuius potestate fuisse proponatur, actionem habere: si donabit, repeti posse, quanto locupletior ex ea donatione pater factus est.

This passage has been overlooked in the recent discussion of the relation of the condiction to the *actiones adjectitiae* by all but Pflüger, 34, who holds the former interpolated (*repeti*) because the remedy should have been *utilis de peculio*, as in the case of theft, which is, however, not an analogy, on account of the complicating influence of noxality, cf. 50. 17. 58; Levy, Konk., 1. 445 *ad* 15. 1. 3. 12. The question is as to the reason for the distinction; Pflüger's statement that the acceptance of a gift is never a *negotium peculiare* is belied by many texts on slaves, cf. 15. 1. 7. 5; Mandry, Familiengüterrecht, 2. 123 n.; Buckland, 188. Furthermore, in case of failure of a gift *m. c.* to a son, the *actio de peculio* is given by Julian, 39. 6. 19, cf. Mandry, *loc. cit.*, n. 4. The distinction between that case and ours is subtle: there the son was quasi contractually bound; here, in expending the gift, he is violating no obligation to the donor. If by consumption he could benefit himself alone it would not even constitute a breach of our prohibition. Since on account of the patrimonial identity this is impossible, the father is held directly for any enrichment which exists for our purposes, cf. 3. 4, regardless of a *versio*, *i. e.*, though the proceeds of the gift remain in the *peculium*. The *datio* theory thus cannot be saved by assuming that *repeti* refers or referred to the *actio de in rem verso* (on which cf. Solazzi, R. I. S. G., 49. 56 n. 1; Betti, *cit.* Rabel, Z., 1926, 477; Buckland, 184 n. 4); the condiction is the only remedy by which our prohibition can be enforced, and the rules of 3. 4 ff. are incompatible with the requirement of a *datio*, or with the supposed principle that the condiction lay only in concurrence with the *actio quod iussu*, Solazzi, *loc. cit.*; v. Mayr, 246 ff.; *contra* Buckland, 32 L. Q. R. 213, who cheerfully allows either action in every case of enrichment. If they were exceptional, the effect of these rules in such an ancient institution as ours may well have contributed to the classical development of the condiction in other fields.

---

59. Paulus *libro secundo sententiarum* Si quis uxori ea condicione donavit, ut quod donavit in dotem accipiat, defuncto eo donatio convalescit.

As Haymann remarks, 72, this case is analogous to that in 12. 1. 20; 39. 5. 33. 1. The latter transaction cannot be characterized too harshly; it seems inconceivable that it should have been taken seriously by Hermogenian. If A delivers to B a coin as a gift with the understanding that B shall redeliver it immediately as a gift, nobody would pretend that there had been two transactions or that ownership had passed. If the same is done with the understanding that A shall owe the money to B, all that has happened is a nude pact to make a gift. There is no imaginable purpose in such antics except to elude the Cincian Law. The only cases adduced by Haymann are quite different: either where three persons are concerned, the donee receiving the present absolutely, or where neither ownership nor perhaps possession but merely the use is retransferred. As for our case, where there is no question of eluding the law, the decision may be explained *favore nuptiarum*, the delivery and redelivery being held equivalent to a stipulation.

---

60. Hermogenianus *libro secundo iuris epitomarum* Vitricus et privignus invicem sibi donare praetexto matrimonii non prohibentur. 1. Divortii causa donationes inter virum et uxorem concessae sunt: saepe enim evenit, uti propter sacerdotium vel etiam sterilitatem,

61. Gaius *libro undecimo ad edictum provinciale* vel senectutem aut valetudinem aut militiam satis commode retineri matrimonium non possit:

62. Hermogenianus *libro secundo iuris epitomarum* et ideo bona gratia matrimonium dissolvitur.

On the Byzantine institution of divorce *bona gratia*, see Finestres, Hermogenian, 1. 505 ff.; Cohn, Z., 1878, 411 ff., followed by Bonfante, 263 ff. In classical law it seems to have designated a case where, although the divorce was unilateral, no penalties were incurred, cf. Vat. Fr., 107; 45. 1. 19, in view of which function Solazzi's suspicions of the term, Bull., 34. 305 n. 3, seem unjustified. If it is true that the *oratio* applied only to death during marriage, *supra* 32. 10; 32. 14, these passages merely explain the possibility of a gift *divortii causa*.

---

1. Divortio facto nec instaurato matrimonio non confirmabitur inter virum et uxorem facta donatio: nec inter patronum et libertam, si ab eo invito divertere non licet, facta donatio separatur, cum inter hos divortium intercedat. perinde enim id quod donatum est habetur divortio intercedente ac si donatum non fuisset.

It is hard to comprehend Solazzi's objections, *loc. cit.*, to this text, which he calls hopeless although it does not seem seriously to conflict with his theories. The statement that the *oratio* does not apply after divorce, even one *bona gratia*, is correct, 32. 14. The words *instaurato mat.* imply agreement with 32. 11, which Solazzi seems to suspect chiefly to find fault with our passage. Understanding *separatur* with Cujas and H. S. as "is different," a common Ciceronian use, the remainder of the text is reasonable. More specifically than any other in the Digest does it state the fact, upheld by those who impugn it, *e. g.*, Levy, 141 n. 3, that divorce was possible in these circumstances.

---

63. PAULUS *libro tertio ad Neratium* De eo, quod uxoris in aedificium viri ita coniunctum est, ut detractum alicuius usus esse possit, dicendum est agi posse, quia nulla actio est, ex lege duodecim tabularum, quamvis decemviros non sit credibile de his sensisse, quorum voluntate res eorum in alienum aedificium coniunctae essent. PAULUS notat: sed in hoc solum agi potest, ut sola vindicatio soluta re competat mulieri, non in duplum ex lege duodecim tabularum: neque enim furtivum est, quod sciente domino inclusum est.

Incredible ingenuity has been expended upon this text; for the literature see Monier, Tignum Junctum, 120 ff., adding Riccobono, 448; Haymann, 34; Lenel, Ed., 3 ed., 330. One suggestion, that of Huvelin, may be discarded at once; it would appear from 29. pr. that in Neratius' day nobody would have dreamt of holding junction with the owner's consent to be furtive. The fact of consent also precludes any consideration of the *actio ad exhibendum*, *supra* 37. Furthermore, the clause *ut detractum . . . possit*, so significant to Riccobono, must be disregarded. In view of our certainty that where the vindication has been lost, recovery is restricted both to the enrichment of the donee and the impoverishment of the donor, the value of the separated timber is irrelevant, corresponding, as it may, to neither requirement. The phrase and perhaps the whole doctrine of the *ius tollendi* originated in the *actio rei uxorae*, *supra* 43. 1, but it is hard to understand why it should be accepted here, yet suspected where it is in point, as in 6. 1. 38. If there is any gloss in our passage it is this, cf. Lenel, Paul, 1039, which renders it probable that a discussion of the dotal action immediately preceded this text. As for the words *quia. . . essent*, the improbability of Riccobono's hypothesis that they embody a gloss upon a separate edition of Neratius is obvious, and the weakness of all the other emendations except Haymann's is brought out by Monier. But if, following

Haymann, *alienatio* is substituted for the first *actio*, the text is quite clear. The theory of Girard and Pernice thus gains support, that the statute mentioned *tignum alienum;* cf. 6. 1. 23. 6. The *duplum* does not show bad faith, but, like the back reckoning under the *Lex Aquilia*, is intended as a substitute for the vindiction to reimburse the owner for any increase of value since the loss. Such seems indeed the only reasonable explanation; if bad faith were required, the action for theft is adequate; if not, it seems arbitrary to allow the liability of a *bona fide* defendant to depend upon the accident of previous theft, *e. g.*, one might build with another's materials without liability for mistake of ownership. The requirement of furtivity may have been introduced after Neratius, or not till Justinian; the fact that the action was placed in the edict after the action for theft does not seem conclusive; the *duplum* may well have led to the idea that the action should be classified as delictal, cf. G. 4. 9, which in turn coupled with the analogy of *usucapio* may be the origin of the need for furtivity. Whether or not the last clause is genuine, Paul was evidently impressed by the penal aspect of the damages, although the praetor might have restricted recovery to the *simplum*, cf. 11. 3. 7. The objection to his note is the exclusion of what seems the clearly proper remedy of the condiction, cf. 31. 1; Savigny, 181 n. *g*. The repetition of *solus* is so inelegant and unpleasant that suspicion is permissible, cf. Lenel, Ed., 3 ed., 331 n. 6; Landucci, St. Serafini, 413. The absence of any mention of the condiction by Neratius is explicable on the ground that Paul would have nothing to say to such a clearly correct remark.

---

64. IAVOLENUS *libro sexto ex posterioribus Labeonis* Vir mulieri divortio facto quaedam idcirco dederat, ut ad se reverteretur: mulier reversa erat, deinde divortium fecerat. LABEO: Trebatius inter Terentiam et Maecenatem respondit, si verum divortium fuisset, ratam esse donationem, si simulatum, contra. sed verum est, quod Proculus et Caecilius putant, tunc verum esse divortium et valere donationem divortii causa factam, si aliae nuptiae insecutae sunt aut tam longo tempore vidua fuisset, ut dubium non foret alterum esse matrimonium: alias nec donationem ullius esse momenti futuram.

For a detailed textual criticism, see Levy, 87. This passage shows most clearly the improbability of Alibrandi's hypothesis

that our prohibition originated in the Lex Julia *de maritis ordinandis*, the earliest possible date of which is 736, Karlowa, 1. 617 ff. The incident here described is dated at the very latest in 736–738 by Teuffel, Z. Alt. Wiss., 1845, 608 ff.; Kirchner's Hor., Sat. 2. 2. 13, where it is remarked that it is the only evidence, after 711, of Trebatius' existence.

---

65. LABEO *libro sexto posteriorum a Iavoleno epitomatorum* Quod vir ei, quae nondum viripotens nupserit, donaverit, ratum futurum existimo.

Cf. 32. 27, 28.

---

66. SCAEVOLA *libro nono digestorum* Seia Sempronio cum certa die nuptura esset, antequam domum deduceretur tabulaeque dotis signarentur, donavit tot aureos: quaero, an ea donatio rata sit. non attinuisse tempus, an antequam domum deduceretur, donatio facta esset, aut tabularum consignatarum, quae plerumque et post contractum matrimonium fierent, in quaerendo exprimi: itaque nisi ante matrimonium contractum, quod consensu intellegitur, donatio facta esset, non valere.

This passage is termed "gibberish" by Levy, 72, who revives Ortolan's theory that the analogy of possession was followed in determining the moment of marriage. A reconciliation of the text with 23. 2. 5 and Paul, 2. 19. 8 seems satisfactorily made by Machelard, 241 ff.; cf. Bonfante, 189. The chief objection to Levy's view is that it is inapplicable to a case where the couple are to enjoy a honeymoon or to live at the house of W. or her father. It seems incredible that the classical jurists were able to escape such cases and cling to ideas of *usus* which were out of date in the time of Augustus. Whenever the parties engaged in the ceremony the moment of common consent must have been decisive, with the addition, due to the influence of the ancient practice, that the *deductio* sufficed if they were apart.

---

1. Virgini in hortos deductae ante diem tertium quam ibi nuptiae fierent, cum in separata diaeta ab eo esset, die nuptiarum, priusquam ad eum transiret et priusquam aqua

et igni acciperetur, id est nuptiae celebrentur, optulit decem aureos dono: quaesitum est, post nuptias contractas divortio facto an summa donata repeti possit. respondit id, quod ante nuptias donatum proponeretur, non posse de dote deduci.

The clause *id est... celebrantur* was suspected by Gentilis, 193, before Lenel, cf. Kr. *ad h. l.*; see also Levy, 71 ff.; Di Marzo, Lezioni sul Mat., 84 ff.

---

67. LABEO *libro secundo pithanon a Paulo epitomatorum* Si uxor nummis a viro aut ab eo qui in eius potestate esset sibi donatis servum emerit, deinde cum eius factus fuerit, eum ipsum donationis causa viro tradiderit, rata erit traditio, quamvis ea mente facta fuerit qua ceterae donationes, neque ulla actio eius nomine dari potest.

The words *ea mente*, perhaps used by Labeo, show clearly the importance of the *animus*, which alone makes possible the decisions in 5. 5; 34; 36. 1 and *passim;* in fact all who attack that conception should add the word *mens* to their researches in the V. I. R. In view of 32. 9 the only justification for the decision is that the donor had a subrogatory or equitable right in the changed form of the *res* just as in 7. 4; 31. 3; 55. It is uncertain whether the decision applies to a W. who knew that the slave was more valuable than his price and was availing herself of the opportunity to make a gift, cf. *supra* 28. 5.

Bei Fragen zur Produktsicherheit wenden Sie sich bitte an:
If you have any questions regarding product safety,
please contact:

Walter de Gruyter GmbH
Genthiner Straße 13
10785 Berlin
productsafety@degruyterbrill.com